British Widows of
the First World War

British Widows of the First World War
First World War

The Forgotten Legion

Andrea Hetherington

Pen & Sword
MILITARY

First published in Great Britain in 2018 by
Pen & Sword Military
Pen & Sword Books Limited
47 Church Street
Barnsley
South Yorkshire
S70 2AS

ISBN 978 1 47388 676 6

A CIP catalogue record for this book is
available from the British Library.

Typeset by Geniies IT & Services Private Limited
Printed and bound by TJ International Ltd, Padstow, Cornwall

Pen & Sword Books Limited incorporates the imprints of Archaeology,
Atlas, Aviation, Discovery, Family History, Fiction, History, Maritime,
Military, Military Classics, Politics, Select, Transport, True Crime, Air World,
Frontline Publishing, Leo Cooper, Remember When, Seaforth Publishing,
The Praetorian Press, Wharncliffe Local History, Wharncliffe Transport,
Wharncliffe True Crime and White Owl.

For a complete list of Pen & Sword titles please contact
PEN & SWORD BOOKS LIMITED
47 Church Street, Barnsley, South Yorkshire S70 2AS, United Kingdom
E-mail: enquiries@pen-and-sword.co.uk
Website: www.pen-and-sword.co.uk

Contents

Acknowledgements

Firstly, I must thank Dr Peter Liddle for starting me on this project and for his work in compiling the collection that bears his name at the University of Leeds. The staff at Special Collections at the university have been most helpful as always, particularly Fiona Gell, Karen Mee, Tim Procter, Matthew Dunne and Hannah Wynne. Professor Alison Fell and the Legacies of War team at the University of Leeds have been a great source of support and encouragement, as has Lucy Moore of the Leeds Museums Service.

I would like to thank all of the staff at the National Archives, Eleanor Johnston at the University of Staffordshire, the staff at the Women's Library at the London School of Economics, and everyone at the Salvation Army Heritage Centre for their help. The staff at Leeds Central Library are unfailingly helpful in retrieving obscure items that have not been loaned in years, and I thank them for all of the trips they have made to the depths of the building on my behalf.

I want to thank Graham Wright and Jackie Coleman for sharing their family stories with me, and Pauline Baldwin for allowing me to use material from her family's file at the Liddle Collection.

On a personal note, I would like to thank my mother, Maureen Hetherington, for sharing my own family's story. Sapper Joseph Lamb was my great-grandfather. My mother is a widow herself and I would like to thank her for bearing her own grief with 'patience and fortitude' and making many sacrifices on behalf of her children.

Lastly, I would like to thank Linda Gilhespy for her incredible patience and tolerance for the many hours I have spent stuck at my desk.

Chapter 1

Lady Visitors and Army Wives

'I could not tell you this morning the insults I got from a visitor.'

Traditionally, soldiers' wives were not well looked after by Britain's armed forces. Soldiers were not allowed to marry without permission, and only a certain number in any one battalion would be granted that honour. These wives were then considered to be 'on the strength' and would be provided for and even allowed to follow their husbands abroad. Should their husbands die in combat during these postings, the wives were allowed to share the regiment's resources for six months before they must either return to England or remarry. Rates of remarriage were accordingly high amongst these women.

The army itself had a poor reputation at home. Recruits during the Victorian and Edwardian eras were often men with nothing better to do rather than those with hearts set on a military career. Soldiers were not looked on kindly by the general populace, being banned from public houses in some places and tolerated, rather than welcomed, in others. Their active service was in far-flung parts of the Empire rather than just across the Channel, so the notion that they were the defenders of the nation was hard to sustain. This lack of respect also applied to soldiers' wives, who were seen as lower-class women with suspect morals. Some of this would change with the advent of the First World War, though unfriendly attitudes towards soldiers' dependants can still be discerned in the way they were treated by some agencies.

Widows and orphans of those killed in action were on their own unless they had been married 'on the strength'. During the Crimean War charitable donations were made by the general public for the relief of widows and orphans of the conflict. These sums were large and a body called the Royal Patriotic Fund Corporation (RPFC) was set up to distribute them amongst the needy. This was the beginning of any organized effort to support war widows financially, though, notably, it did not come from the state. The First Boer War in 1881 saw pensions paid to war widows from the public purse for the first time. The War Office only paid out if a man was killed in action or died of his wounds, and the amount paid was a year's soldier's salary, not a lifetime payment. Once again, this was only for wives considered to be 'on the strength'.

The Second Boer War, which began in 1899, was of a different character to the many small wars fought in the nineteenth century, partly because it attracted a significant number of volunteers to the armed forces from all over the Empire. Press coverage was more extensive, public opinion of a soldier's status changed accordingly and a great deal of fundraising work was done at home to provide for the wives and widows of those fighting in South Africa. Rudyard Kipling composed a poem for the *Daily Mail* in return for a donation to the RPFC and over a million pounds was raised generally from 1899 to 1901. The RPFC sent £5 to every widow and £1 for every child when a soldier's death was reported, the monies being sent direct to the widow via the Post Office. The *Daily Telegraph* raised enough money to administer its own widows' and orphans' fund, which paid £20 to the widow immediately, then an annuity of 5s 9d a week thereafter. After lobbying from the RPFC and others, the state finally and grudgingly took some responsibility for war widows by the Royal Warrant of 25 June 1901, which granted pensions to 'on the strength' widows on a scale according to the soldier's rank, beginning at five shillings a week for the wife, with extra allowances for the children. Widows who remarried did not lose their pensions, but were paid at half the previous rate. The state was still taking no responsibility for 'off the strength' wives, and the total number of Boer War widows eligible for a pension was a mere 3,000.

Charity attempted to fill the gaps state provision was not prepared to reach, and the RPFC worked hand in hand with the Soldiers' and Sailors' Families Association[1] (SSFA) to assist wives while their husbands were on active service. Started in 1885, the SSFA was designed to help the relatives of living soldiers while they were away, providing advice and some financial assistance, largely in the garrison towns of Britain. The Princess of Wales, later to become Queen Alexandra, was patron of the charity, giving it the royal seal of approval. The SSFA operated on the principle that the old Victorian virtue of 'self-help' was to be encouraged at every turn, rather than simple handouts being given to those in need.

Charity was seen as a fitting occupation for the Victorian and Edwardian lady – on a voluntary basis, of course. The ideology behind this was that a woman's 'better nature' could be used to improve the moral lot of the lower classes whilst also distributing financial largesse. For some women this was also driven by a religious imperative, particularly amongst the nonconformist denominations. For example, Eleanor Rathbone, elected as an MP in 1929 and heavily involved in relief work in Liverpool, was the daughter of a noted Unitarian family. Jeffrey Cox studied religious activity in the parish of Lambeth in the late Victorian and Edwardian period and found large numbers of middle-class women engaged in 'visitation' on behalf of the different churches in the area.[2] By the 1890s, it is estimated that there were 500,000 such women engaged in philanthropy.[3] Women trying to enter public life could only do so through this kind of activity in the late nineteenth century. Without the vote or the right to take positions at Westminster and on town councils, women had to find themselves places on school boards and similar bodies as a means of participating in politics. Particularly in rural areas and provincial towns, the same women sat on committees for various different bodies, all concerned with charitable relief of some kind. From the SSFA to the local Boards of Guardians charged with administering the Poor Law there was a great deal of crossover in personnel and, therefore, in the attitudes brought to bear upon the work itself.

Many of the women concerned were products of involvement with the Charity Organisation Society (COS), a body with very strict ideas on where charity should start and end, infused with the spirit of self-help and tough love towards the poor. Founded in 1869, the COS had surveillance of the recipients of charitable relief at its heart and made distinctions between those who deserved charity and those who did not, regardless of the depth of their despair. The fact that the society's original name was the London Association for the Prevention of Pauperism and Crime perhaps gives a better clue as to its intentions than the title by which it soon became known. Double payments were felt to be a particular scourge, and the COS advocated close co-operation between agencies to ensure that claimants were not receiving assistance from multiple sources. This was universally known as 'overlapping' and was to be avoided at all costs. Any material assistance given to a claimant had to be accompanied by 'friendly visitation' designed to have a civilizing influence on the individual being visited. Though founded in London, the COS and its principles spread nationwide, spawning a number of spin-off organizations in the field of 'social work'. Those involved in voluntary work with soldiers' families during the First World War were often infused with COS ideology.

The 'lady visitor' was a familiar figure to the working classes of Victorian and Edwardian Britain, and not one who was universally welcomed into their lives, regardless of their motives. The Fabian Women's Group started a study of working-class families in Lambeth in 1909, which involved paying extra money to them for a period of time for the sustenance of newborn babies. Though this study was not based on COS principles, several of the participant families ended their involvement within a matter of days or weeks after finding that they were expected to have visits from the group as a condition of participation.[4]

A number of studies of working-class communities in Britain were completed in the years before the First World War and are vital reading for anyone wishing to understand ordinary lives at this time. Women writers in particular produced a number of texts that have resonance for the study of the lives of First World War widows. Despite the fact that these studies are unavoidably mediated through the eyes of middle-class women, Lady Bell in Middlesbrough,[5] Maud

Pember Reeves in Lambeth,[6] Eleanor Rathbone in Liverpool,[7] and Clementina Black and her associate researchers around the country[8] left a portrait of working-class women and their families that showed the precarious nature of their daily existence.

Sympathetic reformers often had ideas of a better life for a working-class family that looked like their own, middle-class lifestyle. Even those most keen on widows being given financial assistance wanted that assistance combined with supervision. Ideals of social service were rooted in Victorian sensibilities, not in concepts of the rights of citizenship, and the First World War saw the start of a sea change in attitudes to state aid that would eventually lead, with some stumbling and misdirected steps, to our present welfare state. Pension provision was absolutely fundamental to First World War widows, dictating their everyday existence and informing their life decisions, so this must be the starting point of any study of their lives.

Britain's standing army in 1914 was laughably small compared to that of its German opponents, with most of its strength scattered around the globe rather than immediately ready to respond to the invasion of Belgium. Only 1,100 wives were considered to be 'on the strength' and were therefore in receipt of separation allowances.[9] Reservists who had already served their time in the army and were now back in civilian life were subject to recall to the colours. These men, having been single during their military service, now frequently had wives and children to support. A vigorous recruitment campaign was fundamental to the chances of a successful war and the promise of payments to wives if their husbands enlisted was made in that context rather than out of a sense of moral duty or obligation.

Britain declared war on Germany on 4 August 1914. Two days later, the Under Secretary for War was refusing to give assurances in the House of Commons that wives 'off the strength' would be catered for, either in separation allowances or in pensions. It was not until 10 August that Prime Minister H.H. Asquith gave a promise to the House that all wives would be looked after, and orders were not issued by the Army Council to that effect until 16 August. Separation allowances and widows' pensions would now be available for all wives, whether 'on the strength' or not. The rates of payment were not generous. Separation allowance started at the rate of 11s 6d per week. The widow of a private would receive only five shillings a week on his death, the same as was being given out during the Boer War fifteen years earlier. If she were to remarry, she would receive a one-off gratuity of the princely sum of £13. Additional allowances were payable for a soldier's children, beginning at 1s 6d per week. These rates were as outlined in the Royal Warrant on military pay of August 1913 – no review of the payment rates to satisfy the needs of a nation at war was carried out before their implementation. It was not until late October 1914 that an increase was announced, with a private's widow now to get 7s 6d per week, whilst the remarriage gratuity was tripled to £39, or two years' pay.

For the first time, sailors' wives were also now to receive separation allowances. Sailors had traditionally made allotments from their pay to be given to their wives at home. Away at sea there was not a lot to spend their wages on, as all of their on-board needs were catered for, hence the willingness to provide more generously for their wives at home. It was now seen as only fair that sailors should be treated on the same principles as soldiers in relation to their dependants.

No attempts were to be made to match a soldier's wife's allowance or pension with his civilian earnings, despite representations that this was unfair to those in higher earning occupations. It was deemed too complex to attempt this kind of reconciliation, which would also have been at odds with the concept of military discipline: a man was a soldier now, not a miner, shopkeeper or accountant, and all would be treated equally according to their military rank. A differential rate would also imply that one man's life was worth more than another's – a miner's widow receiving more than a labourer's wife though their husbands may have died side by side. No such considerations applied to distinguishing between officers and men; a colonel's wife would receive £200 a year on his death, whilst a private's widow would have to live on an annual income of £13.

The Royal Warrant of 1913 was clear in its assertion that pensions were not payable as of right to anyone, but were rewards for the service of the husband. The couple had to be married at the time the man enlisted, and also at the time he received the injury from which he died. The death had to be entirely due to military service and not caused by his own negligence, and had to take place within seven years of the original injury. A pension could be withdrawn completely if there was misbehaviour by the widow. Whilst some of these regulations would be modified over the course of the war, these were the core principles on which pension policy would be built. The interpretation of and adherence to those principles caused a great deal of distress to thousands of widows.

Officers' wives were treated differently in that they were eligible for pensions if the man died of natural causes, and were given a scale of pensions that varied depending on the circumstances of his death. If the officer died in action, a larger sum was awarded than if he had succumbed to disease. Certain aspects of an officer's conduct would disqualify his wife from claiming a pension, and as usual, her own behaviour had to be beyond reproach. For an officer's widow, the pension ceased completely on remarriage, though unlike the widow of an ordinary soldier, she could reapply for her pension if she was widowed a second time. Officers' wives did not receive separation allowances at this stage of the war.

Separation allowance levels were set to take into account the fact that a wife no longer had her husband to feed and clothe now he was the responsibility of the armed forces, and were accordingly of a modest amount. Pension payments were even more miserly, being issued on the basis that the family could now live even more cheaply in the knowledge that the breadwinner was not going to return home. Women who were expected to keep a man's home in good order for his eventual return were now expected to cut their cloth accordingly and economize. Separation allowances would continue for six months after a man's death to allow adjustments to be made before the lower pension payment kicked in.

A number of newspapers reported themselves satisfied with the new rate of allowances, seeing the provision for soldiers' families as the removal of an impediment to married men joining the colours and even removing the need for conscription. This optimism was entirely misplaced, both in the idea that war widows would now be well looked after and also in the belief that conscription was now entirely unnecessary. Correspondents to the letters pages often had a different view. Writing to the *Daily Express* in September 1914, an agent of the Royal Patriotic Fund Corporation said: 'This is a very rich country which these men have left homes and families to defend, and surely to leave the dependants to barely exist on such a paltry allowance is contemptible in the extreme.'[10]

The government acknowledged that the arrangements for separation allowances and pensions were imperfect by setting up a Select Committee on Naval and Military Pensions in November 1914. Sitting from December 1914 to March 1915, the committee looked at the whole machinery of pensions and allowances, in addition to the rates of payment. The Select Committee were particularly keen to hear evidence about working-class incomes and family budgets. The Port of London Authority provided real life cases of thirty men previously in their employ who had now been killed in action, listing their pre-war jobs and incomes. The lowest paid labourer amongst the group was earning twenty-seven shillings a week before his enlistment. The War Emergency Workers' National Committee submitted wage details across a wider spectrum of employment, again finding that even for general labourers and gas workers, men were earning an absolute minimum of eighteen shillings a week, and sometimes as much as sixty shillings for the more skilled worker. Miners from the Durham coalfield earned from thirty to thirty-five shillings a week, with free coal and housing on top of that. A war widow's pension of five shillings a week was woefully inadequate for the families of these men. Most of the witnesses to the committee proposed a flat rate pension of £1 a week – five times the payment rate to a private's widow at the time. The Government Actuary went so far as to prepare a cost assessment to the nation of looking after widows and dependants, estimating that £58 million would need to be put aside. If the figure of £1 a week for widows and five shillings per child were adopted, this would double that estimate.[11]

The issue of pensions to the widow of the higher paid worker was not properly addressed until April 1917, when the alternative pension was introduced. If the widow could show that her husband was earning more than the flat rate of pension for total disablement before he enlisted, she could have an alternative pension of half of that amount.[12] There were no separate children's allowances, so it was not necessarily a better deal for many families. Applying for an alternative pension was a complex procedure and it was up to the widow herself, as with any pension claim, to provide evidence to support her application. Early volunteers were at a disadvantage as the rise in wages and general inflation during the war meant that a 1916 conscript may have been earning considerably more than a 1914 volunteer for doing the same job. Obtaining evidence of a husband's pre-enlistment wage was very difficult. Record keeping at many businesses was not particularly detailed in the days before universal taxation, and firms had sometimes closed down by the time the widow would come to make her application. Those paid on piece-work were also at a considerable disadvantage when it came to being able to prove their earnings. The tailoring trade was just one example of an industry arranged on piecework, with many skilled workers paid by the garment, not by the hour. Providing evidence of a man's income in such circumstances was very challenging for his widow. Nowhere near as many widows as were eligible successfully applied for alternative pensions. In 1919 there were 200,000 war widows, of whom only 18,000 had demonstrated that they were eligible for alternative pensions, just 9 per cent of the total. The Ministry of Pensions believed that the real eligibility figure amongst widows was around 25 per cent.[13] It was not in the government's interests for widows to apply; had all those eligible done so, it would have cost the state an extra £18 million per year.

While the 1915 Select Committee were deliberating, problems with the arrangements for all military wives were immediately apparent. Substantial delays in receiving separation allowances from the War Office were reported nationwide. The War Office machinery had been entirely unprepared for the flood of separation allowance applications and was unable to respond in a timely manner. The announcement that the 'off the strength' wife was now to be financially supported took the War Office by surprise. Sir Charles Harris, giving evidence before the Select Committee, said that it had always been 'a cardinal point in military policy'[14] not to recognize 'off the strength' wives. As a result, those members of the British Expeditionary Force hurrying across the Channel had often left no records of their marriage or dependants with the War Office at all. Only 1,100 wives had been in receipt of separation allowance before the declaration of war. Even amongst the regular army that number would soar on the erosion of the on/off strength distinction. Adding to that number the married reservists returning to their regiments and the huge number of new recruits, the War Office was completely unprepared to deal with the influx. The Select Committee heard that in August 1914 the army was taking in as many men in a day as they had been accustomed to recruiting in a year. By November 1914, 500,000 women were claiming separation allowance.[15] It is hard not to feel some sympathy with the overwhelmed army administrators suddenly faced with this problem.

However, the travails of an army paper pusher were nothing as compared with the plight of the woman who was suddenly left bereft of financial support on her husband's enlistment or recall. Stories emerged of women who had been waiting for their separation allowances for weeks or months, despite the intervention of Members of Parliament. Delays in paying separation allowances were the immediate problem, but as the casualties started to come in, those same delays would also affect widows' pensions. Those familiar institutions, the RPFC and the SSFA, were to play their part in easing the distress of those disadvantaged by the war, though not entirely effectively and not without criticism from many quarters. Voluntarism and charitable endeavour would again plug the gaps in state provision, just as they had in the Boer War.

As the War Office could not possibly cope with the level of allowances now being claimed, they drafted in the voluntary services of the SSFA. The SSFA boasted that they had 800 branches nationwide, but had no presence in several major cities, Liverpool and Birmingham being examples. The SSFA were to assist with the administration of allowances and started to pay out monies themselves when the War Office delays were causing hardship to families. The monies were to be recovered from the army at a later date. Sometimes payments given to women by the SSFA were recovered from the women themselves once their separation allowances or pensions were received. The War Office was aware that in some parts of the country, women would not apply to the SSFA for assistance because they believed that what was being given was charity, rather than monies to which they were entitled, be that separation allowance or an advance on a pension.[16] The perceived attitude of some of those working on the SSFA's behalf, as we shall see, will have done little to dispel that myth.

The SSFA issued a circular in August 1914 that set out some of the principles on which they were to work. Acknowledging that the number of families to be helped would far exceed those from the Boer War, the SSFA also declared that the rich would be adversely affected by the disruption in trade caused and would not have as much money to donate to charity. As a result, they decided that it was necessary to restrict the amount of help given, and that no help at all should be forthcoming where a wife had more than 12s 6d a week coming into the household. 'Sobriety and good conduct' were to govern all assistance, which was to be given 'PERSONALLY and WEEKLY'. In some cases, volunteers were told not to give women the money at all, but to pay it direct to a third party, for example, to the landlord who was expecting his rent. The old COS fear of overlapping was rampant in the SSFA's literature, with visitors told to make enquiries with men's employers to see if they were providing assistance to the family.

Eleanor Rathbone had been heavily involved in setting up a branch of the SSFA in Liverpool on the outbreak of war. She claimed that the organization had been instrumental in avoiding 'an appalling public scandal' by stepping in and paying out separation allowances that were not forthcoming from the army.[17] The chairman of the SSFA, Captain George Wickham Legg, was unsurprisingly an enthusiastic advocate of the lady visitor. He claimed that the practice of visiting 'brings people together in a way which nothing else does',[18] establishing a community of interest between the classes. The question of in whose interest this alleged community was established remained a moot point and the use of the SSFA to assist in checking, processing and paying claims was not universally applauded.

The growing influence of the Labour Party had been one of the drivers behind the welfare reforms already introduced in the early part of the century. The introduction of school meals in 1906, old age pensions in 1908 and the National Insurance scheme in 1911 were all products not only of a desire for welfare reform on the part of the Liberal government, but also a desire to neutralize the appeal of the Labour Party to the working-class voter.[19] With forty-two Labour MPs now sitting by 1914, questions were asked in Parliament about the role of the lady visitor and the treatment of soldiers' families. The decision to use the SSFA rather than the professional services of local government caused consternation, particularly amongst the Labour representatives. A direction from the War Office to the local police to check up on women in receipt of pensions and allowances was also heavily criticized.[20] These themes of interrogation and surveillance of women by both state and voluntary agencies would continue throughout the war and beyond.

The Prince of Wales established a charitable fund on the outbreak of war that was designed to alleviate the distress caused domestically by the immediate consequences of the conflict. The dislocation of overseas trade had caused wide-scale unemployment at home as businesses struggled to cope. Many of those losing their jobs were women, and the Prince of Wales National Relief Fund was to assist those suffering as a result. In Leicester, applications to the fund ran at 900 per week in the first fortnight of its operation.[21] This trade collapse was a boon to recruiters, with men suddenly out of work with uncertain prospects finding that the army was delighted to accept their services. The fund was not designed to help those finding

themselves in need as a result of the breadwinner joining up, but the level of distress caused by delays in War Office payments meant that monies were given to
the SSFA to meet those requirements. The *Nottingham Journal* on 14 September
reported a queue of dependants at the local relief office and a caseload of 2,000,
only 200 of which were what was described as 'civilian cases' – the rest were all
wives, widows and other dependants who were not yet in receipt of their allowances.
Those administering monies from the fund on a local level were often the same
personnel engaged in work for the SSFA or other charitable agencies, increasing
the power of the lady visitor. The administration of the fund was criticized from
many quarters. *John Bull*, the patriotic magazine edited by Horatio Bottomley,
echoed the comments of a number of MPs regarding the inquisition by charitable
workers. The paper published an extract from a letter from a sailor's wife who had
sought assistance while waiting for her separation allowance to arrive:

> You would not tell me to go to the POW fund if you knew all. I could not
> tell you the insults I got this morning from a visitor. She told me I had a
> drunken husband and believed that you were drunk when you enlisted.[22]

Others felt that the fund was inefficient in its distribution of relief, with too many
hands involved in allocating money to too few mouths. The three bodies – the
Prince of Wales National Relief Fund, the RPFC and the SSFA – worked hand
in hand, with monies going from the Prince of Wales Fund to the RPFC for the
temporary relief of widows, and being physically administered by the SSFA.
Only £50,000 was initially given to the RPFC by the Prince of Wales Fund. In
late August 1914, the government gave an assurance in the House of Commons
that they were not intending widows and orphans to be looked after by charitable
sources, but paid from public funds.[23] This answer was somewhat disingenuous
when thousands of women around the country would be assisted by charitable
funds, be that in the form of temporary relief, or because they did not fit the criteria applied to a pension application at the time. The government had no qualms
in referring such widows to charitable sources rather than take any responsibility
for their upkeep.

A woman did not have to be married to a soldier in order to be eligible for a
pension. If she was able to prove that he had supported her financially, and she
had children to him, she and they would be able to claim a pension on his death.
However, the burden of proof was very much with the woman herself. She would
often fall at the first hurdle if the man had failed to mention her on his enlistment
papers. This concession was one that reflected the reality of working-class lives at
the time. In an era where divorce was difficult and expensive, couples simply lived

apart and formed new relationships, which could not be legitimized by marriage. Objections were received to paying pensions to what were termed as 'unmarried wives' from a number of sources, including the Church of England and a large number of SSFA members. In January 1915, a meeting called by those protesting against the measure attracted the largest single attendance of any SSFA meeting in history.[24] Though the association eventually voted for assistance being given to such women, it is likely that the attitude towards them from SSFA volunteers at ground level was not particularly helpful. The irony was that an unmarried wife was better off than a wife who had married her husband after enlistment; the original regulations stipulated that those marrying after a man was in khaki were not entitled to a pension on his death, the authorities apparently fearing a tide of gold-digging widows marrying for money, not love.

On the death of her husband, a wife did not automatically receive a pension, but had to make an application and fill in the relevant forms, which were generally sent out to her along with confirmation of her husband's demise. The soldier's nomina-tion of her on his own enlistment papers was not sufficient evidence of her entitle-ment, nor was the existence of the couple's children. A form had to be completed with the full details of the marriage and of the birth of any eligible children, then taken to a Justice of the Peace or a police officer above the rank of sergeant who was prepared to vouch that the information therein was correct. The form then had to be sent to the War Office along with copies of the marriage certificate and any birth certificates. The declaration to be signed by the relevant authority figure also stated that the widow was 'in every respect deserving of the grant of Pension'. The question of whether a widow continued to live up to that recommendation would see thousands of women facing the forfeiture of their pension.

This somewhat tortuous process was not easy for many widows. Many of the application forms that survive show errors on dates and names made by the widow completing the form, often resulting in further delays while the War Office que-ried the information. It was by no means common practice to retain copies of such certificates in a working-class household. A general lack of birth certificates allowed many an underage soldier to join up as it was not expected that he would be able to routinely prove his age in this way. Then, as now, copies of these certificates had to be paid for, the cost being three shillings per copy. The larger the family, the more expense incurred by the widow in providing the certificates. The financial burden of obtaining birth certificates was recognized by the Bradford committees in charge of administering war relief. An arrangement was made with the registrar by which, on presentation of the relevant form from the local education officer, a parent could obtain a birth certificate for the sum of sixpence, rather than three shillings. Once the application was approved, the widow would start to receive her money through the local Post Office, as she had done with her separation allowance. This was the theory, though in practice the transition from separation allowance to pension was not seamless and other agencies often had to step in to assist the widow until the War Office caught up.

The evidence heard before the Select Committee on Pensions of 1915 demonstrated how chaotic and difficult the administration of pensions and separation allowances had been in the first six months of the war. The system of allowances was difficult for applicants to understand, and challenging an adverse decision on pension eligibility was almost impossible for the average working-class woman. The work of Maud Pember Reeves and Lady Bell, in different areas of the country, showed how little a role literacy played in the life of many working-class women. From a survey of 200 ironworkers' houses in Middlesbrough, Lady Bell found that seventeen of the wives could not read.[25] In Pember Reeves' Lambeth sample, the situation was worse, with eight out of forty-two women unable to read and write.[26] The actual number of illiterate women is likely to have been greater as some will not have been prepared to admit this shortcoming to a middle-class visitor. A number of witnesses to the Select Committee gave similar evidence on this point, the Mayor of Manchester saying that widows of the poorer classes were at a great disadvantage in pleading their cases before pensions committees, whilst the Birmingham Citizens' Committee gave evidence that widows found letters from the authorities difficult to understand. It was not just working-class women who struggled to come to a full understanding of the regulations. The Archbishop of Canterbury pointed out that the War Office had specifically asked the clergy to assist parishioners in deciphering the many circulars issued on pensions, 'which were found unintelligible by those for whom they were intended, and I am afraid I may say not less unintelligible to me.'[27]

As soon as separation allowances and pensions began to be paid, the idea was at large that women were somehow incapable of managing that money themselves. The myth arose that they were spending this money on drink or luxuries rather than on the upkeep of their families. The idea that working-class women were poor managers was rife amongst those influenced by the Charity Organisation Society, who saw poverty as a moral rather than an economic issue. This belied the findings of Lady Bell and others, who found that such women were, on the whole, very good managers. A large proportion of men were accustomed to handing over the majority of their wage each week to their wife, for her to run the household budget. The notion that separation allowances and pensions meant that women, for the first time in history, had their own money to spend was absurd. The levels of separation allowances and pensions actually compared unfavourably to the amounts a woman might previously have received from her husband, meaning that there would be very little left over for luxuries or frivolity of any kind.

The recommendations of the Select Committee on Pensions 1915 were to remove responsibility from the SSFA for the administration of pensions and allowances, instead setting up a Statutory Committee of the Royal Patriotic Fund Corporation to perform this task. Many of the day to day functions of the Statutory Committee would be devolved to local committees, on which those from voluntary organizations would continue to play a prominent role. The SSFA were not happy with power being taken from their hands and wanted significant representation on the Statutory Committee both at a local and national level. They railed against more government red tape and the costs of establishing a new structure, but to no avail. The new Statutory Committee assumed responsibility from the SSFA completely from June 1916. By this time, the SSFA had assisted more than 700,000 widows of all wars, and distributed £2.6 million in pensions and allowances.[28] In the end, the local committees often contained those same individuals who had always been involved in the distribution of charity, including SSFA representatives, with the same attitudes towards self-help and the undeserving poor.

The Select Committee made a number of other recommendations that were taken up by the government, increasing the level of separation allowances to 12s 6d for a wife, five shillings for the first child, then lesser amounts for subsequent children. Pension rates were raised to ten shillings a week minimum, with higher amounts if the widow was over thirty-five, and then more again if she was over forty-five, the theory being that it was harder for her to either remarry or obtain work the older she became. Widows who remarried were now to receive two years' gratuity rather than one. Payments to the unmarried wife remained, and the distinction between a marriage pre and post enlistment was removed. A large number of 'khaki weddings' were popularly suspected of having taken place as a direct result.

The Statutory Committee was to decide on questions of fact for pensions for dependants other than wives and children, to act in a judicial capacity in relation to forfeiture cases and where two people were claiming the same allowance, and to supplement separation allowances and pensions in appropriate cases – to 'fill in the gaps'[29] left by the Royal Warrants. The previous assurances that charity would not be expected to step in and support widows were shown to be hollow by the words of the Select Committee:

> We suggest that the Prince of Wales Fund and any other local funds should be invited to supplement the Government rates of allowances and pensions where it appears to be desirable to do so, having regard to all the circumstances of the case.[30]

The sheer number of cases that were not appropriately met by the terms of successive Royal Warrants changed this approach somewhat, with Parliament voting that £1 million should be given to the Statutory Committee to meet these demands. This amount would not be enough to deal with all 'hard cases', and charity would continue to play a big role in the lives of many widows and children.

Lord Kitchener estimated that the total number of war widows from the conflict would be 50,000.[31] Within six months of the outbreak of war, the number of widows was already approaching 5,000.[32] Despite this early evidence, members of the Select Committee appear to have been hopelessly optimistic about the numbers of women who would require assistance. Andrew Bonar Law said, 'However badly the war goes the number of men killed will not exceed at the outside 60,000.'[33] Official statistics estimated in December 1920 that there had been 702,410 British casualties.[34] In 1921, 235,233 war widows were in receipt of pensions.[35] The Pensions Issue Office would accordingly increase its staff numbers from just twenty in January 1915 to 4,262 by March 1919.[36] Both state and charitable aid would be put under a strain that was never imagined at the outbreak of the war.

The demand for pensions, both for widows and disabled men, would see the existing administrative machinery replaced by the establishment of a whole new ministry in December 1916. The Statutory Committee's role was now given to a body called the Special Grants Committee (SGC). The First Minister of Pensions was a Labour man, George Barnes, who had heard evidence as one of the Select Committee in 1915 and had also served on the Statutory Committee. Staffed by penny-pinching civil servants from the Treasury, and assisted by the existing army of voluntary workers on the local committees, any hope that the Ministry of Pensions would right the wrongs of previous administrations and interpret the regulations liberally in favour of pension claimants would prove to be an impossible dream.

Chapter 2

Becoming a Widow

'I didn't read any more – I guessed what was coming …'

Margaret Forster worked as a postwoman in Sunderland in 1915 while her husband Will was serving in France. She had undertaken the sad task of delivering many War Office letters notifying families that their loved ones were dead. In August 1915, she had the disconcerting experience of delivering a letter to herself, announcing that Will was missing. It was six long weeks before further communication was received to confirm that he was in hospital suffering from enteric fever. He recovered, but sustained a shell wound to the abdomen at Passchendaele in 1917, dying of his wounds. Margaret, no longer a postwoman, received news of his death in the form of a letter from a nurse at the hospital where Will was treated. Her whole family were present when she opened the letter:

> 'Dear Mrs Forster, sorry to inform you that …' and while I was reading I saw underneath 'passed away' and I said 'My husband is dead.' My mother said 'Don't talk so daft.' I said 'Will is dead, mother.'[1]

The next day, Margaret received official notification from the War Office, including the paperwork required to apply for her widow's pension.

It was not unusual for the War Office to be the second or third source of the awful news of a loved one's death. Hospital nurses, commanding officers and the dead man's comrades often wrote letters that beat the official notification by a day or two. Men often made pacts with their fellow soldiers that they would send information to their families should one of them meet their death. In September 1917, Annie Allard received two letters in one day concerning her husband George, who was also fighting at Passchendaele.

> When I opened one … it said, dear Mrs Allard, it's a very sad heart that I write these few lines. Prior going into action your husband and I made a pact if anything happened to either of us, you know, one was left, we'd acquaint the next – I didn't read any more. I – I guessed what was coming.[2]

The other letter was from George Allard's commanding officer, confirming his death.

Officers' wives too sometimes heard of their husbands' deaths in a letter from a comrade rather than a telegram from the War Office. Captain Michael Heenan's wife, Lorna, received a letter from his fellow officer, Captain Gillson, to inform her that her husband had been killed by a sniper. The writer's intention was to beat the War Office notification as 'it may perhaps lessen the shock to hear the news from a private source before the official notification is received.'[3]

The crossover of telegrams and private letters often gave a false picture of an officer's condition. Eve Hammond's husband Percy, an officer in the Royal Artillery, had been sent to Italy in 1918, three weeks after their wedding. This posting pleased Eve as the battle in Italy appeared less intense than on the Western Front, but when heavy fighting was reported in the early summer, Eve was worried. However, having received two letters from Percy in the post that morning she was satisfied that he was safe for the time being. When she returned home from work to the house where she lived with her mother and father, the presence of the local vicar and the absence of any prepared meal immediately alerted her to some calamity. The telegram boy had visited that afternoon with official notification that Percy had been killed in action. Eve fainted on hearing the news. Heartbreakingly, at that moment, Percy Hammond's own mother visited her daughter-in-law with a late wedding present for the couple. Eve's mother had to tell Mrs Hammond that her son was dead.[4]

Sometimes the communication from the War Office was to inform families that their men had been wounded, potentially giving a wife the opportunity to visit her husband. Edith Fowler's husband George was badly wounded in December 1917 and evacuated to St George's Hospital in London. A letter to Edith dated 15 December from the nursing sister on George's ward said that he was suffering from tetanus and would like to see her. The sister said that a railway pass could be arranged for her to come to London from the mining village of Normanton in Yorkshire. She described George Fowler as 'so plucky and very bright'[5] and ended her letter by advising Edith not to worry too much about him. Alarm bells should have rung with the nurse's suggestion that Edith should not wait for the railway pass to arrive but pay her own way and seek reimbursement later. At 10.32 on 17 December, Edith received a telegram informing her that George was dangerously ill. She was told that if she did not have enough money to travel to London, she should take the telegram to the nearest police station, where arrangements would be made for her. Two hours later, she received a further telegram to report that it was too late and George had died.

Some wives made long trips to see their dying husbands, travelling all the way to France. The YMCA ran a scheme in conjunction with the War Office whereby the families of those wounded men who were dangerously ill would be invited to visit, if it were safe to do so. The War Office would pay for their travel if they were of limited means, and the YMCA would accommodate them free of charge in hostels close to the hospital where the injured man lay. As many as 150 visitors a day would take part in these trips. Those travelling great distances sometimes arrived too late but were able to see the grave in which their relative was buried. Some were at the bedside when the man died and could actually take part in the funeral.

Notification of death from the War Office gave no detail about the circumstances. This left an aching void for many women who were desperate for any kind of information about their husband. Not satisfied with the letters she had received, Annie Allard started her own enquiries about the fate of her husband. She advertised for months in the *Territorial Gazette*, hoping that one of her husband's comrades could give her further information. Her questions were answered by a man who had been in a military hospital after sustaining injuries in the battle that killed George Allard. He was able to tell her that he had been the last person to see George, who had then been killed outright by a shell.[6]

Letters from commanding officers and others informing women of the death of their husbands were often formulaic, stating that he had been a brave soldier and that his death was painless and instantaneous, whether this was true or not. One shot in the head from a sniper's bullet seems to have been regarded as a 'good death' from the point of view of comforting a family. Those widows who dug a little deeper often found that the reality was very different. Given the endless number of horrendous and painful ways a man could meet his death in the trenches, the likelihood of a clean, neat demise was slim. When Captain Harold Ackroyd was killed in August 1917, his wife Mabel received a letter from his servant, Private Scriven, explaining the circumstances of his death. Scriven wrote that his captain had received a sniper's bullet in the head and was killed instantly, not speaking a word after the fatal shot. After further correspondence with Scriven, Mabel discovered that his version of her husband's death was supposition at best. Scriven admitted that he was not actually with the captain at the time of his death and found his body in a shell hole along with six other casualties.[7]

Not satisfied with the 'sniper's bullet' explanation she was initially given, Lorna Heenan made more enquiries of her husband's superior officer. She received a letter from the Roman Catholic chaplain who officiated at Captain Heenan's funeral. The chaplain told her that Michael was hit in the stomach while inspecting barbed wire and took ten minutes to die. A stomach wound meant a very different experience than a clean shot to the head and was particularly feared amongst combatants. Lorna Heenan may have been better prepared than some widows to bear these details, as Michael was a career soldier who had served in the South African War and had already been badly wounded once in France.

On the death of Captain William T. Dickson of the Inniskilling Fusiliers at a casualty clearing station at Beauval on the Somme, the battalion padre wrote an unusually graphic though sentimental account of his demise to his family back home in Dungannon. Reared in the blood and thunder of Ulster Protestant preaching, Thomas Sinclair, who was also a family friend, did not spare the gore. He explained that Dickson had required the amputation of his leg after arriving at the hospital, having spent the previous six hours bleeding profusely. His other leg also needed to be removed, but he was too weak to survive a further operation. Though the letter was addressed to Dickson's mother, it seems to have been meant for the whole family, including his widow, Elsie, as the writer then gave details of the man's final words:

> He clasped a miniature photo of his wife to the last breath – kissed it and begged that it should be buried with him, which will be done. He answered when I asked him for a message for his wife 'Elsie! God bless her. I hope to meet her in another world.' These were the last words he uttered, and just as the evening Church bells of Beaumont began to toll close by he died.[8]

Any kind of detail brought some comfort and a sense of closure to widows. Ethel Booth's mother, Eliza, had been notified that her husband Norman was missing in November 1916. She was pregnant with her fourth child at the time, and her eldest daughter describes her grief as almost uncontrollable: 'She went on weeping, nearly all of the time.'[9] When the baby, Norah, was born in April 1917, she had an eye condition, which required the application of special drops every fifteen minutes. Baby Norah looked as though she had been constantly crying, and her mother was told by various people that this was due to her own relentless sobbing during the pregnancy. The local vicar helped the family by writing to the Red Cross to see if any further news could be found about Norman Booth's fate. Eventually a letter was received from a former policeman from Huddersfield who had been serving with the same regiment. He said that he had seen Norman put into an ambulance, which had never arrived at the hospital; the presumption being was that it was blown up en route. Despite the lack of absolute clarity as to what had happened, Ethel Booth recalls that the information satisfied her mother and enabled her to move on from her extreme grief.

The British Red Cross started to undertake the task of tracing missing men, sending volunteers into hospitals in London to make enquiries with the wounded.

This aspect of the organization's work increased dramatically as the war went on, with branches established across Europe. With so many men unaccounted for, it is hardly surprising that many widows refused to accept that their husbands were dead. In September 1916, Annie Blackburn received notification that her husband Ernest was missing. Annie was pregnant with her second son, and gave birth prematurely at the shock of this news. The whole extended family started to make enquiries with a variety of agencies, including the Red Cross and the lesser known Queen Victoria Jubilee Fund Association, an unofficial body based in Switzerland that compiled and circulated lists and photographs of the missing amongst prisoners of war in Germany. Ernest Blackburn was included on one of the Jubilee Fund's lists circulated in 1916. Annie also placed notices in the local newspapers, hoping to attract the attention of a fellow soldier on leave or wounded who might have seen him:

> Rifleman Ernest Blackburn, formerly a teacher at the Upper Wortley Council School, is reported missing since September 16th. His wife would be grateful for any news sent to her at 7 Moorfield Avenue, Armley.[10]

Notices like this appeared in the newspapers on a daily basis throughout the war, especially after a major battle when casualties and numbers of missing men soared. The Blackburn family clung to the hope that Ernest may have been taken prisoner rather than killed. This hope burned strongly in the hearts of many women, however unlikely this scenario may have been. Reports did occasionally appear in the newspapers of men believed to be dead who were actually prisoners and had managed to convey messages to their grieving relatives months after their capture. The hope for the Blackburn family was extinguished seven months later, when the same newspapers in which Annie had appealed for information reported that Rifleman Ernest Blackburn was dead.

The announcement caught the attention of Lily Davies, of Scarborough. Lily's husband Harold had served in the same company as Ernest and had been reported missing at the same time. Lily had heard no further news of him and, having now read of Ernest's death, was desperate to know what information Annie had received, and if any proof had been provided to her. 'The suspense is becoming more than I can bear,'[11] she wrote. Lily too clung to the hope that Harold Davies may be a prisoner of war somewhere, believing that many men would eventually return home: 'Even if we have to wait until the war is over I feel a great number will return who have been reported lost.'[12]

Kate Newbert was told that her husband, Sergeant Fred Newbert, was missing, believed killed, in April 1918. Anxious for any news of Fred, she would go to meet as many boats as possible arriving at Hull docks to quiz returning prisoners of war for information. None of the soldiers she met could tell her anything about her husband. She eventually abandoned hope that Fred would come home and remarried in 1923.[13]

Families were undoubtedly encouraged in their hope that a missing loved one was a prisoner of war rather than a casualty by the form that was sent out by the army on the report that a soldier was missing. Army form B 104-83 read as follows:

> I regret to have to inform you that a report has been received from the War Office to the effect that no [rank] [name] [regiment] was posted as 'missing' on the …
>
> The report that he is missing does not necessarily mean that he has been killed, as he may be a prisoner of war or temporarily separated from his regiment.
>
> Official reports that men are prisoners of war take some time to reach this country, and if he has been captured by the enemy it is probable that unofficial news will reach you first. In that case, I am to ask you to forward any letter received at once to this Office, and it will be returned to you as soon as possible.

The letter issued to wives of missing men twenty-six weeks after their disappearance, turning their separation allowance into a widow's pension, was equally ambiguous, stating that the change of payment 'must not be taken as indicating that there is any proof of the death of your husband'. Not only did this encourage families to believe the prisoner of war dream, but it also encouraged them to seek information through 'unofficial' channels, leaving them open to misinformation and fraudsters.[14]

Sometimes the information received from agencies looking for a soldier was innocently incorrect. David Harkness Blakey was one of the thousands of British troops who went missing on the first day of the Battle of the Somme. Blakey, a miner from County Durham, also played rugby league professionally with Leeds, though the war meant that career was a short one. Sergeant Blakey was with the Inniskilling Fusiliers at Thiepval the last time he was seen alive. His wife Sally sought help from the Lord Mayor's War Information Office in Newcastle, a branch of the local war relief fund that liaised between families and official agencies to find missing men. The War Information Office wrote to her in November 1917 with the first eyewitness account of what had happened to 'Davy'. Sally was informed that a fellow soldier had reported seeing Sergeant Blakey hit by a bullet but did not know his condition. This still left the possibility that he had been wounded, not killed.

In February 1917, a further letter was sent with some information from a wounded soldier at Beckett Park Military Hospital in Leeds saying that 'Harkness' was dead. Ten days later, the War Information Office wrote to Sally again, apologizing that they had been given incorrect information – the casualty referred to was not her husband. 'I regret to think that you have been distressed by the intelligence and am afraid it was a mistake of the British Red Cross Society.'[15] At the end of March 1917, official notification was received that David Harkness Blakey was dead, though his body was not recovered.

The widow of Private George Webb had the traumatic experience of seeing her husband turn up alive at his own funeral. When a private by that name died of a disease while training in Glasgow in March 1915, a letter was sent to Mrs Webb in Maidstone to give her the sad news. The whole family travelled north for the funeral, borrowing money against the man's insurance policy on the strength of the letter from the War Office. Dressed in mourning clothes, they attended the Glasgow Necropolis to see their soldier buried with full military honours. As the graveside firing party were about to discharge their weapons, George Webb's mother-in-law saw him stood amongst the mourners. The 'George Webb' being buried was a different man entirely, though of the same age and with an army number just one digit apart.[16]

Like Lily Davies and Annie Blackburn, the bereaved did sometimes write to each other to share information and consolation on the death of their loved ones. In 1915, one bereaved mother, Catherine Meade, received a detailed sketch of the small cemetery at Gully Beach in Gallipoli showing the graves of her son, Second Lieutenant Richard Meade, and a colleague from the 14th Sikh Regiment. Looking at the sketch, Mrs Meade – a widow herself – noticed the grave of a private of the Manchester Regiment situated between the two officers' plots. She traced the relatives of the dead private to share the sketch with them. Thomas Barton was the soldier concerned, a tram driver from Manchester with a wife and four sons, one just a month old at the time of his death. Mrs Meade wrote to Mary Ann Barton:

> I thought you would be glad to know that your husband is resting between two good, brave Englishmen and that the ground has been railed in and consecrated. … Trusting that the little sketch may be a little comfort to you in your sad loss and that God may sustain and help you in your grief and loneliness.[17]

A correspondence then ensued, with Mary Ann Barton sending photographs of her husband and children to Catherine Meade, and a promise made in return to send a photograph of the gravesite should one become available. The social status of the two women was very different – Catherine Meade was the widow of a high ranking officer in the Indian army – yet their suffering brought them together on some level, at least temporarily.[18]

Once a death was confirmed, widows were anxious to retrieve their husbands' personal belongings. This need for some piece of the dead man was understood by comrades, who would sometimes send back small items themselves rather than follow the official procedure. Private Scriven, servant to Captain Harold Ackroyd, cut the buttons from his master's uniform and sent them home to his widow.

Personal effects were not infrequently missing from a body, having been stolen by the enemy before the casualty could be brought behind British lines, or taken by fellow British soldiers. The ordinary Tommy harboured suspicions about the activities of certain members of the Royal Army Medical Corps to the extent that it was said by some that RAMC stood for 'Rob All My Comrades'. For many casualties there was nothing to send home as the body was either completely destroyed or never found. Mary Ann Lamb's husband Joseph was with a tunnelling company in Givenchy in February 1916 when counter mining by German sappers buried him and two comrades under tons of soil and rubble. There was no chance of recovering the bodies or any personal effects in such circumstances. No details of her husband's death appear to have been given to his widow, as she wrote to the War Office several times over the next few years in an attempt to retrieve Joseph's personal effects. In February 1917 she wrote, 'I haven't received any of his belongings, yet it will be a year on 10th Feb [since Joseph's death].' Enquiries were still being made in 1919, when an army form was finally scrawled with the words 'No effects'.[19] All the family had left of Joseph Lamb was a photograph he sent home from a studio on the south coast before he embarked for France.

Items that did make their way home were sometimes too close a reminder of the daily horrors of the Western Front. Annie Allard was disturbed by what she received on the death of her beloved George.

> Do you know what they sent me back? The last letters I had and a piece of heather and some money I'd sent out to him, a registered letter, my photograph and all that, absolutely congealed blood. Together. They sent me that ... .[20]

Wilfrid Cove's wife Ethel was sent the photographs and drawings her husband had with him on his death. Wilfrid had been killed by a shell landing on his billet, and the items she received reflected that end, being significantly charred.

Personal items assumed the status of religious relics in some households. Many homes reserved pride of place for a memento of the departed husband in the form of a photograph, postcard or letter. When the war was over and death plaques and campaign medals were sent out to the families of deceased servicemen, these too would often be on display in a widow's house. Equally, many a widow would hide such things away, unable to withstand visual reminders of her husband's death, or having remarried, feeling that such a display was inappropriate.

For some women the grief was too much to bear: 'I cannot live without Cecil, the world is empty' were the words left on a suicide note by Sybil Griffin, widow of an officer attached to the Royal Flying Corps, who shot herself in November 1917. Cecil was killed in a flying accident in Surrey a month earlier. His young wife had a mental breakdown on his death and was only able to attend his funeral in the company of two nurses. Having been out shopping with her mother, Sybil had suddenly excused herself and returned to her fashionable London address, just off Eaton Square. Shortly thereafter, Sybil was discovered in the smoking room of the house, mortally wounded. The inquest jury returned a verdict of suicide while of unsound mind.[21]

Where a man had earned a posthumous medal for valour, more robust widows had value to the state as propaganda tools. A public presentation of the medal was made to the widow with reports in the newspapers and, sometimes, newsreel footage of the ceremony shown in cinemas nationwide. A presentation by the King, the symbolic head of the nation, linked the national struggle to its smallest combatants and served as a reminder that the whole nation was working as one to defeat the enemy. The stoic widow became a national symbol of steadfastness in the face of tragedy. Captain Harold Ackroyd had been awarded the Victoria Cross for his actions in a battle a few days before his death in August 1917. Mabel Ackroyd and her eldest son, Stephen, received Harold's medals from the King at Buckingham Palace. Five-year-old Stephen was dressed in a sailor suit with a black armband, whilst his mother was in full mourning dress. Corporal James Llewellyn Davies won a posthumous Victoria Cross at Polygon Wood with the Royal Welsh Fusiliers and his wife Elizabeth was presented with the medal at Buckingham Palace in October 1917. Both of these ceremonies were captured on camera.[22]

For lesser medals, the method of investiture seemed to depend on geographic location and rank. Second Lieutenant Albert Beasley's wife Caroline and his son Peter received his Military Medal from the King and Queen when the Royal couple visited the war hospital in Reading in 1918.[23] Sergeant David Harkness Blakey's son Harry received his father's Military Medal at the Gem Picture Hall in Winlaton, County Durham from the head of the local Welcome Home Committee. No cameras were there to record the ceremony. If the deceased serviceman had children, sons were the preferred companion to his widow and, like little Harry

Blakey, were sometimes the actual recipients of the medals. Upon the men of Britain lay the heavy responsibility of defending the nation, and the passing on of the medal signified the transfer of that responsibility to the next generation.

The scale and type of casualties during the First World War necessitated new attitudes to mourning rituals and a break with Victorian funeral traditions. A death in the family was an important event in Victorian England. Funerals were ever more lavish with a great deal of expense being incurred by the bereaved, whether they could afford it or not. Societal rules applied to regulate the behaviour of all mourners, but especially that of widows.

Victorian convention stipulated that a wife was in mourning for two and a half years after her husband's death. She was in full mourning for a year and a day, second mourning for nine months, ordinary mourning for three months and then 'half mourning' for another six months after that. The various stages were denoted by her clothing, moving from heavy crape in the first period through different stages to clothes in half mourning colours – greys, muted lilacs etc. – for the last phase. Two years was felt to be the minimum period of time a widow must spend alone before contemplating remarriage.[24] Of course, these rules could only apply where there was money to pay for this extravagant costume. Working-class women had to modify their mode of dress accordingly. They could not afford to drape themselves in crape and bombazine and wear jet jewellery. It was still a source of pride that a working-class woman could dress in some mourning finery regardless of the detriment to other aspects of the family budget.

An editorial in *The Times* on 31 August 1914 was already questioning whether traditional forms of mourning dress were appropriate in these unique times.[25] Different methods of denoting grief were discussed, including the wearing of coloured armbands. Members of the aristocracy had given the lead, the Duchess of Devonshire pronouncing that if she were bereaved she would not be wearing mourning dress but a white armband instead.[26] *The Times* commented that this stratum of society would set the tone for the lower classes to follow.

The article set off a debate in the pages of the paper as to what should be the appropriate public display to denote that one had lost a family member in the war. Some were concerned that if mourning dress were abandoned, those who were employed in that industry would lose their jobs. It was suggested that black clothing should be donated to poorer families so they could show their grief without bankrupting themselves in the process. Miss Henderson, a Red Cross worker from Sutton Coldfield, wrote:

> The average rich person has not the slightest idea of the immense impor-
> tance that working women attach to mourning. They will even starve

themselves and their children to obtain money for its purchase. To urge them at such a time to dispense with mourning is to add a sting to the terrors of death.[27]

Newspapers across the country carried similar letters, whilst also carrying advertisements for purveyors of mourning dress of all kinds, some of which announced special offers in light of the current crisis. The effect on the national morale of seeing thousands of women dressed in black walking the streets was a significant consideration. One correspondent referred to the universal mourning that was bound to take place during the war as having 'an enervating effect at a time when this will be disastrous'.[28] Unrestrained displays of grief were no longer fashionable or desirable. Soldiers' wills were reported as stipulating that no mourning should take place for their deaths. On a national level excessive displays of mourning would give the enemy a propaganda boost if reported, and could also act as support to those at home who wanted to end the war. On the other side of the conflict, strictures on mourning dress had been suggested in both Germany and Austria for the same reasons.[29] The Tatler in November 1914 made reference to widows of new soldiers being accused of cowardice if they showed their grief.[30] Eve Hammond recalls going to church the day she was told of her husband's death and breaking down, much to the consternation of the rest of the congregation.[31] Reminders of their own losses, or the thought that loved ones still serving may also make the final sacrifice, were too raw for people to process comfortably.

In January 1915, The Tatler's fashion column was still prescribing rules for mourning dress: 'It is now universally acknowledged that it is a mark of respect that must be paid to those near and dear to us who have given up their lives to save our country from German Kultur.'[32]

The magazine pronounced that a widow should wear crape-trimmed dresses for at least eighteen months, and a crape-edged veil over the face for the first six months.[33] The Royal Family continued to follow pre-war practices, ordering that the Court wear full mourning for the requisite number of weeks on the death of distant royals, for example, that of the King of Romania in October 1914. Geoffrey Gorer's mother was the widow of a wealthy antiques dealer who had died in the Lusitania tragedy of May 1915. Gorer himself was at boarding school at the time and was given black ties to wear and crape bands for the arms of his suits, which he found comforting. His mother was 'almost a frightening figure in the full panoply of widow's weeds and unrestrained black'.[34] Gorer said that a woman of her class had no choice but to follow this convention. By June 1916, things had changed. The Tatler, referring to the smart upper classes, said: 'The war widows wear their weeds very lightly; crape isn't done at all, black chiffon being the very heaviest black permissible, and that, as everyone knows, needn't look the least bit mourning-y.'[35]

At the other end of the social scale, Patrick McVeigh's mother wore mourning dress for five years after his father's death in 1931.[36] The McVeigh family were living in the village of Longniddry in East Lothian in a 'colony' of houses built by the Earl Haig Fund for wounded soldiers and their families. Perhaps there was more social pressure to mark the death of the ex-serviceman husband in such an environment as Ella McVeigh wore her widow's weeds until the family moved to Edinburgh in 1936.

Mourning dress continued to be worn to some degree throughout the war and beyond. Some bereaved relatives were reported to be wearing very dark blue garments rather than black, but the armband idea promoted by the aristocratic ladies on the outbreak of war never really gained popularity. In some respect the wearing of mourning dress was the only ritual a widow had left from pre-war times.

The status attached to wearing good mourning clothes before the war also applied to the funeral, it being very important that the dead man was given a 'good send-off'. Lady Bell wrote of a woman proudly announcing of her husband's funeral that she had 'buried him with ham'.[37] She described a funeral as one of the main social opportunities in the working-class community. By the end of the nineteenth century, the upper and middle classes had started to tone down the funereal excesses. However, a number of commentators have remarked on how things that became unfashionable amongst the upper echelons of society took longer to go out of style further down the economic ladder.[38] The extravagant funeral for a working-class man had an aspirational dimension to it.

Most working-class families paid into what was known as a burial club – a scheme that promised to pay the costs of a funeral in return for a small weekly payment. Burial clubs were sometimes criticized by those higher up the social scale, who believed that the working-class woman would be better off spending the money elsewhere.[39] The spectre of a pauper's funeral was overwhelmingly shameful and any provision that could be made to avoid such a calamity would be taken. The 1911 census for the mining village of Trimdon Colliery recorded three insurance agents in a community with only 350 households. The weekly visit from the insurance man to collect his subscription would remain a feature of working-class life for many years. Insurance companies were making such large profits from these communities that they lobbied the government extensively during the debates on the introduction of National Insurance in 1911 to ensure that widows and orphans were excluded from the scheme.

The lack of a funeral would be the most immediate break with tradition for a First World War widow. Unless a soldier died in Britain, any funeral ceremony would be held in the arena of war in which he was killed, with no time for elaborate preparations and no family attendance. In many cases there would be nothing to bury as men simply disappeared. These widows would not even have the comfort of an individual grave for their man, but simply a name on one of the great monoliths like the Menin Gate. Sometimes bodies initially recovered and buried were later lost as the battle lines moved backwards and forwards. This was another difficult concept for a widow to grasp, having been told there was a grave and then discovering that it no longer existed. Annie Allard was told that her husband was buried and talked of having to pay out a guinea for a burial blanket, which still rankled with her many years later. 'He was never buried. And then – they said he was buried, then they said the graves were blown up. And his name – his name was on the Menin Gate.'[40]

The descendants of women like Annie Allard sometimes did receive closure from the recovery of a loved one's remains. Bodies were being discovered in significant numbers years after the Armistice, sometimes by specially designated units and sometimes by civilians, often French and Belgian farmers. Like George Allard, Private Herbert Allcock's body had originally been recovered from the battlefield after his death in October 1914, and his personal effects returned to his wife, Ethel, in Leeds. During the course of the war, the small cemetery at Beaucamps-Ligny where Herbert and some of his comrades had been buried was destroyed by shellfire and the graves lost. In 2009, drainage work on the site exposed the bodies of fifteen soldiers from the Yorks and Lancs Regiment, including Herbert Allcock. One hundred years after their deaths, DNA technology was used to find out the names of eleven of these casualties. Six of the eleven soldiers had left widows behind them in England.[41]

The renewed interest in the First World War occasioned by the centenary of its start prompted the Commonwealth War Graves Commission to embark on a series of renovations in anticipation of the greater number of visitors to the former Western Front. When the road leading to the visitor centre at Thiepval was widened, excavations revealed a number of bodies, which had lain undisturbed for almost a century. One of them belonged to David Harkness Blakey, identifiable by a home-made metal disc with his details engraved upon it. His wife and children were long dead, but other relatives were traced, including his granddaughter, Helen, and great-granddaughter, Jackie. On 8 October 1914, Blakey was buried with full military honours at Connaught Cemetery in front of his surviving relatives.

Individual regiments periodically arranged memorial services for batches of casualties from their battalions, especially if the regiment had recently been involved in heavy action. The 16th Lancers, for example, held a memorial service at St Peter's Church in London in March 1915. The battalion had lost fifteen men in the explosion of a German mine under their trench on 21 February 1915. It is worth noting that the bodies of the officers killed were recovered, whilst those ordinary ranks killed are remembered only on the Menin Gate.

Peter Green, Rector of St Philips in Salford and Residentiary Canon of Manchester, had a regular newspaper column in which he discussed matters of Church doctrine and policy under the nom de plume 'Artifex'. After attending a memorial service at Manchester Cathedral in July 1915 for two battalions of the Manchester Regiment, he wrote about the importance of a funeral to the relatives of a soldier, even if they could not actually place their loved one's body in a grave. Artifex noted: 'It is impossible to visit the relations in such cases without seeing how much they miss the funeral service, and the opportunity of offering some last tribute of love and of respect for the lost husband, brother, or son.'[42]

Some families still had a church service for a loved one, either a special memorial service or a mention in an already crowded service of remembrance in the local church. When Captain William T. Dickson died in July 1916, there was a memorial service at the First Dungannon Presbyterian Church, where William and his family were prominent members of the congregation. Such services were more common for the middle and upper-class soldier than for the ordinary working man – William Dickson was the son of an MP and wealthy linen manufacturer in Dungannon.

Funeral customs revolved around the body itself in the late nineteenth and early twentieth centuries. Cremation was not yet a widespread practice, and indeed, was actively opposed by some religious doctrines. The body was central to funeral rites, especially amongst working-class communities. This persisted well beyond the First World War, with a number of studies of mourning rituals showing the importance of the body well into the late twentieth century. For example, Peter Marris studied a sample of widows in Bethnal Green in the 1950s, finding that burial rites were an important part of the grieving process. He said that the laying out of the corpse and other tasks eased the shock of the loss and helped maintain a link with the deceased.[43] The widows in his study were not war widows, but having all lost their husbands unexpectedly in youth or middle age, had something in common with them. Geoffrey Gorer's 1969 study noted that presence at the deathbed of the family member was much more prevalent amongst the working classes. In addition, 'paying respects' by visiting the body after death was still something undertaken by many working-class mourners.[44] Writing about the North Yorkshire fishing village of Staithes in the 1970s, David Clark found that a number of established funeral practices from the nineteenth century and earlier were still going strong.[45] The resilience of these traditions amongst the working classes speaks of their importance to both the immediate family and the wider community.

For First World War widows there was nothing to be done for the dead other than to mourn their passing. They would never see the corpse of their husband, or in many cases even know the full circumstances of his death. They would be deprived of the funeral and all of the rituals involving other members of the community that went alongside it, especially in working-class areas.

It is not only the lack of a funeral that would have deprived widows of those killed on active service of comfort, but also the lack of a gravestone. A focal point for the expression of grief and respect for a loved one was important. Gorer found that a lot of ritual connected with the gravestone of the deceased remained important in the late 1960s. He described the members of his sample study who had opted for a burial visiting the grave very regularly and tending the plot or leaving flowers. This, of course, is the reason why many families bereaved by a death abroad opted to have a commemoration of their loved one inscribed on a family grave in their hometown. In practical terms it was impossible for the vast majority of widows to visit their husband's actual grave in whichever theatre of war he fell.

The importance to a widow of her husband's last resting place was understood by those with whom he served, and comrades would often write to reassure the widow on the circumstances of his burial. Wilfrid Cove's wife received a letter from her husband's commanding officer telling her of the ceremony that took place in the village of Vlamertinghe:

> The funeral was attended by all men in the battery who were able to be there. The body was wrapped in the Union Jack and received all honours due to the heroic death. ... I am having a special cross put up on the grave and flowers planted on it.[46]

In relation to Captain Michael Heenan, his colleague Second Lieutenant Manning wrote to his wife that her husband was buried in 'as pretty a little spot as you can imagine'. Manning told Lorna Heenan, 'His grave is where it should be, amongst soldiers like himself who have given their lives for all that is so well worth fighting for.'[47]

Lieutenant Manning's view was not shared by every bereaved family back in Britain. The announcement that British war dead would remain buried in the country where they fell caused a great deal of controversy. The practicalities involved in repatriating so many men would have been daunting, and for large numbers of families there would have been no body to bring home. The American government's decision to allow families the choice of having their loved ones repatriated stoked the flames of debate in Britain. Seventy per cent of bereaved American families chose to have their relative's body returned to US soil. Canada also allowed the repatriation of bodies, but only if the soldier was buried in Britain.[48] If American and Canadian soldiers could be taken all the way across the Atlantic, why could not a British soldier travel the short distance across the Channel? An organization called the British War Graves Association was founded in 1919 to pressurise the government into changing their policy and bringing the bodies back home for burial. Largely composed of bereaved parents, the association wrote letters to MPs and newspapers on a regular basis setting out their arguments. The Imperial War Graves Commission (IWGC) was now consolidating scattered burials and the association felt it was a small step to bring those bodies back to England rather than taking them to a new cemetery in France or Belgium. The association believed that British war graves abroad would not be respected or properly cared for. The pristine condition of all Commonwealth War Graves Commission cemeteries on the former battlefields today is quite different from the nightmare vision presented by the British War Graves Association.[49]

Widows were urged to think of the greater good in this time of national emergency and not give in to grief. The fact that many women had lost their husbands was seen in the press as somehow making the loss easier to bear. The *Leeds Mercury* declared in 1919, 'When the loss has been universal, the bereaved woman is better able to face the future with spirit.'[50] Following the Battle of Jutland in June 1916, *The Times* reported that the estimated 2,000 widows were 'bearing their loss stoically. Mourning is tempered by pride in the lost one's gallant end.'[51] The bravery and reserve of British women was favourably contrasted with the behaviour of those in Germany. A correspondent from Hamburg reported in the early months of the war that, 'Unlike Englishwomen they [the bereaved] do not restrain their grief in public. They weep as they walk along the streets. It is very distressing.'[52]

Those who were not able to 'bear up' felt themselves that they were letting the side down in some way. Lily Davies, who had no children, felt she had no right to give in to worry when she learnt of Annie Blackburn's situation: 'When I read your letter Mrs Blackburn I felt a real coward as your case is so very much harder than mine.'[53]

Women were encouraged to think of their men as martyrs for the British cause. Queen Mary herself issued a special New Year's message to women, especially the bereaved, in January 1915. The Queen exhorted women to bear their sacrifice with 'patience and fortitude' and to be consoled by the fact that 'those who are near and dear to you have died like heroes for their King and country.'[54] The message was not always taken to heart. Lily Davies spoke for many widows when she wrote, 'We are told to believe that everything is done for the best, but it's hard to think so at the time when we women have to take blows like these.'[55]

The pressure to put on a brave face for the sake of the nation, either in abandoning mourning dress or not showing outward signs of grief, must have been considerable. Eliza Booth was told – and appeared to believe – that it was her fault that her infant daughter had an eye condition. The ideal widow was the plucky recipient of a brave husband's medal, not the eternally weeping woman who made others feel uncomfortable. A piece of doggerel that appeared regularly in the in memoriam columns of newspapers all over the country summed up the attitude to mourning to be encouraged during the war:

> *I mourn for you, dear husband,*
> *But not with outward show,*
> *For the heart that mourns sincerely*
> *Mourns silently, and low.*

Chapter 3

Working Widows

'Friends rallied round ... I went out to work ...'

The loss of the chief breadwinner had long been recognized as a crucial event that could drag a family below the poverty line. The pre-war studies already referred to all showed that working-class families were mostly one illness or accident away from penury. For many families the death of a husband in the First World War would be that calamitous event.

Women were forced to economize from the moment their man donned the uniform. Separation allowances in many cases did not meet the level of income earned by the man in civilian life. Some women immediately gave up their homes, moving in with relatives or to smaller accommodation to try to keep a roof over their heads. Margaret Forster had given up her job in the local paper mill when she married in 1912.[1] When her husband joined up in August 1914, her separation allowance only amounted to 12s 6d per week, considerably less than her man's wage as a miner. It was impossible for Margaret to maintain her own household on this amount, so she moved back in with her parents. Edith Fowler moved in with her in-laws in Normanton once her husband George had joined the army, partly to take advantage of free childcare by her mother-in-law so she could go out to work.[2]

This trend added to the difficulty of overcrowding, which had been endemic in working-class housing without the pressures of war. Miner Joseph Lamb, his wife and three children lived in one room in their house in Trimdon Colliery, County Durham in 1911, and were by no means the most pressed for space in the village. Lady Bell reported that around a third of the small households in her study of ironworkers and their families in Middlesbrough in 1907 were taking in lodgers, earning a wife two or three shillings' profit a week.[3] The hard decisions forced upon women by the inadequacy of state provision once their men had joined up made this problem worse. William Angus, Acting Medical Officer for Leeds, noted in 1915, 'Overcrowding has arisen in some cases from the soldier's wife and children going to live with parents, and giving up the home till the husband returns.'[4] There were suggestions that women were being urged to give up their homes by members of agencies to which they applied for financial help. In Bradford at the outbreak of war, the Lord Mayor organized a Ladies' Visiting

Committee to help evaluate and alleviate economic distress. Reports came back to Mrs Annie Hoffman, chairwoman of the committee, that some of her lady visitors were advising applicants for relief to sell their furniture and go into smaller houses, and in some cases into lodging houses. Mrs Hoffman, whilst doubting the rumours were true, gave her ladies a gentle reminder that they were to continue 'doing all in their power to carry out the wishes of the committee to enable applicants to keep their furniture and homes together'.[5] The Bradford Ladies' Visiting Committee included the wives of three former mayors of Bradford who were unlikely to ever experience such hardship themselves.

When the husband did not return, women who had given up their homes were unlikely to be able to afford to run their own household again. Pension payments were deliberately set at a lesser level than separation allowances, as a widow was expected to make economies and potentially move to smaller accommodation. One widow noted in a sample provided to the Select Committee on Pensions by the Liverpool branch of the SSFA in 1915 had been accustomed to spending 12s 6d a week on rent for the eight-room house in which the family lived when her husband was alive.[6] This was the exact amount of the basic pension she would now receive for herself and her child. It is impossible to see how this woman could possibly remain in this superior accommodation now her husband was dead. In many cases moving to a smaller house was simply not a practical solution. For some it was impossible to downsize any further. At the other end of the SSFA's scale in Liverpool was a widow with three children living in two rented rooms in a sublet house in a 'low neighbourhood' for two shillings a week rent. Housing shortages made things worse and it was well known that widows with children were not attractive tenants to most landlords. The amalgamation of households sometimes concentrated tragedy, particularly in naval towns where a disaster for one ship could devastate a whole community. The first casualties of the war were at sea, not on land, and the sinking of HMS *Amphion* on 6 August 1914 left 130 families mourning. Newspapers reported at the end of the month that there was a house in Golden Lion Lane in Harwich where there were now three war widows.[7]

Keeping a house of their own was a struggle for many widows. Some tried to make ends meet by taking in lodgers, adding to the overcrowding problem. For those in receipt of a war widow's pension, the presence of lodgers in the house would potentially cause problems with the Ministry should rumours reach them that there was a closer relationship with the 'lodger' than the widow acknowledged. The forfeiture files, as we shall see later, are full of cases of women taking in lodgers, whether they were legitimate or not. The location of the McVeigh family home near a newly constructed golf course gave Ella McVeigh the chance to make extra money on short lets to caddies and sometimes whole families wanting a seaside break. The McVeigh children would cram themselves into the rest of the house when the paying guests arrived.[8]

Once the war was over, some companies previously lauded for allowing wives to continue to occupy workplace houses when their men enlisted quickly backtracked on this promise. There were strong rumours that some mining companies had been engaged in this practice during the war itself, asking soldiers' widows to leave their houses so that more workers could be accommodated. It seemed that the patriotic promises made at the outbreak of the war had been quickly forgotten. In some colliery villages after the war, widows were allowed to remain living in the properties rent free, whilst elsewhere nominal rents were charged. However, it was common for a landlord to cease to maintain the property in these circumstances. Other house owners were not so generous and were anxious to have property returned to them so that more workers could be accommodated. If widows did not vacate the properties voluntarily, ejectment orders were sought from the local courts. The Morpeth magistrates came under fire from the local veterans' group for the regularity with which they issued eviction notices to war widows and former soldiers. The Ashington ex-servicemen's organizations went so far as to have a protest march through the town against the practice in August 1919.[9] Margaret Fife of Hetton in County Durham appeared before the courts to fight an eviction application in 1929. Margaret's husband William had been killed in action in 1917 and she had remained in the house after his death. The landlord claimed the house was in a terrible state. Margaret denied this and pointed out that the landlord had not carried out any repairs on the property since 1917. The court found for the landlord, provoking Margaret to say, 'Thank you gentlemen. That is what a soldier's widow gets.'[10]

The facilities in the average colliery house were far inferior to those of the new council houses that were now being built as a response to the housing shortage. War widows (along with ex-servicemen) were given priority on the council housing list in a number of areas. However, the rent for a council house was much more than the pit owners were charging war widows; in 1928, the average rent for a council house in County Durham was ten shillings a week, whereas a colliery house could be occupied for only two shillings a week. There was also no guarantee that the council house would be in an area in which the widow was prepared to live. Kinship links were vital in maintaining the family unit and it would be unattractive to the widow to have to move any distance from her friends and relatives.

In the first rush of patriotism, many employers had made provision for a proportion of a man's wages to be paid to his family on his enlistment in the services. Liverpool Corporation, the Post Office and a number of railway companies were cited as examples before the Select Committee on Pensions in 1915. Edward Hope, former Mayor of Manchester and owner of a brewing company, gave five shillings a week to the families of his men who enlisted, and estimated that around a quarter of employers in the city had made similar arrangements. Manchester Corporation were said to be paying a more generous figure of half an enlisted man's wages to his wife for the duration of the war. Leeds City Council operated the same arrangement; teacher Ernest Blackburn wrote to the local Board of Education checking that his wife would be entitled to half of his salary before registering under the Derby Scheme in 1915.[11] Payments to a widow from an employer on the death of her husband were often not generous and had conditions attached; the Post Office paid out a year's salary to the widows of employees killed in action, but only if the man had more than five years' service in their employ. Payments pledged to widows from smaller employers were sometimes not forthcoming due to a simple refusal to make good on the promise and sometimes because the firm no longer existed years after the outbreak of the war. Some companies made a distinction between men who had volunteered and those who had been conscripted, with the families of the latter being denied any payments either for subsistence during the man's service, or upon his death. The War Emergency Workers' National Committee warned the Select Committee on Pensions in 1915 that such contributions from employers could not be relied upon to support the wives of soldiers as it was 'an act of grace dictated by a sense of patriotism ... it is not and cannot be a general rule.'[12]

The payment of a war widow's pension did not remove the need to work. Margaret Forster, despite moving in with her parents, still could not live on her separation allowance, so applied for a job as a postwoman, earning around £1 a week. She then obtained employment at a munitions factory in Newcastle, where she worked filling shells with cordite. This work made her ill, so she left and took a job in the offices of an insurance company. She continued to work there after her husband's death in 1917 to make her contribution to the household finances.[13] Margaret was not unusual in taking a job when her husband enlisted; of 155 wives of men previously employed by Birmingham Tramways but now in the armed forces, only fifteen were still 'at home' in 1915. The others now worked in a range of industries from brass founding to shroud making.[14] The significant rise in the cost of living caused by the war undoubtedly hit hard in working-class communities, forcing these women back into the labour market. The Select Committee of 1915 heard that prices had risen from their pre-war levels by 25 per cent by January 1915.

Self-employed men were at something of a disadvantage as there was no employer to grant their wives an allowance once they were in the armed services. Their wives had to depend on separation allowances alone, and even if the man returned from the war unscathed, the business may not have survived. Wives of self-employed men sometimes tried to keep the business going in the hope that their husband would return after a short period and life would go back to normal. The situation was acknowledged by a number of trades associations; in 1918, the butchers of Leeds clubbed together and paid ten shillings a month each into a fund to support dependants of those in the trade who were called up and to reinstate in business those who came back. When Leonard Greenwood was conscripted in 1916, his wife Alice took on his greengrocer's business in Todmorden, going out with horse and cart to do his rounds. Wilfred Cove from Pinner was a bank clerk but also owned some houses, which he rented out. His wife Ethel looked after the rental business while he was away, writing to him about the tenants and repair work that needed doing on the properties. Mary Jane Savage assisted her husband Norman in his business as a dairyman in Leeds before the war, and once he was called up, ran the whole show herself. All three of these men were killed and it seems that Alice Greenwood and Ethel Cove relinquished their husbands' businesses at that stage. Alice remarried a fellow Methodist called Percy Sharratt in 1920, whilst Ethel Cove moved to Southend-on-Sea to be with her parents. Mary Jane Savage, however, carried on the dairy business, latterly with the assistance of her eldest son. The Savage name appeared in the trades directories of Leeds as milk dealers until the mid-1940s.

Some women had taken up war work partly to keep their minds occupied while their men were away. Patriotic literature described war work as 'the best antidote to worry'.[15] Work was an equally welcome distraction for widows in their grief. Margaret Forster threw herself into her work at the insurance office after the death of husband Will. As she remembered many years later, 'Friends rallied round ... I went to work.'[16]

Some employers had traditionally terminated a woman's contract once she married. The Civil Service had a 'marriage bar' into the 1930s, and teaching was another profession that was not always open to a married woman. Widowhood opened the possibility for a return to work. Gladys Lethem had left her teaching post in Leeds when she married John Lethem in 1916. As John was already serving in the Royal Field Artillery on the Western Front, the couple never set up home together, Gladys remaining with her parents. John Lethem was killed in December 1917, and in January 1918, Gladys returned to teaching. She reported to her family that she didn't find the first day as hard as she expected.[17]

The whole question of widows going out to work had been hotly debated throughout the war years and particularly afterwards, when men were returning to the labour market in great numbers and finding positions hard to secure. War widows' pensions were not designed to support a widow for life without the need for her to consider working. Prime Minister Herbert Asquith had himself expressed this view, saying during a Commons debate on the issue in November 1914, 'We all have to work.'[18]

Widows, however, were traditionally seen as an enemy in the workplace, not only because they would take the place of a man, but also because they were regarded as a danger to the living wage for everyone. The idea was that, because widows were already in receipt of money in the form of a pension, they would be prepared to take employment for lower wages, thereby distorting the labour market and lowering salaries for everyone. This myth was not new – it had appeared in the 1840s in debates about widows being given Poor Law relief, yet it still had currency in the popular imagination.[19] A number of the delegates giving evidence before the Select Committee on Pensions in 1915 supported the idea of widows being a disruptive element in the labour market. Robert Smillie, president of the Miners' Federation, felt that widows would be unfair competition and also that they would be taken advantage of by those employing sweated labour. This view was supported by others who gave evidence, including Dr Marion Phillips of the National Women's Labour League. A pension of £1 a week – ironically the title of Maud Pember Reeves' study of the amount required to keep an average family in Lambeth five years earlier – was felt by Smillie and other witnesses to be enough to keep widows at home. The recommendation of the Select Committee was that the rate for a basic widow's pension should be half of this amount, meaning it was inevitable that many women would have to work. Even this figure was higher than some wanted – the National Union of Women's Suffrage Societies (NUWSS) expressed the view that a childless widow should not be granted a pension at all. Though undoubtedly pursuing an agenda towards having women in the workplace as part of the drive for equality and, ultimately, the vote, the NUWSS used unfortunate language in their statement to the Select Committee, saying that a childless widow 'should not be shelved with a pension' because it would be 'demoralizing for her to become parasitic on the nation'.[20] The notion of the war widow as some kind of parasite is a particularly unattractive metaphor for an organization campaigning for women's rights to use.

Many widows, of course, did work during the war, being heavily involved in all areas of industry in support of the war effort, from shipbuilding to clerical work. After the death of her husband in March 1918, Rose Knight left rural Whissendine in Rutland to move to lodgings in Leicester and look for work. Rose managed to obtain employment in a factory operated by Mellor Bromley who, like many manufacturers, had turned their hand from peacetime production to munitions – the factory had previously made knitting machines. After the Armistice, when munitions work was no longer available, Rose was lucky enough to find a job at Pearson Brothers & Campbell, a shoe factory in Leicester. She then moved on to a similar position with Evans & Co, who were good enough to provide her with a reference when she found herself in difficulties with the Ministry of Pensions in 1925.[21]

Large numbers of women worked throughout the war in various government departments, including the Ministry of Pensions. However, once the war was over, women found themselves out of work, sometimes very quickly. The day the Armistice was declared, the thousands of women working at the Barnbow munitions works in Leeds were told that their employment was terminated. The Royal Dockyards had been heavily reliant on female labour, but once men started to be discharged from the services they were employed in the place of women. In the spring of 1919, 1,500 women were made redundant from the dockyards at Portsmouth. Government departments in general tried to replace women with returning men. Local War Pensions Committees followed suit – the Bradford Committee, for example, decided in September 1919 that all of its female workers would be replaced by discharged servicemen.

The agreements made between trade unions and the government during the war, which had allowed so much interference in established industrial practice for the benefit of the nation, included an acknowledgement that such control was temporary. The Restoration of Pre-War Practices Act of 1919 was the price the government had paid for imposing restrictions on the movement of labour. The act simply stated that any recognized trade practice that had been suspended during the war should now be reinstated, with prosecutions for those who did not comply. Recognized trade practices had inevitably worked to the detriment of women in traditional areas of male employment before the war. It is no surprise that within a year of this legislation the number of women in the labour market had fallen significantly. Ex-servicemen's organizations were chiefly concerned with getting men back to work at the expense of women. Though they did make protests about war widows being dismissed from their employment after the war, the ex-serviceman would always take priority in their campaigning and they would not protect the widow to his detriment.

The sacrifices made by working women during the war were not given the same status as those of men in uniform, despite the dangers and health problems associated with munitions work. Hundreds of women were killed around the country in explosions at munitions factories, and exposure to the chemicals involved had a deleterious effect upon their health. Margaret Forster recalled that the women in the munitions factory in Newcastle where she worked were to spend six weeks working with cordite and six weeks in a different department to try to minimize the poisonous effects of the explosive. Even this balancing act was not enough for Margaret, who developed stomach trouble, which would not resolve itself until she left the factory and obtained work in an insurance office.[22]

A week after the Armistice, 6,000 women workers marched to the House of Commons in protest at their summary dismissal. A limited scheme of unemployment benefit was introduced, but it was less than the wages most women would have been earning during the war and was also limited to thirteen weeks. If an offer of employment, no matter how unsuitable, was turned down, the benefit was stopped. It was reported in Leeds that 10,000 women had been drawing the benefit in March 1919, but by June this had come down to a mere 400. As the local newspaper pointed out, this was not due to the fact that the rest of these women now had jobs, but was down to the work of the Local Employment Committee 'which reviewed all the cases and dealt with them',[23] removing the benefit from anyone who would not return to domestic service. Being a servant was a far less attractive option than factory work to many women, involving as it did lower rates of pay and a constant reminder of one's place on the social ladder. There were other local initiatives to alleviate the problem; authorities in Leeds organized training courses for women who had been engaged in war work and had now lost their jobs. By 1920, 455 women had been trained and found jobs in industries in the district.[24] This was, of course, nowhere near the amount of effort that was being expended in the retraining of ex-servicemen.

A training scheme had been introduced across the country for war widows in 1917 to find them a place in the labour force in selected occupations in which there was felt to be a nationwide demand. The scheme involved the Ministry of Pensions paying for the relevant training, and also giving the widow a maintenance allowance should she be able to prove that the training necessitated living away from home, giving up her current employment or incurring childcare costs. The lesser importance of the war widow as opposed to the disabled ex-serviceman was made absolutely plain in the instructions issued to the Local War Pensions Committees who were to forward applications to the Ministry. The booklet stated the following:

> The training of widows is on a somewhat different footing from the training of disabled men. In the latter case the State deems that it owes a duty to the man to provide him with the means of regaining the highest measure of industrial capacity that his disablement allows. ... In the case of the widow the State is not replacing an earning capacity which has been lost in its service, but offers to assist the widow to add to her income where her domestic needs made a remunerative occupation desirable in her own interest or in that of her children.[25]

By the death of their husbands, war widows had absolutely lost an earning capacity in service, and many of them would not have been looking to work at all if their men had not been killed in action, but the Ministry of Pensions did not view the situation in that way. As with most forms of assistance to widows, the training programme was seen as doing widows a favour, not meeting a moral obligation.

The list of occupations considered suitable for such applications included home helps, gardeners, cooks, dressmakers, laundry workers, hairdressers, midwives, nurses, sanitary inspectors, health visitors, infant welfare officers, pharmacists and school teachers.[26] Preference was to be given to those applying to retrain as midwives, as this was an area in which there was felt to be a national shortage. It is noteworthy that domestic service of all kinds was heavily represented in the list. In addition to the list of allowed occupations, there was a list of areas in which widows should not be encouraged to train, specifically because they were not to be put in competition with disabled men. The occupations to be avoided were:

> All branches of munitions work; massage; shorthand typewriting and other clerical work; dental mechanics; dispensing; motor driving; dyeing; glass blowing; hand-made lace industry; jewellery trade; watch and clock repairing; musical profession; lower grade laundry work; millinery; sight testing; toy making.[27]

A number of these jobs had been traditionally carried out by women, whilst others had seen a great intake of female labour during the war, which was now to be dispensed with.

In common with every kind of assistance provided to war widows, the training allowance was not a right. The Local War Pensions Committee had to satisfy themselves that the training was of the right sort and that the widow was of the right sort before forwarding the application to the Ministry. The maximum allowance to be paid for the training itself was 7s 6d per week, whilst the maximum maintenance allowance was 12s 6d per week. Both amounts were limited to thirteen weeks' duration. This was in addition to the pension the widow was receiving, and only those in receipt of a war widow's pension were eligible to apply.

Widows with children were only to be considered if the committee were satisfied that proper childcare arrangements could be made and 'that afterwards, the duties entailed by her occupation will not materially interfere with the still more important duties of the home.'[28] The instructions made it clear that women with several children or very young children were not to be given the training allowance unless there were 'special circumstances' that warranted it.

The November 1918 edition of the *War Pensions Gazette* noted that the widows' training scheme had now been in place for a year. In that time only 311 widows had applied for training and 147 applications were granted – less than half. Only forty-nine widows had actually completed a course of retraining by this time. The Ministry declared that the slow take-up of the scheme was because employment opportunities still existed for women in the general labour market without the need for special assistance; the inadequacy of the training scheme itself was not acknowledged as a reason for its limited appeal.

War widows with children were seen as doubly selfish by going out to work; they were not only potentially taking the place of a man, but were undoubtedly neglecting their children at the same time. Some Local War Pensions Committees wanted widows to obtain their permission before taking work outside of the home, whilst those Poor Law Guardians who were prepared to offer relief to war widows did so on the basis that no such work was undertaken. It was not made easy for widows with children to go out to work. Day nurseries did exist but were limited in number and also charged women to look after their children, negating the advantage of earning a wage. For its own workers, the Ministry of Munitions did fund some nurseries where there was a demonstrable need, but this was in wartime only. In Leeds, site of the huge Barnbow munitions complex, which employed 16,000 women in addition to many other factories around the city devoted solely to war work, the Ministry had only five day nurseries. This was a pitiful number for a city that traditionally had high levels of employment across the gender divide and was one of the key hubs of wartime production.

Widows with children found themselves in a perfect storm of scrutiny given the growing obsession with the fitness of the nation as evidenced by the health of its children. The Boer War had highlighted the poor physical condition of many of those who had tried to enlist, particularly those from urban, working-class areas, and the idea of national efficiency fuelled many of the welfare reforms already introduced before the start of the First World War.

Mothers were the bedrock of the nation, charged with the responsibility of rearing healthy and robust young citizens to allow Britain to compete effectively with other nations on all levels, including waging war. 'Mothercraft' was the new skill that, it seems, women – especially working-class women – needed to be taught. The Mothercraft crusade was well established before the First World War, but the outbreak of hostilities heightened its importance. By 1915, there were around 600 Mothercraft clubs all over the country, assisted by grants from the Local Government Board and the Board of Education. National competitions were held to demonstrate proficiency in the domestic arts, with mothers judged on the condition of their homes and babies. The knowledge demonstrated was meant to 'spread and permeate the crowded masses of the ignorant and the negligent'.[29] Eleanor Rathbone was one of many campaigners sceptical about the new science, pointing out that no amount of advice could take the place of meeting the practical needs of a working-class family. Writing in her pre-war report on Liverpool widows, she said:

> If the well-to-do people who enlarge upon the incompetence of the English working woman and undertake to teach her 'Mothercraft' had to lead her life under her conditions, how many of them could stand the strain for a week?[30]

The Mothercraft agenda was given centre stage with the establishment of National Baby Week in 1917. With the main event in London, classes, clinics and competitions were held nationwide to promote infant welfare and efficient childcare. Discussing the event in a meeting at the Guildhall a month before its start, Lord Rhondda announced that if 'the greatest virility and the greatest competence' were to be achieved amongst the people of the Empire, 'they must see that they started with healthy babies.'[31] Union man Ben Tillett, fighting against the general tide somewhat, said that the authorities must 'play the game by all mothers in the country instead of preaching at them.'[32] This was a forlorn hope. Though campaigners like Anna Martin would write scathingly of Baby Week and its ability to improve the lives of working-class children, the general mood in the press was that mothers needed to improve.

A syndicated columnist writing under the name of Lily Rose Clyne penned an article that appeared in a number of newspapers in January 1919, headlined 'Selfish Mothers'. Clyne claimed that working during the war had 'robbed some women of the knack of bringing up their children properly',[33] citing incidents of children being left alone while war widows went out to socialize in the evenings after working all day. The Reverend F.M. Kelly told the Edmonton War Pensions Committee that he had interrupted a gambling den of teenagers at the home of a war widow who was out working, and that teenage daughters of war widows were regularly prowling the streets late at night. He expressed the view that these evils were entirely due to widows working outside the home. His belief was that there was no need for such women to work, as the war widow's pension was more than enough to live on. Shamefully, the rest of the committee agreed with him and resolved to send a letter to the Ministry asking that war widows obtain permission from them before taking up work.[34] War widows were now wedded to the state, which was providing for them, and in the opinion of Reverend Kelly and his Edmonton colleagues, should also be controlling their activities.

The reality was that the pension was not enough to live on for many women and certainly left no room for luxuries, nor did it give them the ability to build up any kind of savings for emergencies. There were also thousands of bereaved wives who were struggling on without access to a war widow's pension due to the strict eligibility rules, or the fact that their pension had been taken from them for some alleged misconduct.

In 1920, the newly established National Council of Social Service (NCSS)[35] produced a report on the condition of the families of widows around the country. Using an initial survey of 400 families, the aim of the report was to examine the effects of widowhood on a household's standard of living and to look at wages earned by widows alongside other sources of income.[36] The work was undertaken with a view to informing a general discussion that was then taking place about the introduction of civilian pensions for widows.

Using a scale of average weekly earnings, adjusted for the significant levels of inflation that had occurred during the war, the NCSS report found that war widows with no source of money other than their pensions were living on half of the family's pre-war income. Twenty-two per cent of the sample fell into this category, with two examples in particular illustrating the dire situation in which some families found themselves. The husband in one household had been a docker, earning the equivalent of 104 shillings a week before the war; his family were now surviving on a war pension of 20s 5d per week. In a family where the husband had been a 'holder up' – a riveter's mate employed in shipbuilding – the household income had plummeted from 133 shillings a week to just thirty-seven shillings.

If a widow was lucky enough to obtain employment, the situation was better, but the lucrative factory work that had been available to women during the war itself had largely disappeared in many areas of the country. Female munitions workers during the war could earn upwards of £2 a week in some factories. Now most of the war widows in the study who worked were employed in domestic cleaning of some sort, where the average wage was around seven shillings a week. The NCSS reported that only 10 per cent of the women in the sample had worked during their husband's lifetime – the number now working after a husband's death was just over 78 per cent.

Many widows, especially those with young children, did not take work outside of the house. Some took on home work, making small articles on a piecework basis for an employer. Others found sometimes ingenious ways to earn money while remaining at home. Mary Mason's father had survived the war, though had a lingering chest complaint from being gassed, for which he received a nominal disablement pension. Tiring of appearing before medical boards to have his condition reassessed, he threw his paperwork on the fire and refused to attend again. When he died in 1933 he was not in receipt of a disablement pension, though it seems likely that the condition that killed him was a result of his war service. With three daughters to support, his wife Sarah now had to earn some money of her own. She started with the traditional work of a widow, taking in washing. A widower with a household of sons had asked her to do their laundry and news of her efficiency at the task spread around the neighbourhood of Hunslet in Leeds, providing further customers. War widows were no strangers to the pawn shop, but in Sarah Walker's case they became her customers rather than the other way around. Sarah arranged with the local pawn shop that she would wash unredeemed pledges in exchange for having her pick of the items. Towels and tablecloths were the items she sought most eagerly, as these could be sold on for a few pence once they were clean. Sarah managed to acquire a damask tablecloth, which she did not sell on but hired out to locals for weddings and funerals at a shilling a time.[37]

The children of war widows were often working to make their small contribution to the family finances. During the war, local authorities in certain areas of the country granted large numbers of exemptions to allow children to leave school at an earlier age than usual and work, especially in agricultural areas at harvest time. In 1915, it was reported that 45,000 fewer children were on the books of the country's schools than would have been expected.[38] Some were at home looking after younger siblings to allow their mothers to go out to work, but many were working themselves. Children as young as seven were out working outside of school hours, selling papers, running errands and generally doing anything that might result in a few shillings to take home. One 13-year-old in Manchester was noted as working forty-eight and a half hours a week selling papers, in addition to going to school.[39] In some areas, 'half timers', as such children were called, were an established part of the industrial landscape, and those sitting on local committees charged with looking after their welfare were sometimes the direct beneficiaries of their labour.

Patrick McVeigh and his siblings all had to work at a young age. Their father had died after the war from a condition he developed while a prisoner in Germany. His mother was left with five children to raise on a total pension of twenty-seven shillings a week. Patrick started a paper round at the age of seven, whilst his elder sisters, aged ten and eleven, were out delivering milk. Hard decisions had to be made as the rent on their house was ten shillings a week, leaving only seventeen shillings for all other expenses. The eldest daughter was forced into domestic service, the calculation being made that the five shillings a week that would be lost in the form of her children's allowance could be replaced by approximately seven shillings a week in wages. The child herself would also receive free board and lodging at her employer's. Patrick's mother pawned her wedding ring and watch in order to pay for her daughter's new uniform.[40]

Ethel Booth was one of many children who had to cut short her education in order to earn a living. She had won a scholarship to the local grammar school and had plans to continue her education. The death of her father changed everything and she had to leave school because her mother could not afford to keep her four young children on the widow's pension she was receiving. Ethel went to work at a local photographer's studio for a mere five shillings a week and always regretted having to give up her hard-won place at grammar school: 'We ought to have had more help so I could have continued.'[41]

The children of war widows sometimes lost out on education and other opportunities in order to play their part in the fight to keep the family above the poverty line. However, the working widows in such households were already making huge sacrifices themselves to provide for their children and everyone had to make a contribution. The NCSS report concluded:

> It requires no special measure of sympathy to appreciate something of the struggle with poverty and ill health that in too many of these cases is added to the sense of personal loss on the death of the husband. Nor is it easy to overlook the evidence of courage and determination with which the struggle is in many cases faced and overcome.[42]

Chapter 4

Charity and Self-help

'My dear little children cannot go to school as they have not got boots to go.'

Work was not always an option for war widows. Both Eleanor Rathbone and Seebohm Rowntree told the Select Committee in 1915 that work was simply not available for women in many areas of the country. In mining areas, married women traditionally did not work; their husbands earned comparatively good wages and there was little opportunity for employment beyond the pit in the average mining village in Durham or South Wales. The poor living circumstances of some widows caused a breakdown in their health, which prevented them from taking any part in the labour market even where work was available.

Widows who were not able to obtain employment and were not in receipt of pensions or could not make them stretch to cover the family's expenses had to find other sources of income. Around 35 per cent of the National Council of Social Service's sample widows were in receipt of Poor Law relief, either in addition to or instead of a pension or earnings.[1] Seeking Poor Law relief was not done lightly. For some widows, 'going on the Parish' was unthinkable and the shadow of the workhouse was something that haunted the lives of many working-class families for decades. It is noteworthy that, during the war, when a number of workhouse buildings were converted to military hospitals, some soldiers protested at being treated there. Until the passing of the 1918 Representation of the People Act, a male recipient of Poor Law relief lost his right to vote. The message that seeking parish relief was something shameful was heard loud and clear by those in need of assistance. The NCSS noted that acceptance of Poor Law relief was 'generally felt to involve a loss of self-respect'.[2] The level of scrutiny that would have been applied to a war widow seeking relief, already under the general supervision of the Local War Pensions Committee, would have been intolerable to many. The degree to which the home visit was resented in some households can be seen by the report of a London widow who 'refused to show the bedrooms at all and suggested that a search warrant be brought in future.'[3] The correlation between the lady visitor and the police is one that was clear in the mind of this particular recipient of Poor Law relief.

The attitude of Poor Law Guardians to widows varied around the country. The NCSS noted that in some areas, outdoor relief was not given to widows at all and they were forced to enter the workhouse with their children. Other boards would only give outdoor relief if a woman agreed to give up the care of some of her children. One researcher noted that the policy of her local board was to offer to take the widow's children into the Poor Law schools if she had more than two.

A survey of the policies of providing relief to widows and children was carried out by the Ministry of Health in 1919. The enquiry was prompted by a desire to see if Poor Law Guardians had complied with a direction given to them by the government in 1914 that they should not wait until families were completely destitute before helping, and should try to keep families together rather than put them in institutions. Their conclusion was that the circular had been largely ignored. Some Guardians would give nothing to able bodied widows, expecting them to work, whilst those who did give financial aid did not do so at a sufficient level to be of real assistance. Some areas were giving widows as little as five shillings a week. This was not a new feature of outdoor relief. The Royal Commission on the Poor Law in 1909 had found that the worst cases of inadequate relief granted in the years immediately preceding the report were for widows with children, and when Eleanor Rathbone conducted a survey of outdoor relief paid to widows in Liverpool four years later, the situation had not really improved.[4]

Some Boards of Guardians gave very little to widows on the understanding that other charities might step in and meet their needs. Eleanor Rathbone found that where such resources did exist in Liverpool before the war, it was not in the form of a regular income stream, but rather in what she described as 'stray windfalls' – occasional meals given to poor children, or old clothes donated to a family. She was scornful of this approach to welfare, saying that 'No one surely can seriously maintain that the "children of the State" ought to be driven to live by cadging on their neighbours.'[5] In a time where candidates were elected to the local boards and Poor Law relief came from the local ratepayers, there was a definite personal interest in keeping the Poor Law bills low. A number of Boards of Guardians expressed the opinion that the war widow's pension was insufficient, feeling the strain of having to take up the slack for such families. The Ministry of Health report noted that some boards were 'only too pleased' to have the family's income supplemented from other sources, sometimes imagining that these sources existed rather than making proper enquiries. The report described boards as being too keen on 'the old economic doctrine that the pauper should not be better off than his or her outside neighbour'.[6] This might be an old doctrine but one that we still see today in debates on benefits. Of course, it was a completely illogical doctrine to apply to widows; as the report notes, the availability of relief was hardly likely to encourage widowhood. However, harshness to widows was partly designed to encourage the living husband to make adequate provision for his family on his death so that the Poor Law authorities did not have to contribute at all.

The Ministry of Health report, despite its criticism of less than generous Boards of Guardians, was full of the same old prejudices and value judgements about working-class women. It reproduced the classification system for widows, which came direct from the 1909 Poor Law Commission report, categorizing them into four types, Class I being 'capable, trustworthy' women, with Class IV described as 'people guilty of wilful neglect, sometimes drunkards or people of immoral character'.[7] The 1909 report made it clear that respectable behaviour should be a prerequisite for obtaining Poor Law relief. Ten years later, this stance had not changed.

The Ministry of Health report of 1919 stressed the need for careful supervision of every widow to whom outdoor relief was granted, and had no qualms about the removal of children from the 'lower' category of widows. The report noted that in London, from December 1918 to February 1919, a total of 3,093 widows and deserted wives were receiving relief from the Board of Guardians. From this number, 2,429 were described as being 'allowed' to keep their children, meaning that 664 families had children removed as a result of seeking Poor Law relief. One particular case is described in detail:

> One slovenly, irresponsible woman who refused to part with her children was refused other forms of relief and finally three were taken into the schools. The baby left with the woman died and the house went from bad to worse.[8]

The fact that the woman's circumstances deteriorated after the removal of her children is not stated as a criticism of the policy, but of the woman herself. It is no surprise that many widows in dire financial straits would try all other avenues before considering approaching the local Board of Guardians for assistance.

Patrick McVeigh describes his mother as coming under pressure to have some of her four children cared for in an institution.[9] Reducing the number of children in the house, either to allow a widow to work or simply to cut her immediate household costs, was a tactic suggested by a range of agencies, from the Poor Law Guardians to the Local War Pensions Committees. The Charity Organisation Society had long pursued the policy of placing some of a widow's children in care institutions so she could cope better with those she had left. The availability of war widows' pensions actually contributed to a decrease in the numbers of children who were accommodated in homes as widows now had a source of income, however meagre, to help them look after their children. However, for some women, keeping the family together would prove to be impossible and the Poor Law schools or private charities were used to accommodate children, hopefully temporarily.

The term 'orphan' rarely had the exact connotations used today and the majority of children in homes in the early twentieth century were not orphans at all. The Walmsley Orphan Home in Leeds was one of a number of private children's homes in the city around the time of the First World War. Renamed the Home for Friendless Lads, in 1916, seventy-six boys were admitted, only two being true orphans and a number having both parents living. The home had established a special dormitory to accommodate soldiers' sons as 'it was found that some of the wives of soldiers were either too ill or too careless to attend to the needs of their children.'[10] Some employers set up their own institutions to look after 'orphan' children. The Metropolitan and City Police Orphanage had been established in Twickenham in 1870 to care for the children of deceased police officers and accommodated those children whose fathers had swapped blue serge for khaki. As it could only take a maximum of 200 children at any one time, some maintenance payments were allowed to police officers' widows with children to help them keep the family together and remove the need for them to be placed in the orphanage.

A considerable number of war widows who sought to have their children accommodated outside the family home did so because they were not in receipt of pensions. *Our Waifs and Strays* was the monthly magazine of the Church of England Society for Providing Homes for Waifs and Strays. The society had been founded in 1881 and used its monthly magazine to fundraise generally, but also to bring specific cases to the attention of its readers and ask for sponsorship of those children. There are numerous examples of cases in which a war widow was not eligible for a pension and could not afford to keep her family together. A typical example comes from 1916, the case of 'George E.D.', aged ten: 'One of five children whose father, a private in the army, died as the result of an epileptic fit. His widow is ineligible for a pension and is quite unable to maintain her five little ones.'[11]

It was often younger children who were the subject of accommodation by the authorities as they prevented a widow from working, but were too small themselves to contribute to the family income. Asking for assistance to pay for the upkeep of 'Margaret E.B.', aged four, *Our Waifs and Strays* said, 'with one child taken, mother hopes to get work in an arsenal.'[12]

Women unfortunate enough to have their pensions removed by the authorities found it very difficult to maintain their families without the payment of their allowances. Beatrice S. had resisted the removal of her six children as being an inevitable consequence of the removal of her pension. Described by her sister as a good mother, within six months of her pension being taken for misconduct she could no longer afford to maintain the household. In 1925, the Local War Pensions Committee wrote to the Special Grants Committee to report on her case, saying, 'Mrs S. is now voluntarily relinquishing the pensionable children.'[13] Beatrice's four youngest children were sent to local orphanages.

Once a child was accommodated in an orphanage, it was often difficult to have them returned to the care of a parent, especially a widow. Though not a war widow, Kathleen Dayus lost her husband in the years following the war, and finding herself in deep financial difficulty, reluctantly gave her children to Barnardo's until she was earning enough to reunite the family. Though her financial position improved fairly quickly, it took her eight years to have her children returned to her care.[14] Private charities like Barnardo's were harder to challenge than the Board of Guardians, and were able to set their own rules on contact with children once the parents had relinquished their care. Again, the shadow of the Charity Organisation Society can be detected in the attitude of Barnardo's, which was that poverty was a moral issue and that removing a child from the influence of its family was the way to ensure the cycle was broken. Control over all aspects of the child's life was relinquished, from decisions over vaccination to which religion the child would follow. Barnardo's even sent boys to work in munitions factories for a period of time during the war, without the consent of their parents. The charity made much in their advertising of the estimated 10,500 former Barnardo's boys who had joined up to fight. What was less publicized was that 6,000 of those boys had been child emigrants to Canada in the years before the war and had joined the Canadian forces, some of them, no doubt, with a view to receiving free passage home to England. Only one in six of those young emigrants had been true orphans, and a number of them had been sent to Canada without the consent of the living parent.[15] The longer a child was away from its family, the harder it would prove to adjust on its return; Kathleen Dayus describes a very difficult relationship with her daughters when they were eventually restored to her care.

A widow's family network was often vital to the economic survival of the household. From providing free childcare so the widow could work to more immediate aid like free board and lodging, the extended family was an important source of support. For many women, that assistance came from the maternal side of the family rather than that of their husband. Ethel Booth's father, Norman, was one of fourteen children. When he was killed, only one of those siblings offered any assistance at all, and even then it was minimal. The uncle concerned was a wholesale clothier and fairly well off in comparison to Ethel's father. At the time war broke out, the Booths had been in the process of buying their own home with a mortgage from the Halifax Building Society. Uncle Henry's sole contribution was to speak to the building society and arrange for the loan to be converted to a lower, interest only repayment mortgage.[16]

A feature of working-class life noted as far back as Edwin Chadwick's Poor Law report of 1834 was the generosity of the poor towards the poor. Maud Pember Reeves noted that in Lambeth before the war, people knew the realities of extreme poverty and would help out friends and family in times of trouble to make sure they did not fall into this trap.[17] This unofficial assistance was apparent in the daily lives of war widows and their families. Friends and neighbours would often provide support even when they were far from rich themselves. This might range from passing on food or clothing to providing free child-minding to allow a widow to go and earn a few shillings, or paying the widow to do small tasks the family could have done themselves. Patrick McVeigh remembers his mother being visited by a man who had been a prisoner of war with his father. The man and his wife, by no means rich, had a smallholding a few miles away and pressed his mother to take a ten shilling note to put in the family coffers.[18] On a more formal level, in mining districts at the outbreak of the war, committees had been formed and those men still working were paying into the colliery offices to provide a fund to supplement pensions and allowances for those families of miners in khaki. The Dearne Valley Colliery Patriotic Fund was one of many such organizations. Towns and villages also established their own individual funds to help the families of the bereaved.

The idea that women had no idea how to look after money, expressed frequently when separation allowances were introduced, resurfaced again in relation to widows' pensions. Widows were accused of spending their pensions on frivolities or being poor at budgeting, rather than simply poor. The COS and its followers saw poor women as wasteful and ignorant of how to run a household. A woman's character, not the amount of money coming into the household, was regarded as the ultimate deciding factor in her ability to manage a budget. With this idea at the heart of a significant amount of the voluntary work that took place during the war, a simple increase in the amount of money allowed to widows was never going to gain favour with those entrusted to administer relief. Eleanor Rathbone, who would not have aligned herself with the COS, nevertheless shared some of their views on the principle of supervision when it came to allowing relief to women. She believed that granting monies without strict supervision was almost as bad as not granting adequate amounts at all, and advocated the use of more female visitors to monitor widows.[19]

The *War Pensions Gazette* of September 1917 printed a suggestion from one of the 'Lady Clerks' of the West Ham War Pensions Committee that a fund should be organized for widows to pay into and then draw lots for money to spend on their children's boots. The clerk said, 'The women who are bad managers (I do not blame them, but their number is legion) cannot possibly arrange their allowance to leave any margin for these necessary articles.'[20] How she thought such bad managers would have any spare money available to put into a fund for this purpose is a mystery.

Boots were one of the most frequently mentioned articles that widows had trouble obtaining. The expense of boots was a feature of a number of pre-war studies of working-class life. Lady Bell noted that women often went without shoes altogether, wrapping their feet in rags to make sure that their man had a pair of work boots.[21] The Lambeth women in Maud Pember Reeves' study sometimes had no shoes, meaning that they rarely left the house and shopped at night when no one would notice the state of their feet.[22] The man of the house often spent hours repairing children's boots to avoid the need to buy new pairs that the family could not afford. The Women's Industrial Council report on married women's work before the war found that for a working woman, 'the premature collapse of a child's boots is a disaster that disturbs all her calculations.'[23] Without their husband to repair and pay for the boots in the first place, many widows struggled to provide shoes for their children. The Select Committee on Pensions in 1915 were told that children in mining families in the Lanarkshire district of Scotland were 'very badly off for boots, and were it not for the fact that they were strongly shod previously they would now be barefoot.'[24]

Boots were often mentioned in pleading letters from widows to the Ministry of Pensions. Mary Jane Griffiths had nursed her husband Thomas since 1915, only to see him die in 1918 of a heart complaint caused by his war service.[25] He had been unable to work since his discharge from the army and according to his widow had been unable to speak for the two years leading up to his death. Despite being entitled to a portion of her husband's pension, Mary Jane's money was not forthcoming from the Ministry. She had been left in debt from his funeral and was eight weeks behind with her rent. Her daughters, aged seven and ten, also needed new boots. She wrote: 'The burden of nursing my husband has told on me with being up with him night and day I hope you will send me something through for my children's boots going to school wet feet twice a day.'

Having received no response and no money, matters worsened for Mary Jane and she was forced to resort to the Poor Law Guardians for support. She wrote again to the Ministry:

> I would be much obliged if you would kindly give me some direct information as to what I shall have as I am in very needy circumstances and my dear little children cannot go to school because they have not got boots

to go. I have to appear at the Guardians next week and it will come to [*sic*] late. ... I am writing to ask you if will kindly let me know by return because it's impossible to go on like this.[26]

Shortly thereafter, her pension did arrive, amounting to a mere 26s 3d a week. This was not enough to keep the family in anything like comfortable circumstances and Mary Jane Griffiths had to seek employment. The final letter on her file is from August 1918, when she writes asking if it is acceptable for her to do some work for the government without losing her pension as her current allowance was 'taking all towards the living'.

Mary Mason describes shoes as having been 'a constant worry' to her mother.[27] In recognition of the problem, the local newspaper, the *Yorkshire Evening Post*, started a campaign called 'Boots for the Bairns' to provide poor children with footwear.[28] The appeal began in 1921, when the local school attendance officer found large numbers of children were not going to school because they had no shoes to wear. The newspaper had taken up the cause, and from the charitable donations received, 12,000 pairs of boots were distributed that winter.[29] Collecting boxes were placed in shops and workplaces and an annual pantomime was held to raise additional funds. Schools were responsible for handing out the boots, and to qualify a parent had to prove to the headmaster that he or she was either a widow or unemployed. Mary and her sister Jessie were two of the lucky recipients. Boys were given grey woollen socks with patterned tops and lace-up leather boots, whilst girls had black lace-up shoes and long black lisle stockings. Mary recalled:

> It wasn't a stigma for the boys because all boys at that time wore grey patterned socks and boots. Not so the girls. My sister and I and all the other girls were easily recognized as being recipients of 'Boots for the Bairns' with our black lace-up shoes and long black lisle stockings and endured many taunts from children whose parents could afford more fashionable footwear.[30]

Mary, however, brushed off such remarks and was grateful for the boots. 'What a wonderful charity it was and how thankful we were to be warmly shod for the winter.'

In 1933, the year Mary's father died, 5,671 pairs of boots had been given out to needy children in Leeds.[31]

Boots were not the only item that a widow would struggle to provide for her family. The Birmingham Citizen's Committee presented evidence to the Select Committee in 1915 on the budgets of widows in their area before the introduction of pensions.[32] The breakdown of weekly expenditure by those widows reliant on Poor Law relief to any extent showed that there was no room in the budget to buy clothing. Despite increases in pension payments, four years later, new clothes were still a luxury in many homes. The Ministry of Health in 1919 reported that the traditional 'Sunday clothes' were often lacking from a widow's household.[33] Often pawned on a Monday and retrieved on payday, Sunday clothes allowed working-class families to take part in social activities like attending church. They were, however, a luxury that some widows could no longer afford. For some families this meant the end of their church attendance, which was felt to be important for children. The same report also noted that, amongst poorer widows, the household did not contain fireguards because they were too expensive.[34] At a time when houses had open fires, this was a significant safety concern if there were children in the house.

The household of Sarah Bradley in Barnsley suffered a heartbreaking tragedy due to the lack of a fireguard. The wife of a miner who was killed on the Somme in 1917 while part of a tunnelling company, Sarah Bradley was just twenty-five when she was widowed with three children to raise. Her pension monies had been stopped for some reason in November 1918, and she was in dire financial straits. In February 1919, Maggie, the eldest child at eight years old, caught her pinafore on the open fire at their house in Waltham Street. Sarah had gone to a neighbour's house, ironically to try to borrow some money to buy more coal, when her other daughter, Lily, ran in to report 'Maggie is burning!'[35] The neighbour did her best to extinguish the flames, but poor Maggie Bradley died shortly thereafter.

Resorting to private charity was a heavy decision for a widow struggling to maintain the household. Taking 'handouts' of any kind was only slightly above applying to the Poor Law on the scale of working-class respectability. Charities proliferated during the war to the extent that they eventually had to be regulated by law. Assisting Belgian refugees, providing hot drinks to troops in the trenches,[36] or retraining disabled men as poultry farmers – no charitable objective was too obscure if it could be connected with the war. Every day seemed to be a 'Flag Day' and several businesses set aside a day when all profits from sales would be given to war charities. Newspapers had separate advertising sections for charitable appeals and some set up their own funds. *The Times* Fund raised money for the British Red Cross and the Order of St John. By the beginning of July 1918, the paper proudly announced that a total of £11 million had been raised so far.[37] By that date, 6,700 war charities had successfully passed the registration requirements.[38]

For war widows, a range of charitable options existed, though with no guarantee of a successful application being made, and no reassurance that the relief of a family's distress would be anything other than temporary. Charities could make their own rules as to the grounds on which assistance was provided and the threat of yet another lady visitor undoubtedly put many widows off the idea of applying for help. The COS fear of double claiming and fraud was strong in the minds of many administering such funds. Many local relief committees organized at the start of the war operated on the same principles as the Bradford European War Fund, which stipulated that their Ladies Committee should ensure that 'every household receiving help from our fund may be visited and advised how to make present incomes go furthest.' The registers of the COS and the City Guild of Help were to be consulted as 'in this manner co-ordination of help would be secured and overlapping prevented.'[39] It was the practice of the fund to have a police officer visit the household of anyone applying for assistance.

The whole idea of charity was difficult to accept for a class of women who were starting to believe that the country owed them a debt. The NCSS said of the attitude to the war widow's pension amongst its sample:

> It is felt to have been earned as a right, and for service rendered to the State. Indeed, it is recognized that even when the pension has been granted the State is still the debtor, the State rather than the pensioner is under obligation.[40]

For those women who were unlucky enough not even to be in receipt of pensions, the feeling of injustice and resentment of having to resort to charity must have been considerable.

The country's 'official' charity for war widows and others suffering hardship from the war was the Royal Patriotic Fund Corporation. The fund dealt with cases where pensions had been refused and would consider granting weekly allowances in appropriate circumstances. At the start of the war the RPFC was also giving war widows £5 on the death of their husband and an additional £1 for each child in the household. By 15 January 1915, 5,360 widows had received this gratuity.[41] This was stopped in 1916 when the Ministry of Pensions came into existence and started issuing similar grants. The RPFC's own history unsurprisingly praises their endeavours and the assistance they provided to widows. From 1904 to 1953, £477,900 was paid out by the fund in regular weekly allowances to dependants of war casualties who had been deemed not eligible for war pensions.[42]

However, the fund was not always sympathetic to the claims it received. The Bradford War Relief Committee forwarded the case of Alice Florence Milner for the attention of the RPFC in February 1916. Alice had postponed her original marriage date to her husband John when war was declared and he joined up. They eventually married in November 1914. Two weeks later, Private Milner went to France. He went missing in the battle for Hill 60 in May 1915 and was now presumed dead. Due to the fact that they had married after his enlistment, the War Office had decreed that Alice was not entitled to a war widow's pension. She had been surviving on 17s 6d a week provided by her husband's former employers, but this was not a permanent allowance. Alice herself was no longer able to work because she suffered from cataracts in her eyes. At the time the Bradford Committee contacted the RPFC, Alice Milner had been without any income for six weeks. The decision of the RPFC was that she was not eligible for any assistance. The idea that the RPFC was the 'safety net' for those widows not covered by the Royal Warrant does not appear to have held true in many cases.

The Soldiers' and Sailors' Families Association was not keen to help widows once pensions had been introduced. When the war was over their attitude was confirmed in documentation sent out to their own committees. In August 1919, one such circular stated of widows, orphans and other dependants that they were 'adequately provided for under the existing scale of pensions, and it is only under very exceptional circumstances that assistance from the association should be necessary.'[43] No decisions on helping widows were to be taken locally; instructions were issued stating that head office should be given full details in order for them to make the final call.

Charitable funds for widows and orphans were sometimes headed by the wife of a prominent military man. For example, the British and Foreign Sailors' Society started a special fund under the name of Lady Jellicoe, wife of the Admiral of the Fleet, to cater for the needs of the families of sailors in the Mercantile Marine.[44] The fund assisted those who were eligible in making applications for pensions or grants, and made advances to women in anticipation of pensions being payable. Where pensions were unavailable, the fund sometimes paid allowances themselves and could also assist in educating sailors' sons for naval service. The fund was clear in its advertising that such assistance was given 'not as a charity but as a right', though it did also state that help was given only after 'careful and sympathetic investigation'.[45] Pensions for the Mercantile Marine did not come under the usual Naval and Military Pensions acts, but were dealt with under the War Risks Compensation Scheme.

Another potential source of assistance for widows was the Salvation Army. Founded in the East End of London in 1865 by William Booth, from its inception widows and orphans had always been a significant constituency for its ministering aid. The war gave the Salvation Army a new pool of potential customers in the form of war widows. In November 1915, the Salvation Army announced the establishment of a new network of 'Widows' Counsellors' to be in operation nationwide. The ambition was to have a counsellor in every town and village in the country, and by 1917 there were 1,000 advisers. Membership of the Salvation Army was not a prerequisite to qualify as a counsellor, but applicants, male or female, had to be 'godly, sympathetic and wise'.[46]

Described as 'a unique departure in social service',[47] the aim of the Widows' Counsellors' network was:

> To provide within the reach of every widow, without charge of any kind, without any obligation to believe all that the Army believes or to go to The Army Meetings (glad as we should be to see her), honest and unselfish counsel as to herself, her children, her wages, her debts – if there are any – her prospects, and everything else that is vital to her welfare.[48]

In March 1920, the Salvation Army newspaper, *The War Cry*, reported that 1,300 widows had taken advantage of their counselling service during the course of the previous year.

In addition to advice, money was also sometimes given to widows to assist with temporary difficulties with the aim of allowing a woman to keep her whole family together. This contrasted with the attitude of some other charitable organizations who would rather see children given over to the workhouse and a widow released to earn her own living than have the whole family continue to drain the resources of Poor Law relief. The Salvation Army also involved themselves in cases where widows were in danger of forfeiting their pensions, offering to act as advisers and trustees to guide a woman onto the right path and satisfy the authorities over her future behaviour. A series of meetings were arranged nationwide to which widows were invited to have tea and listen to speeches. In some locations, hundreds of widows attended to avail themselves of the Salvationists' services, or at least to have a free meal.

In August 1914, local authorities were empowered to provide free school meals to 'necessitous children' even on non-school days under the Provision of Meals Act. Parents had to apply to the local authority and show that the family could not afford to pay before a child could be fed for free. The Chief Medical Officer noted that some parents were too proud to apply, not wanting their children to be labelled as 'necessitous'.[49] Another deterrent beyond the simple social stigma may have been the increased levels of scrutiny that would be endured by a family applying for this benefit. In Leeds, children receiving free school meals were continually monitored as to their height and weight and were regularly visited at home. Dr Bolton, School Medical Officer for Leeds in 1915, arranged classes in 'Mothercraft' for the parents of undernourished children. Despite protestations to the contrary, the lingering suspicion remained that malnourishment was somehow the fault of the mother, not of the economic situation of the family. These classes took place in the afternoons so it is hard to see how a working mother, of whom there were very many in the city, could attend. The take-up of free school meals is an indicator of the inferior financial position of many widows. In 1920, Dr Blake in Portsmouth looked at the cases of 200 such 'necessitous children' and found that 50 per cent of them came from the families of widows.[50]

Every welfare innovation or charitable donation seemed to involve increasing levels of scrutiny of the working-class woman. The manner in which separation allowances and widows' pensions themselves were administered gave further opportunities for the lady visitor to intervene. A brief fightback against the endless stream of visitors took place with the establishment of the Mother's Defence League in 1919, which campaigned for mothers' rights and against the over scrutinization of the working classes. The league saw lady visitors as disproportionately directed at lower income families, noting that health visitors were not seen in London's fashionable Park Lane. With writer and libertarian G.K. Chesterton as its president, the league invited those women who were oppressed by 'Cruelty Men', 'Health Ladies', 'School Board Men' and others to seek advice from them on the legal rights of such visitors to enter their homes. The lady visitor, a volunteer with no practical knowledge of her own, who presumed to lecture a working-class woman on how to run her home, was a particular target of the league. The organization ran out of steam in the 1920s after being prosecuted by the National Society for the Prevention of Cruelty to Children (NSPCC) for its unfair portrayal of the society.

Eleanor Rathbone's study of pre-war widows in Liverpool discovered most of them living in abject poverty. Rathbone and her committee found that over 72 per cent of her widows were 'living under conditions of grinding poverty, incompatible with healthy and happy life and almost certain to lead to physical degeneration and industrial inefficiency'.[51] Forty-five per cent of children in the sample were living in dirty, insanitary houses, many without furniture. Those war widows who did not receive a pension faced the prospect of falling back to this standard of living and had to try a range of charitable funds to keep their homes together in the absence of any state assistance. It is little wonder that William Hayes Fisher, MP and Vice Chairman of the RPFC, claimed, 'It is a matter of almost life and death to the widow whether she and her children get the pension or not.'[52]

Chapter 5

Officers and Gentlewomen

'I was so wanting to get him away to a good Boarding School.'

Not all First World War widows suffered the grinding poverty seen in the previous chapter. In an army that was based on a strict class hierarchy, officers were usually from middle and upper-class families where finances were not an issue. Even in the trenches, an officer had a servant to take care of his daily needs. This class bias was the reason behind the absence of separation allowances for officers' wives at the start of the war, with officers felt to be financially secure enough to have made provision for their families without the assistance of the government. The scale of the casualties on the Western Front meant that this class of individuals was soon exhausted, necessitating promotion from the ranks and swift commissions for those enlisting in Kitchener's New Army. Such individuals did not always come from the previously accepted 'officer class' and were not as able to provide for their families while they were serving their country. The introduction of separation allowances for officers' families was inevitable.

The death of the new officer was just as likely to mean economizing on the part of the widow as it would for the wife of an ordinary Tommy. Rather than the common cry for boots that was often heard from working-class war widows, those higher up the social scale were most concerned with providing their children with an education.

Henry Harris had been in the army for over a decade as a gym instructor when he was given a commission in December 1914. Unfortunately, he soon developed abdominal problems, which would plague him for the rest of his life. He was discharged with a disability pension in 1919 and moved to the village of Grayshott, where he led the local Scout troop. In April 1923, Henry shot himself with his service rifle and was found in the Scout hut by one of his young charges.

Henry Harris had not been fit enough to work after his discharge from the army and had instead spent his time undertaking various voluntary activities. However, there were certain social expectations of the family of an officer that had to be paid for. The couple's son was being educated at a fee-paying day school and his mother had ambitions for him to go to public school. Emily Harris, unlike the wives of many officers, had to work to supplement her husband's disablement pension. She was earning £150 a year according to the forms she now sent to the Ministry to claim a war widow's pension and struggled to make ends meet while awaiting a determination. She had to borrow the money to pay her son's school fees and wrote to say that she would have to remove him from school if her pension application was refused. By the end of July 1923, she had still heard nothing, and had been without any allowance for three months. She wrote again to the Ministry:

> My earnings are not permanent. My Health is failing and unless I can get away for a Holiday I may have to lose my present post.
>
> I was so wanting to get him away to a good Boarding School.
>
> I cannot make ends meet as things are. We broke up our home in 1914 at the outbreak of war, and I am now compelled to live in two Furnished Rooms, the rent of which is £1 10s exclusive of light and fuel.[1]

Somewhat surprisingly, given the circumstances of some other suicide cases that were rejected, Emily Harris did eventually receive a war widow's pension, being granted £120 a year for herself and £30 for her son. If this amount was not enough to satisfy her ambitions of getting young Henry into a good school, she would have to seek further assistance from the Ministry of Pensions, or from a charitable source.

The Royal Patriotic Fund Corporation provided educational opportunities for the children of deceased servicemen. This education was often of a military character, with funded places at Wellington College and the Royal Naval School being offered to boys. The RPFC had set up two schools of its own, the Royal Victoria Patriotic Asylums, for both girls and boys, but financial mismanagement meant that one had been sold off before the Boer War. A Roman Catholic Orphan's Fund was established for girls to receive a convent education. The RPFC's policy was that it would accept applications for children to be funded to attend any school, provided that there was some assurance that their father would have been in a position to provide a similar level of education had he lived. Alternatively, if it could be shown that sending the child away to school would allow the widow to obtain employment that would significantly improve the family's prospects, consideration would be given to making a grant.

The Special Grants Committee was empowered to make grants to widows to pay for their children's education, but again the class of the child's father would come into play. Funds to send a child to public school would only be considered if that was the level of education the father would have been able to afford. The SGC was not an agent of social mobility. Day school fees were not to exceed £25 a year, whilst boarding school fees up to £50 a year could be paid. These amounts were hardly likely to cover the costs of the most prestigious public schools. In all cases, the fees were only payable if satisfactory reports were received on the 'conduct and industry'[2] of the child concerned. In the seven months from September 1917 to the end of March 1918, the SGC gave out almost £3,000 in educational grants from a total spend of £172,240.[3] By 1936, 28,000 children of deceased and disabled officers and men had been in receipt of education grants of some sort at a cost of around £2 million.[4]

Some public schools set up funds under their own administration to provide education grants to the children of fathers killed in the war. These funds were for the children of former pupils, not of the average soldier, ensuring that those assisted would still be of the right class, regardless of their financial status. Public school educated casualties were considerable, with over 1,000 deaths from the ranks of old Etonians alone. Officers' children could apply for various scholarships via the deceased officer's regimental association, the Officers' Benevolent Department of the British Legion, or the Imperial Services College, Windsor, which had Her Royal Highness Princess Alice as patron.

Assistance was sometimes given to widows to pay for their children's education by their husband's former employer or professional body. On the death of her husband William, a former bank clerk, Ethel Cove utilized one of these funds, which was set up by the banking industry. Confusingly named the Bank Clerk's Orphanage, it did not consist of a bricks and mortar building and it was not necessarily for orphans. It was a monetary fund established in 1883 to provide for the education of children of banking staff upon the death of an employee. Unsurprisingly it became oversubscribed during the war, especially after the introduction of conscription. The usual marriage and birth certificates had to be provided and Ethel wrote to the Ministry of Pensions in April 1917 asking for the return of her certificates so she could prove her status to the fund. Her application was successful and Marjorie Cove was sent to Bray Court, a private preparatory school near Maidenhead. William Cove, despite his middle-class status in the civilian world, was nothing more than a gunner in the Royal Garrison Artillery and served as batman to his commanding officer. Ethel was granted a pension in line with his army rank. The 22s 11d a week she was receiving for herself and her two daughters would clearly not stretch to funding any form of private education.

The Lloyds Patriotic Fund was a potential source of assistance for the widows of naval officers. Shortly after the outbreak of war, the members of Lloyds Register collected £117,000 to be distributed to those suffering loss during the war. The original intention was that it should be for employees of Lloyds who were killed in action and for the children of naval officers who were killed or maimed in the conflict. As it turned out, there were very few Lloyd's employees requiring assistance, so most of the money went to the families of naval officers. In 1916, £3,993 was given to 108 widows and five officers who applied to the fund. Twenty-three widows from the Battle of Jutland made applications to Lloyds for assistance, with the families of those killed in the Battle of Coronal and the sinking of three cruisers by a German U-boat in September 1914 also assisted. The fund also gave education grants to a naval officer's children.

Poverty is a matter of perception in some cases and the upper-class widow may also have had to economize. Romantic novelist Barbara Cartland lamented that her mother was reduced to having just one servant after the death of her father, Major James Cartland, in May 1918. This financial downturn did not appear to impede his daughter's status as a leading socialite in 1920s London.[5] Clare Sheridan was a cousin of Winston Churchill, and her wedding in 1910 had attracted a crowd of the well-to-do, including the Crown Prince and Princess of Sweden. Her husband Wilfred was a descendant of playwright Richard Sheridan, and his father lived at Frampton Court in Dorset, an estate of 11,000 acres. After Wilfred's death, Clare was told her father-in-law could not afford to make any financial provision for her and her children, and she was reduced to living with her parents. Her father continually teetered on the edge of bankruptcy and put Clare under pressure to remarry, reminding her that her widow's pension did not cover the expense of keeping her and her two children under his roof.[6] Clare Sheridan turned to her sculpture to support herself, making busts of her famous friends and relatives and, after a secret trip to Russia in 1920, of leading Bolsheviks too.

Debrett's Peerage & Baronetage of January 1916 said that 800 members of the aristocracy had been killed in the war by 1915. A list of aristocratic casualties published in February 1916 showed that the heirs to forty-five peerages had already been killed.[7] In October 1914, the Royal Family suffered their own tragedy with the death in action of Prince Maurice of Battenberg, youngest grandchild of Queen Victoria and first cousin to the King. The early upper-class casualties were mostly career soldiers or those who had retired only to be called to defend King and country once more. They were often members of Guards regiments, traditionally the smartest and most fashionable regiments, and the hardest to get into if you were not of the right sort.

Death is no respecter of class, and wealthy families had stories just as tragic as those of their poorer neighbours. Captain Charles Bland had rejoined the army on the outbreak of war after a distinguished career that included honours in the South African Wars. Educated at Marlborough and Sandhurst, Captain Bland had joined his father's old regiment, the King's Own Scottish Borderers. His wife Isabella gave birth to a daughter the day after her husband was killed at Pilkem Ridge in April 1915. Lieutenant Colonel E.W. Benson, formerly of Winchester College and Oxford University, was the son of a baronet. Benson returned to the front within twenty-four hours of his wedding in June 1916 to his bride Muriel. She never saw him again as he was killed three months later at Delville Wood. Pamela Greer was widowed in July 1917 when her husband Eric, son of a baronet and the youngest lieutenant colonel in the Irish Guards, died in Belgium while she was pregnant with their first child. Nine months after the birth of her daughter, whom she named Erica, she herself was dead, a victim of the influenza epidemic of 1918. She was just twenty-three years old.

The wartime pages of *The Tatler* were full of pictures of glamorous war widows of the upper classes, often pictured in their expensive widows' weeds. One of the more unusual subjects for the magazine was the Right Honourable Mrs Geoffrey Pearson, who was better known by her maiden name, Ethel Lewis. She had married her husband in 1909, he being the son of Lord Cowdray of Midhurst and she being the daughter of a pub landlord. The social disparity got worse: not only was she of lowly origins, she was also an actress. In case those issues would not give the Pearsons enough concern, the Right Honourable Geoffrey was just eighteen years old when they married. Ethel Lewis was a member of the D'Oyly Carte company and was described as 'one of the most beautiful girls on the English stage'.[8] Perhaps unsurprisingly the couple kept their marriage secret from Geoffrey's family for some time, and the details were not reported in the newspapers until a year after the ceremony.

Lord Cowdray's objections to the marriage may not have been on the grounds of class. The Pearson family were originally from Bradford and had made their money in the civil engineering business. Despite all of the accoutrements of the upper classes, Lord Cowdray was very down to earth; he was proud of his Yorkshire roots, and never sought to abandon his strong Bradford accent. Lord and Lady Cowdray had progressive views on topics such as Home Rule for Ireland and votes for women,[9] and he would later play a significant part in the war by being appointed first chairman of the Air Board. The family's problem with the marriage appeared to be the tender age of the couple. When news of the wedding was finally out, they insisted that the lovers live separately until they were older. Ethel was sent to a Continental finishing school to receive the education that her upbringing had precluded her from experiencing, whilst Geoffrey was sent off to work. When war broke out, he enlisted immediately. Unusually for a man of his class, Geoffrey – known as 'Jeff' – did not serve as an officer, but as a lowly private. Within a few short days he was in France with the Army Service Corps as a motorcyclist. A month later, he was dead, shot while trying to escape from German trenches where he and a companion were being held captive.

The Right Honourable Mrs Geoffrey Pearson applied for a widow's pension. The officials processing the documents could hardly believe that they were dealing with an application for such a pittance from someone of her perceived social standing. When the original application neglected to include her marriage certificate, the record keeper for the Army Service Corps wrote to the War Office, 'In view of this lady's position, is this pension to be proceeded with please?'[10] Ethel also wrote to see if she was entitled to any back pay on behalf of her husband, as she claimed he only ever received thirty shillings in the month he was in khaki, whereas he should have been getting six shillings a day. In September 1915, she eventually received confirmation that she would receive a pension for herself and their daughter of fifteen shillings a week. Geoffrey Pearson's will listed assets of almost £6,000 in 1914.

Charity work was the preferred 'occupation' of the upper-class woman, and the proliferation of charities during the war presented extra opportunities to such women to 'do their bit'. War widows were no exception. Upper-class widows were to be found on all kinds of committees and in charge of fundraising endeavours nationwide. Ethel Lewis performed at benefit concerts for various soldiers' funds in the Midlands, including the Smokes for Wounded Soldiers and Sailors Society. Run by her sister-in-law, Lady Denman, this campaign distributed 265 million free cigarettes to injured Tommies and Tars during the war. Ethel also co-hosted a charity auction in Covent Garden with Lloyd George's daughter to raise funds for Welsh troops.

With the Queen setting an example with her involvement in a number of women's voluntary organizations, her frequent visits to the wounded and her efforts to help the food shortage by growing vegetables at her royal residences, it was very fashionable to be able to say one was engaged in war work. The commitment of some upper-class women was restricted to opening fundraising fetes and visiting the wounded one afternoon a week. *The Tatler* opined that, despite frequent appeals by the War Office, large numbers of women were doing nothing at all: 'if every sixth one is doing war work that's putting it at an indulgent sort of estimate.'[11] Some upper-class widows, however, were more genuine in their efforts.

Hospital work appeared to be particularly attractive to the aristocratic war widow. At the outbreak of hostilities, the War Office was inundated with offers of accommodation for wounded soldiers in country houses and other establishments all over the country. Buckingham Palace itself was suggested as a hospital, but was not easily adaptable to the needs of a surgical establishment. Many of the offers were to house officers only, as ordinary Tommies could not be trusted to behave in an English stately home. Over 3,000 auxiliary hospitals were opened in Britain during the war, a great number of them based in properties belonging to the wealthiest class in the country. *The Tatler* of 17 January 1917 said that nursing was so fashionable that 'even queens are taking to it now. ... while their name is legion those maidens and matrons who've got into nursing garb, anyway long enough to be photographed in it.'

Millicent, Duchess of Sutherland, had set the example for aristocratic nursing abroad, embarking for the Continent early in the war with her own entourage of duchesses, without waiting for official sanction. The Millicent Sutherland Ambulance, a group of eight nurses and a surgeon, had some notable adventures in France and Belgium in the early days of the war before being sent home by the Germans via Holland.[12] Undaunted, the Duchess then established a Red Cross hospital at Malo-Les-Bains, near Dunkirk, which operated throughout the conflict and offered 100 beds to wounded soldiers. Suddenly those fashionable ladies who were accustomed to going to the chic resort of Le Touquet for 'the season' were instead donning hospital garb and heading to the French coast to help the wounded.

Diana Wyndham worked at Millicent Sutherland's hospital from December 1915 to July 1917. She was the niece of Prime Minister Herbert Asquith and daughter of Lord Ribblesdale. In 1913 she had married Percy Wyndham, an Eton and Sandhurst educated officer in the Coldstream Guards. Lieutenant Wyndham, twenty-seven years old and described in the press as 'a fine, manly young Englishman',[13] was shot by a sniper in November 1914. When not nursing in France, Diana Wyndham took part in a range of charity events at home, raising money for the Red Cross and other war-related good causes.

Most upper-class nurses were recruited under the auspices of the Voluntary Aid Detachment, set up by the Red Cross in 1909. A VAD's nursing skills were often fairly basic at the beginning of the war and the work was unpaid, hence the proliferation of women from the ranks of society's better-off families. Barbara McLaren wrote in 1917 of the VADs that 'a large proportion' were 'women accustomed to lives of luxury and ease, to whom the hard and often unattractive work has been a new and difficult experience'.[14] There was resentment and tension between the new voluntary nurses and the established professional body. VADs were felt to be attracting unfair attention and praise and also potentially undermining the efforts of the nursing profession to be taken seriously and accorded appropriate status. On their part, VADs sometimes felt that the trained nurses were unfairly prejudiced against the new recruits and that the profession was generally inhospitable to outsiders.[15] A history of the VAD published during the war was keen to stress that all work was done in a great spirit of co-operation between the classes. The writer claimed that, for the VAD, 'there is no question of kindness or charity. It is the paying of a great debt, a mere matter of common honesty, a privilege beyond price.'[16] By the end of the war, 60,000 women had served as VADs in auxiliary hospitals.

A list of commendations issued by the War Office on 18 October 1917 for women involved in nursing services ran to three whole pages of *The Times*, many aristocratic women being amongst the names of the honoured. The list included the name of Lady Elcho, daughter of the Duke of Rutland. Lady Elcho's husband, Hugo Charteris, was an Eton educated barrister with a commission in the Gloucestershire Hussars. Lady Elcho had followed her husband's regiment to Egypt, where they were fighting the Turkish army. In April 1916, Lord Elcho disappeared in action. In May, Lady Elcho returned to England. In June 1916, information was received by the British Red Cross that Lord Elcho was in a Turkish prisoner of war camp at Damascus. Lady Elcho sent parcels to the camp on a daily basis. During this period of uncertainty, she kept up her public appearances and charity work. One gossip column described her at one of these events, saying, 'she looked ill and bore traces of having endured much.'[17] In July 1916, word was received that Lord Elcho had, in fact, been killed in action at Katia on Easter Sunday morning.

Following her husband's death, Lady Elcho devoted herself to nursing wounded officers. The Duchess of Rutland converted her mansion at 16 Arlington Street, Mayfair, London, into a hospital for officers, which opened in 1917. Though of comparatively small size with about thirty beds, the Rutland Hospital was fully equipped with an operating theatre. White chintz was attached to the walls of the house to hide the gilding and protect it from damage. The Duchess herself was matron, and Lady Elcho and her sister, Lady Diana Manners, were said to assist in operations on a daily basis. Lady Diana had undergone some formal nursing training at Guy's Hospital. The hospital was regularly visited by other royals and aristocrats, including the King and Queen, and the Duchess of Sutherland herself, doyenne of the high born hospital workers. One of the Prime Minister's sons, Arthur Asquith, was once a patient at Arlington Street. A number of the VAD nurses at the hospital were war widows.[18] In 1918, Lady Elcho moved on to Escrick Park near York, the home of Lady Wenlock, at that time another officer's hospital described in *The Sketch* as 'the Mecca at which every "smart" VAD hopes to arrive'.[19]

Rather less glamorous than plumping the pillows of lightly wounded officers in stately homes as imagined by *The Sketch* was the contribution made by Lady Gough, widow of Brigadier General John Edmond Gough VC. Part of a famous military family, Eton and Sandhurst educated John Gough had won his Victoria Cross in Somaliland. Dorothea Gough was also from an army background and the couple had a 6-year-old daughter. As a high ranking officer, Brigadier General

Gough might have been seen to be in much less danger than an ordinary soldier, but in February 1915 he went to inspect the trenches of his division and was mortally wounded. Gough was given the posthumous award of Knight Commander of the British Empire and Lady Gough received it on his behalf at Buckingham Palace in December 1916.

In 1917, part of the Marquess of Townsend's seat at Frognal, Kent was converted into what was known as the Queen's Hospital at Sidcup. The hospital was especially for officers and men who had suffered severe facial injuries, and for the next twelve years would undertake groundbreaking work in the field of facial reconstruction, with over 12,000 major operations carried out. Rehabilitation for these veterans was very important, with the psychological effects of this kind of injury being significantly worse than for those who had lost a limb. Reconstructive surgery was in its infancy and these men faced a long and difficult journey back into society. Training in new professions was a vital part of the work of the hospital and the premises included a toy making workshop and courses on a wide range of skills that could lead to employment opportunities.[20] Lady Gough's contribution was to run classes in writing for the men at the hospital, encouraging them to put their experiences down on paper, partly as an exercise in literacy but also as a psychological step on the road to recovery. Six examples of the essays produced from her classes survive, and are graphic and enthralling descriptions of life on the battlefield.[21]

Another more unusual hospital was the Coulter Hospital in Mayfair, where war widow Lady Juliet Duff was in charge. The Coulter Hospital was for officers and was situated in a mansion owned by a baronet who donated it to the War Office for the duration. The money raised to equip the hospital was provided by an intriguing American woman called Charlotte Herbine. It was as a result of her efforts that the hospital received its name; Mrs Herbine was a spiritualist and her spirit guide was called Dr Coulter. She was well connected, being particularly close to the Earl of Sandwich, who had a great interest in all things psychic and reportedly had skills of his own as a spiritualist healer. When the King and Queen visited the hospital in March 1916, Mrs Herbine greeted them as hostess.

Lady Juliet Duff was close to the Royal Family, her stepfather having been treasurer of Queen Alexandra's household. When she married Robin Duff, a racehorse owner and heir to a slate mine fortune, in 1903, she was driven to the church from Buckingham Palace in the Royal carriage. The King and Queen attended the wedding in person. Lady Duff lost her husband in October 1914 when he was serving on the Western Front with the Life Guards regiment. Lady Duff had been a key fundraiser for Charing Cross Hospital before the war and continued that interest with her work at the Coulter Hospital. She was also one of the aristocratic women behind the Women's War Economy League, which was established in 1915. The stated aims of the league were to reduce waste and unnecessary expense with a view to assisting the war effort. Their manifesto suggested the following rules:

> To reduce spending on imported goods and anything which could be considered a luxury.
> To resist all efforts to introduce new fashions.
> To give up all unnecessary entertaining.
> No motor cars to be used unless for charity work.
> In no case to employ men servants unless they are ineligible for public service.

Of course, this meant nothing to the average woman, who did no entertaining and could only dream of owning a motor car or employing servants, but the league declared that an example must be set by those who could afford to economize.

One war widow who was particularly active on the hospital home front was Marion Hughes-Onslow, known to her family as 'Min'. Marion was the wife of Major Denzil Hughes-Onslow, an officer from a wealthy family with a tradition of military service. Denzil had been schooled at Charterhouse and Sandhurst and had already enjoyed a successful career in the army by 1914. The life of the Hughes-Onslows pre-war appears to have been a happy round of hunting, shooting and fishing. Charity work, of course, played a part and the major was a local councillor in Ballantrae, where they had two country estates, and was also on the local school board. Marion was also involved in opening fetes and supporting church fund-raising activities both in Scotland and at their Dorset home, Colliton House in Dorchester. Though retired from the army, Denzil returned to the colours when war broke out. Marion went back to Scotland to live at one of the houses there as the couple gave Colliton House to the War Office as hospital accommodation. The house became a VAD hospital, with wounded Belgian soldiers the first to use the premises in early 1915. Initially having around sixty beds, a further sixty were added in 1917 with the assistance of a number of marquees placed in the grounds of the house.

Major Denzil Hughes-Onslow was killed at Mametz Wood on the Somme in July 1916. Marion responded by throwing herself into her work, this time converting her home at Laggan House in Ballantrae, Ayrshire into another auxiliary hospital. She was living in the family's other home at Balkissock, a few miles away, but was herself the commandant at Laggan House VAD hospital. The War Office generally gave an allowance per patient to those who provided hospital accommodation during the war, but Marion did not ask for any funds in relation to the fifty beds provided at Laggan House. The premises were used as more of a convalescent home than a hospital, meaning that expensive medical equipment was not necessary. The first soldiers arrived in January 1917, and hundreds had passed through by the time the war was over. Some idea of the size of the house, and the wealth of the Hughes-Onslow family, can be gauged by the fact that in peacetime the premises required twelve servants to keep it running.

In addition to looking after wounded soldiers at Laggan House, Marion Hughes-Onslow was active on a number of committees in the Ballantrae district, including the Local War Pensions Committee. Her two eldest sons were also on active service and survived the war. In July 1920, she was presented with the CBE by the King at Holyrood Palace in Edinburgh in recognition of her war work. Marion contributed a significant amount of money to construct the war memorial at Ballantrae for the thirty-nine local men lost in the conflict. She also paid a proportion of the costs of a new public hall in the village, which included a roll of honour tablet in her husband's name.

Mrs Charlotte ('Lottie') Walrond was the wife of Lionel Walrond MP. She had worked tirelessly to ensure her husband's election to his parliamentary seat and was well respected in his Tiverton constituency. Lionel Walrond was keen to do his bit in the war effort and had enlisted in 1914. He was given a commission in the Royal Army Service Corps and went to France, where he worked as a railway transport officer. Lottie was very active in recruiting in Devon, trying to encourage farmers' sons to join up. A crack shot with a rifle, she was keen on hunting and shooting and took part in retriever trials to raise money for the Prince of Wales Fund. She later sold her pack of retrievers and donated the proceeds to the British Red Cross. She herself was from a wealthy family, part of the Coats thread manufacturing company in Scotland.

Shortly after the outbreak of war, the Walronds gave their house, Bradfield Hall, to the War Office to use as convalescent hospital, Lottie herself being the commandant. Newspapers reported the idyllic surroundings in which the wounded would find themselves:

> The men are free to roam over all parts of the beautiful grounds and to enjoy themselves with golf, fishing or boating on the expansive lake, or the many other pleasures with which Bradfield abounds.[22]

Unlike many of the stately homes offered as hospitals, Bradfield was for all ranks, not just officers. Devon newspapers reported that Mrs Walrond had arranged and paid for the wedding of a soldier convalescing at her home before he returned to the front. Joshua Rigby of the Gloucestershire Regiment married his sweetheart,

Edith Gardener, at Bradfield. Mrs Walrond had the chapel decorated with flowers from the estate's gardens in red, white and blue, and also provided the bridal bouquet. She transported the bride to the ceremony in her own carriage, and, dressed in her Red Cross uniform, gave her away. Two nurses acted as bridesmaids. Mrs Walrond also paid for the reception at Bradfield and the couple's brief honeymoon in Exeter. Giving a speech at the reception, Mrs Walrond said: 'The only thing that makes life worth living is having the affection of someone who is going to share the ups and downs in life, and be sympathetic and understanding.'[23]

Private Rigby would survive the war; Mrs Walrond's husband would not be so lucky. Unfortunately, his always delicate health broke down and, returning to England to convalesce, he died of tuberculosis in November 1915. He was one of twenty-two Members of Parliament to die on active service during the war and he left two sons, aged ten and six. Unlike so many widows who were denied a funeral service for their husbands, Lottie Walrond went through two such ceremonies, one on the family's Scottish estate, where her husband died, and another ceremony back at Bradfield, where he was interred.

Lottie Walrond's war work did not cease with her husband's death. She maintained her position as matron at Bradfield and founded a communal kitchen in the local village. She was honorary secretary of the Melbourne House Training Home in Exeter, part of the town's organization for Friendless Girls.[24] She was also an enthusiastic supporter of the Women's Land Army and of the idea generally that women were capable of running farms in peacetime as well as times of war.

Elizabeth Coey, known as Elsie, was from a prominent family in Northern Ireland, her father being Deputy Lieutenant of County Antrim. In 1912 she married William Tillie Dickson, son of an MP and heir to their prosperous linen business in Dungannon. Educated at Uppingham, William was very active in local politics, being a staunch supporter of the Ulster Volunteer Force (UVF) and among the first to enlist in their ranks at the outbreak of war, serving with the Inniskilling Fusiliers. Elsie Dickson was close to her in-laws, especially her sister-in-law Jessie, who was the same age. Jessie Dickson had been nursing since the start of the war, going out to the hospital established by the UVF Nursing Corps at the fashionable Pyrenees resort town of Pau. Six months after the death of her husband, Elsie Dickson followed Jessie's example, both women now nursing at the Hôpital Temporaire d'Arc-en-Barrois. Established by British nurses, the hospital dealt with French casualties and had a number of upper-class women on the staff, including Kathleen Scott, the widow of Antarctic hero Robert Scott.

Annie Michie, a trained nurse and a matron at the Hôpital Temporaire, was delighted with the work of the Dicksons and in April 1917 wrote to Mrs Dickson senior in Dungannon. She praised Elsie Dickson in particular, saying she had worked 'perfectly splendidly',[25] especially considering she had no previous experience in nursing. Matron said of Elsie, 'She is kind to the patients and yet holds her own with a certain dignity which one cannot help admiring.' The work she was doing at the hospital, Matron felt, 'must have helped to take her mind off her life long sorrow and if possible to deaden the pain caused thereby.' No doubt many of the widows of all classes now working for the war effort hoped for the same outcome.

Lorna Heenan, wife of Captain Michael Heenan, had occupied herself with war work in Dorset before her husband's death in 1916. She had worked on the local recruitment register, visited war hospitals, cooked midnight meals for munitions workers and learned how to fix cars by working in a local garage business.[26] She later reportedly accompanied the Army of Occupation on the Rhine after the Armistice as a policewoman. In 1928, she cited this experience in order to be appointed as female liaison officer to the Dorset Police Force.

Eton educated Lieutenant Ivan Sprot served with the Cameron Highlanders and was killed in France in October 1914. Ivan Sprot's widow, Nancy, was the daughter of renowned Edinburgh eye surgeon George Berry, who was knighted during the war. Her father's medical connections no doubt assisted Nancy in finding a position with the First Aid Nursing Yeomanry, known as the FANY. Largely composed of upper and middle-class women, the FANY were not granted official status by the War Office until 1916. The first members of the FANY to nurse in the First World War did so attached to the Belgian army in 1914. They worked throughout the war, driving ambulances and other vehicles on the front and assisting the wounded. Nancy Sprot became an ambulance driver in France, first going overseas in May 1916, and was mentioned in Sir Douglas Haig's despatch of 1919 for her work with the FANY on the Western Front.

The wealth and status of widows like Marion Hughes-Onslow and Lottie Walrond allowed them to act in ways that were not available to the ordinary woman, who did not have a spare house to offer as a hospital, or the luxury of being able to take work unpaid. War work did not stop wealthy widows from taking part in many of the usual social activities, though opportunities for balls and suppers were very much reduced. Diana Wyndham, clad in very smart black garb, found the time to accompany her father to court in 1915 to see the Brides in the Bath murder case, quite the fashionable thing to do at the time.

Marion Hughes-Onslow's obituary in *The Times* stated that after the death of her husband, her life 'was devoted solely to the welfare and happiness of others', describing her as 'a model of perfect selflessness, eager charity and personal devotion to others such as will live in the memories of those privileged to bear witness'.[27] The publicity given to rich war widows must be placed in context of the aristocracy being seen as setting the tone for the rest of the country. This concept had been apparent in the crusade against mourning dress and, as we have seen, was the underlying ethos of the campaign against waste started by the upper-class ladies of the Women's War Economy League. The coverage of the aristocratic widows' efforts conveyed the impression that the whole country was in the fight together. *Tatler* portraits of fashionable women in nursing garb, subtitled 'A War Widow', showed readers that this was what a war widow could look like, this was work a war widow could do. She was not restricted to wearing widow's weeds and shutting herself away, and indeed had a duty to engage in activities to help the war effort. War widows, like all women, were not only required to help repopulate the country after the war; they were needed to do their bit during the war too. The publication of books like *Women and the War*,[28] with its foreword by Asquith himself, was designed to encourage women from comfortable backgrounds to take up war work, from nursing to munitions.

The First World War is often seen as heralding the end of the privileged lifestyle enjoyed by England's aristocracy. The high death rate amongst officers deprived estates of their rightful heirs, whilst taxation levels previously unseen in Britain made a significant dent in the family coffers. Lottie Walrond had to economize after the war, giving up her house in Aberdeenshire and eventually selling off parts of the Bradfield estate. When Marion Hughes-Onslow died in March 1933, she left her property to her sons. Estate duties no doubt bit into the inheritance and by June that year large amounts of antique furniture and other personal property were being auctioned off at Laggan House, including two motor cars and the contents of the wine cellar.[29]

Surveying the damage done to the ranks of the upper classes as early as September 1914, *The Tatler* said:

> Sometimes they're too heartbreaking, aren't they, these sacrifices of our people? With the light of their lives gone out, how to go on, how to look up, how to face the world at all – that will be the hardest part of all for some of us.[30]

Chapter 6

Misbehaving Husbands and Inquisitive Wives

*'Forgive the trouble I may cause you but I am nearly broken heart-
ed to know nothing of him.'*

A death or disablement in service did not guarantee a pension for a man or his
widow. Problems for widows arose because in principle a pension was awarded for
the service of the husband, not the benefit of the wife. Successive Royal Warrants
specifically excluded pension payments for those who died or were injured at their
own hand or due to their own negligence or misconduct. The refusal of a pension
on these grounds was a source of potential embarrassment and shame for families,
and was one of the reasons cited in evidence before the 1919 Select Committee on
Pensions for keeping Pension Appeal Tribunal hearings closed to members of the
public.[1] As late as 1921, the Ministry of Pensions were considering not even telling
widows that their claim for a pension had failed due to their husband's misconduct. The idea was not taken further as it was felt a widow would certainly appeal
if she was not told the facts, the implication being that the shame of a misconduct
allegation would otherwise deter her.[2]

Accidental deaths in service would appear to be a fairly straightforward proposition; if a man was killed in an accident while engaged in military service, a widow
should be eligible for a pension. Unfortunately, where it came to paying out government money, nothing was ever straightforward and a number of widows found
themselves bereft of support due to hard interpretations of the Royal Warrant.

If an accidental death was held to be the result of any misconduct or negligence
on the part of the man, no pension would be granted to his widow. One such case
was that of James Stansbie, who died in January 1915 after a fall. Stansbie was a
serving soldier at the time and the incident happened in an army camp. However,
he was undergoing field punishment at the time and was confined to the guard
room. Stansbie had climbed up to a shelf above the door and refused to come
down when challenged by his guards. He allegedly fell to the floor and died the
next day from his injuries. Hannah Stansbie had four children to support, but
once her separation allowance was at an end, she received no widow's pension.
She was told, rather disingenuously, that her husband's death had occurred while

he was off duty, meaning that she was not entitled to a pension. Failure to tell widows the truth about their husband's deaths was a common feature of many of the 'doubtful' cases during the war. The hope from the authorities was that widows would just accept letters at face value, make no further enquiries and disappear from the scene. Hannah Stansbie did not disappear and engaged various local agencies around Birmingham to pursue the case on her behalf, including the Birmingham Citizens' Committee and the local branch of the SSFA. Despite this intervention the Ministry of Pensions stood firm in their refusal. Hannah Stansbie did not give up, writing consistently over the next two years, claiming, 'While I am waiting my dear ones are wanting.'[3] Her persistence eventually saw her wring a 'special allowance' of twenty shillings a week out of the Special Grants Committee for her children, but no pension for herself.[4]

The question of whether a man was on or off duty was often decided to the detriment of the pension claimant, though the distinction was a fine one. Two road accident cases illustrate the approach taken to the point. On 11 August 1914, Captain James Arrowsmith of the Northern Cyclist Battalion was riding his motorcycle the short distance from Hartlepool to Seaton Carew to inspect a post when he was involved in a collision with another vehicle. The inquest heard that Arrowsmith had been run over by a steam motor wagon, which turned right across his path. No one saw the actual incident occur, the wagon driver simply feeling the impact. A verdict of accidental death was returned. Arrowsmith had been a court clerk in civilian life, secretary of the Durham County Rifle Meeting, and was described as one of the best rifle shots the county ever had. After reading the inquest report, the War Office granted his widow and three children a pension.[5]

Ernest Roscoe was managing director of a theatrical sign making company in Leeds called Gawthorpe's. A prominent figure in local politics, he was an enthusiastic supporter of the city's recruitment drive, instrumental in the establishment of the 17th Battalion of the West Yorkshire Regiment, the Leeds Bantams. He himself joined the battalion, becoming its adjutant. During training in Skipton in June 1915, Roscoe and a number of other officers were granted permission to drive to Ilkley to see a film about the Bantams. Returning to Skipton in the dark, the driver of the vehicle misjudged the road and crashed. Ernest Roscoe was flung from the car, fracturing his skull. He died at Skipton Hospital shortly thereafter and was buried with full military honours. An inquest heard that neither the passengers nor the driver were drunk and the incident was seen as a tragic accident. Application for a pension was made on behalf of Lieutenant Roscoe's grieving widow, Edith, and the couple's young son. The application was refused as he was not on duty at the time of the accident, despite being on an officially sanctioned trip. After appeals on her behalf from Ernest's brother, a one-off gratuity was eventually granted to Edith of a year's officer's salary – hardly a fitting recompense for the loss of a husband and a lifetime's earnings.[6]

The War Office made a distinction between accidents that happened on British shores and those that took place overseas, granting pensions whether a man was on or off duty if he was abroad at the time and there was no negligence on his behalf. The Ministry of Pensions, once established, adopted the same approach, but took the view that the War Office had been too lenient in such cases. A memo of March 1917 noted that the War Office had a 'tendency to admit almost any accident not clearly due to the man's fault if it happened to occur across the Channel.'[7]

The distinction between home accidents and those that took place abroad created undoubted injustice. Whilst poor Edith Roscoe was refused assistance, the family of Lieutenant James Holmes were dealt with more leniently, despite the circumstances being very similar. Holmes was stationed in Egypt in 1918, and, along with some colleagues, was granted an afternoon off. They hitched a lift to Port Said on an army truck and arranged for the same driver to take them back to base later that night. On the return journey, one of his fellow officers decided to take the wheel from the original driver, subsequently crashing. Lieutenant Holmes was killed instantly. His death was ruled to be attributable to war service and a pension was granted to his dependants.[8]

During George Barnes' tenure as the first Minister of Pensions, a settled policy was arrived at on accident cases that mostly reflected the broad approach that had been taken to date. Barnes softened the formula by stating that men on home service who were going to or from military duties, i.e. returning from leave etc., when they were killed should be entitled to have their families looked after as long as there was no negligence on their part. This 1917 amendment of course came too late for many widows.

In the case of home service deaths, inquest juries seemed to do their best to help the grieving families. In cases where there might have been negligence, the benefit of the doubt was given, verdicts of 'accidental death' being recorded, which may have influenced the Ministry of Pensions into providing financial support to the widow.

On 1 November 1918, Martin Roach of the Royal Defence Corps arrived in Galway with his unit. Seventeen days later, his body was discovered sitting in the mud of the dockway by an employee of the local Guinness stores. Roach's superior, Lieutenant Glover, told the inquest that he had been instructed by his commanding officer that everything possible should be done for the widow and family. This was a clear nod to the jury that they should find the death accidental. They obliged accordingly, the coroner remarking that there had been a previous incident at the docks due to lack of a guard rail. Having studied the inquest report in the local paper, the Ministry granted Mrs Roach her pension.[9]

A special category of cases involved those who were killed accidentally while undergoing military punishment. Examples included a man who was killed by a lorry while being marched under guard from one location to another. Were these cases to be dealt with as accidents during military service that were not of the man's own fault, or was the fact that he was undergoing punishment at the time fatal to his widow's pension? The Ministry were unsure, acknowledging that on the one hand the death was not due to the soldier's misconduct, but on the other that:

> it is repugnant to treat the widow or dependant of a man killed who is under punishment for showing cowardice before the enemy or for deser- tion, in the same way as the widow or dependant of a man who has met his death while performing an act of conspicuous gallantry.[10]

In 1917, it was decided that in such cases a widow would not receive a full pension of 13s 9d per week, but a reduced amount of ten shillings.

The most extreme case of misbehaviour on the part of a soldier would incur the ultimate wrath of the military authorities – execution by firing squad. A total of 346 British and Commonwealth soldiers were executed by their own comrades in the First World War. If the number of married men was in line with the general casualty statistics, one would anticipate that around ninety of those men would leave widows behind them.[11] These women would not be entitled to a pension under the terms of successive Royal Warrants.

The question of a family's knowledge of the details of their disgraced husband's death was a live issue throughout the early years of the war. Part of the ritual of court martial and execution involved the reading out of the miscreant's name, crime and sentence at the roll call of his fellow soldiers. This public shaming was seen by the army as an essential deterrent to desertion, as if the threat of being executed itself were not enough. This practice meant that it was never possible to keep such cases secret from the wider public, as soldiers would talk and the news would get out. In those circumstances, the army took the view that blunt truth was required in communications with the families. Where a soldier had been executed his family were sent a letter informing them of that fact and the reason for the sen- tence being passed. The communication was described in the House of Commons as 'a polite letter which is sent, stating a necessarily brutal fact'.[12] The horror of receiving such a letter is unimaginable. Not only had the loved one died, but he had died in such circumstances as would preclude the widow from participation in memorial rituals and from financial support. No pensions would be payable to dependants and the soldier would have been deemed to have forfeited his right to any campaign medals. The daughter of Private Harry Farr, executed for desertion in 1916, recalled her mother receiving this communication at the Post Office and immediately shoving it into her clothing out of sight, telling no one.[13]

The case of Private George Everill of the North Staffordshire Regiment comes from this phase of the war. His entry in the Commonwealth War Graves records indicates that he was killed in action, whereas his military service record shows the uncomfortable truth that a court martial convicted him of desertion and ordered his execution in September 1917. Everill was thirty years old and had a wife and children living in Hanley, near Stoke. He enlisted in August 1914 and from 1916 onwards was constantly in trouble with the military authorities for various offences of insubordination. His disciplinary problems culminated in the final charge, which was that he had disobeyed the direct order of an officer to proceed to the trenches. Instead, he had left his battalion and gone missing until being found in a village behind the lines. He had only been missing for six hours, but his previous disciplinary record counted heavily against him and this time he received the ultimate punishment.

In April 1918, his personal belongings were returned to his wife Lily, back in Hanley. All of his surviving war records make it crystal clear that he was shot for desertion. Given the army policy at the time, his wife would certainly have been made aware of this fact. It does appear as though the truth about George Everill may well have been kept quiet in the local community; the Hanley war memorial list of names proudly has the name of G. Everill amongst his 11,000 comrades from the town who served.[14]

Jesse Short was a miner living in Felling, County Durham at the outbreak of war. He had already accrued a dubious military record in his native Wales, deserting twice and being discharged twice as not being able to become an efficient soldier.[15] In October 1914, he enlisted again in the North East, claiming never to have been in the army. He was accepted into the Durham Light Infantry, this time for a mere ten days before being discharged again because his teeth were not up to scratch. In November he tried one of the designated 'Tyneside Irish' battalions of the Northumberland Fusiliers and was accepted. He had a wife, Dinah, and two infant daughters.

In 1917, he was identified as a ringleader of the infamous mutiny at Étaples, the detested training camp on the French coast. Short was said to have been the key player in an attempt to cross the bridge out of camp, inciting his fellow soldiers to assault the guards blocking their way. He was arrested and sentenced to death, the only soldier involved in the mutiny to suffer this fate. Jesse Short's gravestone in Boulogne Eastern Cemetery bears the inscription 'Duty called and he went forward. Ever remembered by his wife and children.' Dinah Short would have been the recipient of the blunt communication from the army giving her the facts. She would not have been able to obtain a pension for herself and her daughters, nor would she be entitled to any medals her husband had earned during his service. The cruelty of leaving such families bereft of financial assistance is striking.

However, Dinah Short and Lily Everill's economic distress may have been short-lived. The government had been under pressure from Poor Law Guardians who had essentially been taking up the slack in these cases, providing financial support to women who could have been living on a war widow's pension if their husbands had been killed in action. J.M. Hogge, Liberal MP for Edinburgh East, and other backbench colleagues had persistently raised the problems faced by the widows of the executed in the House of Commons, attacking not only the inability to obtain a pension, but also the form of letter written to the families in such cases. Both of these aspects of the process were now to change.

The year 1917 was a difficult one for the Allies. Failure to make a breakthrough on the Western Front had been coupled with a distinct cooling of support for the war at home. More days were lost by strikes in 1917 than in any other year of the war. In addition, the Bolshevik Revolution in Russia had caused further instability and the fear that such action may spread and undermine the war effort. A number of quiet concessions were made to working-class interests at this time. Wage demands were often met and food subsidies were introduced. It is against this background that the decision to allow widows of executed men a pension should be viewed.

The change happened quite quickly. At the end of June 1917, John Hodge, then Minister for Pensions, wrote: 'A time may come when the State will feel it has a special duty towards the unfortunate dependants of such men, but that is not yet.'[16]

Just four months later, that time did come, no doubt to the surprise of the minister. Hodge had argued that if anything was to be granted, it should be on a two-tier system so that dependants of those who had died in disgrace did not receive as much as those who died in more valiant circumstances. He wrote to the Cabinet stating that he wanted:

> a distinction which, while not placing any dependant of a man shot for cowardice at any monetary disadvantage as compared with other dependants, would have established beyond doubt that pensions as such are a reward for service and not merely grants paid in compassion to the relatives of a deceased soldier.[17]

Quite how he squared the concept of no monetary disadvantage with paying depen-dants of the executed less than other widows is a mystery. His representations came too late as the matter had already been decided. The widows of executed men no longer had the added distress of resorting to the Poor Law to stigmatize them further. On 4 December 1917, newspapers reported that widows of these men could now apply for full pensions under Article 11 of the Royal Warrant – the standard clause that granted pensions in cases of war deaths. The new approach would apply retrospectively. An illustration of the disjointed manner in which the Ministry's policies were decided was that no one had thought to reconsider the cases of men who had died accidentally while in military custody. Their widows were still receiving the lesser pension of ten shillings a week until April 1918, when their amounts were raised to the standard level.[18]

The issue regarding the form of letter from the army was strangely just as prob-lematic. The army took the view that the letter should not be changed, that families should know the truth and that shame was an inevitable consequence of the ultimate sentence. Pensions were granted to dependants of the executed before the army could be persuaded to change its notification letter. In the light of questions that were being asked in the House about the legitimacy of such executions, the gov-ernment no doubt felt pressure to soften the blow to families somewhat. The new letter would no longer contain the details of the crimes and sentence, but just utilize the bland phrase that the executed soldier had 'died on service'. It was to express some regret, but not include the standard message of sympathy from the King and Queen; there was still a concern to maintain some kind of distinction between an ordinary casualty and an execution. The wording was finally agreed and distributed in an Army Order in January 1918.

Up until the last minute the army tried to have the War Cabinet change their mind about the letter. They argued that any dilution of the facts would have a ten-dency to undermine army discipline. Lord Derby called the new procedure 'more cruel than kind'. He obviously believed that such families had no right to mourn in the traditional manner, saying that if they were not told the truth, working-class families would incur considerable expense in buying the trappings of mourning, 'elaborate In Memoriam cards containing the deceased's photograph and some verse of poetry as to a heroe's death [sic]'.[19] He felt that the truth could only be concealed for a few weeks, until letters would arrive from fellow soldiers with the full facts, and that this was 'a double catastrophe for the widow and family'.[20] He was told it was too late, as Parliament had already agreed the change.

The new approach is reflected in the case file of the only married man of the three officers executed during the war.[21] Second Lieutenant James Paterson enlisted in the Essex Regiment in April 1915 at the age of twenty-three. He had a few minor disciplinary issues in his early army career and was removed from duty due to injury on three occasions in 1916. The last two of those injuries were gunshot wounds to the hand, often considered as notorious shirkers' injuries. However, there is no evidence that suspicion attached itself to Paterson's wounds and he was given a commission in September 1917. While away on leave, he married his sweetheart, Alice, who lived in Leytonstone.

Six months later, Paterson absconded from his regiment in France. While AWOL, he committed several offences of cheque fraud and was circulated as wanted by the military authorities. He remained in France, hiding amongst the local population until he was apprehended in Calais on 3 July 1918. The encounter ended in tragedy when Paterson shot and killed Sergeant Collison of the Military Police rather than be arrested. Paterson escaped and his photograph was now distributed to the military police. No enquiries appear to have been made with Alice back in Leytonstone – she herself was writing to the record keeper of the Essex Battalion to ask for news. Oblivious to her husband's desertion, she had previously been notified that James Paterson was simply 'missing'. She had continued to write to him, seeing all of her letters returned 'not known'. James Paterson was eventually apprehended and court-martialled in September 1918; the inevitable result being a death sentence. At 6.27 am on 24 September 1918, that sentence was carried out as he was shot by firing squad. His wife was not informed of his death and was still writing letters, which went unanswered.

Eventually, in late October 1918, her brother took up the cause, writing direct to the War Office begging for information. He described Alice as 'quite unable to bear this awful strain any longer, what with the anxiety of no news coupled with the fact of no financial assistance coming to her from her husband.' Eventually the new style one-paragraph letter was sent to Alice that month, simply stating that J.H. Paterson had 'died on service' in France on 24 September 1914.

Uncomfortably for the War Office and contrary to the hopes of those redesigning the letters, Alice Paterson, in common with many war widows, still craved facts. Writing to the War Office at the end of November 1918, she sought further information about his death. She wrote, 'Forgive the trouble I may cause you but I am nearly broken hearted to know nothing of him.'[22] The War Office were not completely without compassion for her circumstances as, clearly, her husband's misdemeanours were not of her doing. Several versions of a letter to her were painstakingly compiled, the original making it clear that James Paterson had been executed for desertion and murder. However, the letter eventually sent to Alice omitted all reference to the murder of Sergeant Collison. The writer said that it had been hoped she would not make further enquiries after being told of her husband's death, but now that she had, it was with 'extreme grief' that the 'sad facts' must be reported to her that he had been executed for desertion 'and other crimes'. The letter concluded, 'I am directed to offer to you yourself the deepest sympathy in your great sorrow.'[23] Alice was silent thereafter.

Alice Paterson would now be entitled to the pension that was denied her fellow widows for the first three years of the war. The amount she received could have been significantly reduced because, perhaps unsurprisingly, James Paterson had an outstanding debt to the officers' outfitters and bankers, Cox & Co. The firm quietly agreed with the War Office not to pursue the not inconsiderable sum of £56 that was owed. Amongst the personal belongings returned to his wife was a champagne cork.

Despite the amendment to the standard letter, it is likely that wives of the executed would have discovered the truth about their husband's deaths from one source or another. It is difficult to imagine that all of the women concerned would simply have taken the army description of 'died on service' at face value and not made further enquiries. Undoubtedly some did and others will have discovered the facts from local gossip or comrades who returned home and imparted the sad news. The views of those who had served alongside the executed were often far more sympathetic than those of their army superiors. These men had endured the same horrors as their executed comrades and understood the pressures involved. Controversy was occasioned amongst many local committees in the years following the Armistice over the issue of which of the dead were eligible for inclusion on war memorials.[24] In 2006, the 306 First World War soldiers who were executed for cowardice or desertion were officially pardoned. This was ninety years too late in many cases, and did nothing to alleviate the suffering and shame the families had endured.

Some soldiers were unable to cope with the conditions under which they were forced to serve and took their own lives. The widows of these men were not necessarily eligible for pensions and their cases show a great degree of inconsistency on the part of the administration. Suicide was, of course, illegal in England at this time. Those who tried and failed were liable to prosecution and imprisonment until the law was changed in 1961. The state had always placed penalties upon those who committed suicide, usually to be served by their families in the form of the denial of the usual Christian burial rites and the potential seizure of the deceased's property. Inquest juries often returned a verdict of 'temporary insanity' as this avoided the unpleasant consequences that may follow a finding that the individual had deliberately and calculatedly taken their own life. This did not mean that they believed the person was truly insane, but that just for that moment, their grip on lucidity had slipped to the extent that they took their own life. From the mid-nineteenth century onwards, nine-tenths of suicides attracted this verdict from inquest juries.[25]

Inquest verdicts caused a potential problem for the military authorities in deciding whether the wife of a man committing suicide was entitled to a war widow's pension. If a man in the forces was deemed to be suffering from 'temporary insanity', then it was difficult to say that the insanity had not been caused by his war service. The army does not seem to have investigated these cases in great detail at the start of the war, confining itself to checking the inquest verdict, if one took place. Unless it could be proved that the man was insane when he joined up, the army was accepting liability in cases where an inquest had returned a verdict of temporary insanity. However, as the war went on, the increasing number of such cases and the seeming lack of any settled policy provoked an investigation by the Ministry of Pensions. A case where a man with a history of mental problems in his family killed himself after only a few days' service came to the Ministry's attention and years of discussions then took place over the correct stance to be taken.[26]

Inconsistencies in the approach to suicides were clear from the thirty cases sent to the Ministry in this survey. Some apparently meritorious cases were refused, for example that of Private Goddard, who had served in France until sent home wounded but was back on duty at the time of his death. Goddard had shot himself when taking a comrade's rifle down from a rack, leaving a wife and three children. The incident could easily have been an accident as there was no evidence of suicidal intent, but because the owner of the rifle insisted that it had not been loaded when he left it, Goddard was listed as having committed suicide. His widow was told she had no claim to a War Office pension at all.[27] Other cases were granted when the policy would suggest they should be turned down. Gunner Bigham killed himself after serving a period of detention for going absent without leave, but a pension was granted to his wife and children. Company Sergeant Major J. Young was about to be charged with an offence of being found in a brothel when he shot himself. After an initial refusal, his widow's claim was allowed.[28]

Sometimes it appears that the question of eligibility was decided on the basis of the needs of the potential recipient of the pension, rather than on strict liability grounds. Private Robert Ellender reportedly killed himself due to worries at home over his wife's infidelity rather than anything specifically occasioned by his war service. However, in addition to his wife, he had six children to support who would now be a burden on the state in some way, so an Article 11 pension was granted.[29]

The Ministry felt that the army's approach to the issue of temporary insanity was far too lenient. A verdict of temporary insanity was a sympathy verdict by a jury, not a medical diagnosis, and the Ministry felt that tighter interpretations were required. The Ministry decided that where there was no evidence of particular strain other than just being called up, no contraction of an illness that might have caused problems to a man's mental health, and no foreign service, pensions should not be granted 'and certainly not where there is evidence of possible con-genital insanity'.[30] This left a man's whole family history to be investigated, in addition to his own behaviour, before any grant of pension under Article 11 could be made to his widow.

This level of scrutiny applied to officers as well as men. When 2nd Lieutenant Alexander Bell cut his own throat with a razor while being treated in hospital for dysentery in 1919, the inquest jury held that he had killed himself while of unsound mind owing to a disease contracted on war service abroad. Despite this clear indication that a pension would be payable to his widow, the Ministry would not authorize any such payments until a full investigation into his military conduct had taken place. The investigation was directed to discover 'whether the officer's services were satisfactory, and whether there is any reason to connect his death with anything detrimental to his character as an officer'.[31] Only when a satisfactory reply was received was a pension authorized to his widow, Florence.

The case of Private Deeming was brought to the attention of the Ministry due to a protest made by the Atherstone Board of Guardians. Deeming had shot him-self in September 1915 after five months' home service, and his widow, Isabella, was granted a full pension. The Atherstone Guardians protested against this in the strongest possible terms, claiming that Deeming had shot himself to avoid foreign service. His civilian behaviour was placed under the microscope, with the Guardians claiming that he was a drinker who was in trouble with the police before enlisting. The accusation of unworthiness was extended to his wife, with claims that she also liked a drink. The intervention of the Guardians saw his widow's claim for a full pension rejected. However, George Barnes, Minister of Pensions, granted Isabella Deeming a pension under Article 15 of the Royal Warrant – a temporary allowance of fifteen shillings a week, until twelve months from the end of the war. It was made clear that this was subject to her good behaviour.

The temporary pension was a classic ministry fudge where a difficult issue arose. Even Barnes himself acknowledged it was 'illogical', but it was increasingly used in cases of suicide from 1917 onwards. After ordering a review of cases, Barnes seemed incapable of making a decision, leaving it to a more junior ministry official, Matthew Wynne, to come up with a formula to be used. Wynne explained 'the sui-cide formula' as follows, with pensions to be granted in the following circumstances:

Article 11 – suicide, if from insanity traceable to the strain of active ser-vice or some exciting or unnerving cause directly connected with military service.

Article 15 – suicide, if not coming under the above and not from deliber-ate evasion of duty or justice.[32]

This reversed the burden of proof that had been used by the army in deciding such cases; instead of insanity being presumed to be caused by military service unless there was evidence to the contrary, it now had to be *directly* traceable to war service. If it was not, and the Ministry could not find a loophole to deny the claim completely, the most the man's widow would receive was fifteen shillings a week for the rest of the war, with no extra allowances for any children. Fifteen shillings was, of course, much less than a wife was likely to have been getting in separation allowance. In this way, the Ministry still found a way for the state to punish a suicide.

The issue was to come into stark focus in 1919, with these widows approaching the end of their period of entitlement to their fifteen shillings a week. The *News of the World* took up their case, with their 'Pensions Expert', Thomas Ogilvie, writing sympathetic articles and also taking matters up directly with the Ministry, campaigning for equal treatment with Article 11 widows. The paper claimed to have received 1,232 letters from widows receiving temporary pensions, and had interviewed 300 of these women. Ogilvie claimed that:

> homes which were at one time well-furnished are now bare and empty; little children whose faces once bore the look of perfect health are now pale and drawn. … Others, again, are in the workhouse and the children distributed in various institutions.[33]

He quite rightly questioned why the widow should suffer when the husband's death was nothing to do with any misconduct on her part. The future for such widows promised 'nothing else but a sky laden with clouds of deepest poverty'.[34]

In a letter to the then Minister of Pensions, Sir Laming Worthington Evans, Ogilvie wrote:

> Only this week I spoke to a widow who was playing the violin in the London streets. She has a pension under Article 15 and 4 children to maintain, and the widow herself is suffering from consumption, and not being able to maintain her children, she is forced to resort to such humiliating means to earn a livelihood. She was displaying a huge placard with the words 'A grateful country'.[35]

The newspaper's campaign was unsuccessful. The Ministry would not separate the widow from the actions of her husband, refusing to accept the proposition that a man who died in less glorious circumstances should be granted the same consideration as one killed in action. The best they were prepared to do was to point out to the newspaper that the new Appeals Tribunals could now hear applications from widows who had been refused pensions under Article 11.

In fact, some of the suicide appeals were headed off at the pass, going before an Entitlement Board to be considered administratively instead. A number of decisions by the board from March 1920 seem at odds with the 'Suicide Formula', unusually being decided in favour of the widow. There was a belated acceptance by the Ministry that the introduction of conscription had changed the landscape. If the government was to force large numbers of men who did not choose military service to take part in the war, they would have to accept that not all of those men could cope with such demands, and compensate the widow accordingly. This was one of the points that had been made by the *News of the World* the previous year, and at that time rejected. Medical experts had now advised the Ministry that they could not insist on proof of some exceptional stress on a soldier over and above the everyday constraints of service. Conscripted men were often older than volunteer soldiers, with different life experience and expectations. They had not chosen military life and would find any sudden change in their daily routine to potentially have 'a profound nervous effect',[36] meaning that only a few days' service could cause enough mental imbalance for them to take their own lives. This was the new approach to be taken and was clear from the cases accompanying this file where widows appealed against the refusal of Article 11 pensions.

The cases included that of a man who cut his throat with a razor in his West Hartlepool billet when notified to report for parade the next day, another who had hung himself after six days' service, and a further unfortunate who had deliberately placed his head on a railway line. The widow of the last man had been granted a temporary pension under Article 15, but wrote to the authorities:

> What with the anxieties of the war and my husband's absence, great responsibilities have been placed on me and the 15s allowed me has not been sufficient to enable me to look after my children as they should be.[37]

All of these grieving widows were now granted Article 11 pensions.

The new approach was of no help to those widows who had their cases turned down in the preceding six years. Unless an appeal was lodged, the cases would not be reconsidered. No doubt many widows were ignorant of the appeal provisions and even those who were aware may well have preferred to let sleeping dogs lie rather than rake up the pain and shame of their husband's suicide.

Post-war suicides presented a whole new set of problems for the widows. A widow would have to show that her husband's suicide was a direct result of his pensionable disability in order to succeed in a claim. The Ministry laid down some general thoughts about such cases without, as usual, wanting to establish any settled policy. The existence of a disability due to service that would cause a man to be depressed was held to be a point in the widow's favour, as was previous mental instability while in service due to pressures of war or separation from home.

Horace Hackett, formerly of the Manchester Regiment, had killed himself in 1924 after suffering badly from the tuberculosis for which he was in receipt of a disability pension. On the basis that the tuberculosis had become very much worse in the last six months and had caused him to be depressed, his widow Clara was granted a pension under Article 11.

There was, however, no consistency in the approach to post-war suicide cases. There appears little to distinguish the case of Horace Hackett from that of Donald Ross, yet the attitude of the Ministry was completely different. Ross was an old soldier who had been called up from the reserve again on the outbreak of war. He had served in France until evacuated in April 1915 due to the severe bronchitis that would eventually see him granted a 100 per cent disablement pension. In 1929, Donald Ross cut his throat with a razor and died. He had been suffering particularly badly from his bronchitis at the time and could no longer stand the pain. The case would seem to fit squarely within the criteria for post-war sui-cides being granted – Ross was suffering from a pensionable disability that caused him to become depressed, but the Ministry refused his widow's pension claim. Thomasina Ross challenged the decision at a tribunal. She was supported by her local GP, who had treated her husband and told the tribunal: 'I think the poor man only did what I should have done under the circumstances.'[38] The tribunal agreed and granted her a pension.

The further the war disappeared into history, the harder it was for widows of suicides to prove that the act was a direct result of war service. Applications for pensions in the later suicide cases that remain in the archives were often rejected. Robert Roberts had received gunshot wounds to his neck and hand and also lost three toes as a result of his war service. He struggled to obtain work to support himself and his eight children during the Depression and had spent much of the eight years prior to his death in hospital. In 1939, he drank aconite and died. The inquest jury heard that he was paranoid that the world was against him and believed that the Germans were still after him.[39] His widow's claim for a pension was refused. Unfortunately, like many widows, Mrs Roberts did not appeal, so it is not possible to see the Ministry's reasoning for the refusal, but it is perverse in the face of the available facts.

The way in which the Ministry of Pensions dealt with the 'doubtful' cases over the years has all the hallmarks of their general approach to problems during and

George Fowler.
(Reproduced with permission of Special Collections, University of Leeds)

Edith Fowler and daughter, Marjorie.
(Reproduced with permission of Special Collections, University of Leeds)

Eliza Booth and her children, Henry, Arnold and Ethel.
(Reproduced with permission of Special Collections, University of Leeds)

Norman Booth, middle row second left, and the men from the Brighouse Co-Operative Society Carriers. *(Reproduced with permission of Special Collections, University of Leeds)*

Ernest Blackburn. *(Reproduced with permission of Special Collections, University of Leeds)*

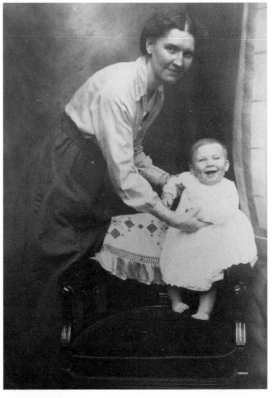

Annie Blackburn and son Stanley, in 1916. *(Reproduced with permission of Special Collections, University of Leeds)*

Thiepval Memorial. Ernest Blackburn's name is among the 100,000 inscribed here. *(Photo: Andrea Hetherington)*

Sally Blakey and her children. Harry would receive his father's Military Medal. *(Courtesy of Jackie Coleman)*

Joseph Lamb, 1915. *(Courtesy of the Hetherington family)*

John and Gladys Lethem's wedding. *(Reproduced with permission of Special Collections, University of Leeds)*

Wilfrid Cove and 26 Siege Battery – The Somme Boys. *(Courtesy of Pauline Baldwin. Reproduced with permission of Special Collections, University of Leeds)*

Wilfrid Cove's two children, Marjorie and Betty. The photograph was found on his body after his death. *(Courtesy of Pauline Baldwin. Reproduced with permission of Special Collections, University of Leeds)*

War Pensions Gazette, April 1920. 24,892 people were employed in the administration of pensions by May 1920, many of them women.

The Women's Migration Scheme, as pictured in the publication *Empire Reconstruction*. *(Courtesy of the Salvation Army Heritage Centre)*

Mrs. Commissioner Lamb, J.P., bidding good-bye to a War Widow and her family. The Army had arranged their passage, obtained situations, and secured their new Oversea home.

It was seen as the duty of women to populate the British Empire. *(Image taken from the publication* Empire Reconstruction, *courtesy of the Salvation Army Heritage Centre)*

A War Widow and her family—all desirous to assist to strengthen and build up the Empire overseas

War Cry, 12 February 1916. Children of soldiers and sailors from Hackney and their widowed mothers attending a Salvation Army tea party in 1916. *(Courtesy of the Salvation Army Heritage Centre)*

Widowed mother and her sextette of happy children who were also included in the joyous party

War Cry, 7 July 1923. Emigration figures never reached the heights imagined by the Salvation Army after the war. *(Courtesy of the Salvation Army Heritage Centre)*

The Salvation Army assisted grieving relatives to visit cemeteries on the Western Front after the Armistice. *(Photograph courtesy of the Salvation Army Heritage Centre)*

A HALLOWED SPOT.—Salvation Army Officer kneeling by the grave of a fallen soldier in France, with the widow who travelled from England under The Army's care

St Barnabas pilgrimage to the Menin Gate, 1927, as pictured in the *Daily Sketch*.

The Menin Gate memorial. *(Photo: Andrea Hetherington)*

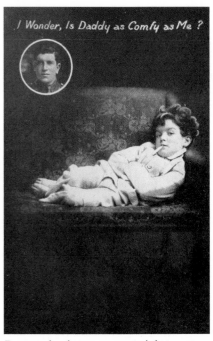

I Wonder, Is Daddy as Comfy as Me ?

Maud Wright with husband Reginald and son Edward. *(By permission of Graham Wright)*

Postcard printers were quick to exploit the market of families writing to soldiers abroad. *(Author's own collection)*

Headingley War Memorial, outside St Michael's Church. Maud Wright did not submit her husband's name for inclusion on the memorial. *(Photo: Andrea Hetherington)*

after the war. They firstly ignored the issue, then researched it and waited for advice while widows and children suffered from their inactivity. They then established a formula that was not strictly followed by their own officials, only to quietly change their approach at a later date without necessarily making any general announcement. Individuals at the Ministry then continued to put purse strings over public justice and refuse cases that should have been granted. Lack of consistency was endemic at the Ministry, even admitted by their own bureaucrats. In 1917, Matthew Wynne wrote:

> We cannot claim complete consistency and it would really be impossible to secure it in respect of cases occurring at fairly wide intervals and decided by different persons – or even by the same person. But rough justice is done.[40]

Many observers would disagree with that assessment.

Chapter 7

Widows and the Law

'For the sake of him who laid in France.'

One area in which war widows' interaction with the state can be traced is through their brushes with the criminal law. Various cases that came before the courts involved war widows as defendants and the fact was always remarked upon in the press reports. Some widows had a previous history of criminality whilst some had been driven to offend by the financial circumstances in which they found themselves. Magistrates around the country took different approaches to dealing with these unfortunate women and it was something of a lottery as to whether prison sentences would be imposed.

Sometimes magistrates could show a great deal of sympathy and humanity to a war widow in distressed circumstances. This was certainly the case of the Dewsbury bench who dealt with Susannah Dent, a war widow who was said to have abandoned her 5-month-old baby. Already the mother of one child, Susannah had given birth to a baby after a relationship with a man who had now abandoned her. She feared that the Ministry of Pensions would find out about her baby and stop her pension for misconduct as a result. In order to try to conceal the pregnancy she had travelled to the Isle of Man to give birth. On her return she left the baby in an alleyway, waiting until she saw someone take the child in before abandoning it completely. The police gave her a good character reference, as usual making a point of the neat and tidy condition of her house. The magistrates of Dewsbury appear to have understood her position entirely, dealing with her by way of a simple binding over to be of good behaviour for twelve months, and on the same day the Board of Guardians decided that the child should be returned to her care immediately.[1]

Some offences were clearly borne out of the struggle of single parenthood. Hilda Duff of Buckingham appeared before the magistrates for not sending her child to school. On closer enquiry, it seemed that the issue was not that the child did not go to school but that she did so in such a state as to cause the school nurse to send her home again. When there was no improvement in the child's condition, Hilda was prosecuted. Her only response to the allegation was that she 'did her best' as far as the child was concerned. The bench announced that 'as she was a war widow they would give her another chance,'[2] but fined her five shillings.

War widows appearing before the court often blamed their misdemeanours on their uncontrollable grief. Catherine Powell of Hartlepool was widowed in July 1916 when her husband Albert died of his wounds in hospital in Rouen. Finding herself in trouble in November that year she claimed that the arrival of a photograph of her husband's grave upset her so much that she drank two bottles of stout and proceeded to steal a box of chocolates. Her story was somewhat undermined by the fact that she had a number of previous appearances before the local courts. Catherine was trying to raise three children on a pension of twenty-three shillings a week. The Hartlepool bench found her more in need of guidance than punishment and placed her on probation for two years.[3]

Lily Carnell appeared before Guisborough Magistrates' Court in 1918 on charges of neglecting her children. Lily had lost her husband Frank two days before Christmas in 1914 and had six children to support. The family appear to have had some previous association with the Salvation Army, indicated by the fact that one of the children was christened Bramwell Booth Carnell. Warnings had been given to the parents in 1913 over the state of the children. The NSPCC finally embarked on a prosecution in 1918, having given Lily more leeway than usual due to the death of her husband. Lily was not slow to appeal to the court's patriotism, asking for a further opportunity to reform 'for the sake of him who laid in France'.[4] The bench was unimpressed and Lily Carnell was sentenced to three months' imprisonment. The court also ordered that the children be adopted by the local Board of Guardians. The only crumb of comfort for poor Lily was that her solicitor succeeded in having her serve a sentence without hard labour, on the understanding that this would save her widow's pension from forfeiture.

The presiding magistrate or judge sometimes made pronouncements in cases where leniency was exercised, specifying that this was entirely due to respect owed to the widow's dead husband, not to the widow herself. Such was the case for an unnamed Liverpool widow appearing before the stipendiary magistrate of the city in 1919. Charged with the offence of being found on enclosed premises with the intention of stealing, she was lucky enough to have an ex-soldier come forward and testify on her behalf. The man had lost an arm during his war service and the court was greatly affected upon hearing that he was the pal of her deceased husband and had made a deathbed promise to him that he would take care of his wife and children. The magistrate decided to fine the woman rather than send her to prison in recognition of her husband's service to his country.[5]

Sometimes the appeal for the sympathy of the court on the basis of war bereavement backfired. One plucky lad appearing before the court in Doncaster for the theft of fruit declared that he was the son of a war widow who had been left to bring up nine children. Unfortunately for him, his tale of woe was scuppered when his father appeared in court.[6]

Crimes against property were then, as now, punished more heavily, often resulting in prison sentences. Millicent King had a stash of jewellery hidden under the floor of her lodgings in 1923 when the police investigated some thefts from a restaurant where she was employed as a cook. She was said to be a war widow with five children to support on a pension of £1 16s 8d a week. She was sent to prison by the Brighton magistrates for a period of two months with hard labour.[7]

Florence May Gladdis from the Isle of Wight was another widow who found herself in court for theft from her employer. Charles Gladdis, a carter before the war, had been killed on the Salonika front in 1917, while Florence was pregnant with what would be their fourth child. Left with three pre-school age children in addition to her newborn baby, Florence struggled to cope. In 1923, while working as a charwoman for a doctor, temptation overcame her and she stole a ring. Her criminal endeavour was doomed to failure in her small community when she attempted to pawn the stolen property. The pawnbroker became suspicious when Mrs Gladdis couldn't give him a straight story as to how she had come into possession of the ring and he called the police. Florence had been sent to prison two years earlier for failure to send her children to school and the magistrates did not spare her on this occasion either, sentencing her to two months' imprisonment with hard labour.[8]

Immoral sexual behaviour by war widows was always censured by the courts, particularly while the war was in progress. Mrs Jackson of Guisborough appeared before the court on a charge of running a disorderly house in February 1916. Police witnesses testified that they had the premises concerned under observation and had seen a number of men attending the house at all hours. Two other women were also involved in the enterprise. An aggravating feature appears to be that Mrs Jackson's husband had only been dead a matter of weeks when the police first had cause to warn her about her behaviour. The prosecution also made much of the fact that Mrs Jackson had two children. Once the bench had satisfied themselves that there were family members to take care of the children, the widow was sentenced to a month's imprisonment.[9]

Occasionally widows used their court appearance to vent their frustration for the way they were treated by the pension authorities. Elsie Lees was widowed in April 1918 when her 25-year-old husband Norman was killed in Belgium. Elsie was taken to court in Dewsbury in December 1919 for non-payment of her rates. She declared that she was in arrears due to a backlog in payment of her war widow's pension and laid the blame squarely with the government.

When writing to attempt to hurry them along she had received a reply from the Ministry of Pensions that merely said she would receive her payment in due course. As she defiantly declared before the magistrates, 'That is what the government cares for soldiers' widows.'[10] The Dewsbury bench, sensible as ever in their dealings with widows, ordered that the arrears be paid, but not until her pension was brought up to date.

Cases that seem to have routinely attracted custodial sentences were those involving any fraud upon the Ministry of Pensions. The concept of duty to the taxpayer to ensure that their monies did not end up in the wrong hands was a strong one and often remarked upon by those sentencing the fraudsters. Esther Knight of Whitstable had five children to support on her own after the death of her first husband, and failed to declare her remarriage. She claimed £228 in pension payments to which she was no longer entitled and was sentenced to a month's imprisonment.[11]

Mabel Bell, a 27-year-old munitions worker, appeared before the Old Bailey in January 1917 for fraudulently claiming a war widow's pension, and also for bigamy. She was the widow of Lieutenant Ernest Ashcroft of the Devonshire Regiment, killed in September 1915, and was, therefore, entitled to a pension. The complicating factor was that Mabel's marriage to Ernest had taken place at a time when she was still legally married to another man. In 1909, Mabel had married Edward Bell, who was nine years her senior. She immediately followed him to Burma, where he worked in the Indian Civil Service. Mabel left Bell in 1911 for a soldier in the British Indian Army called Captain Ransford. The new couple came to England, living as man and wife to all intents and purposes, and had a child together. Mabel started to run a small tea shop in Aldershot.

Captain Ransford was sent to France early in the war, meeting his end in late October 1914. Though the War Office officially listed him as missing, unofficial sources had communicated the facts of his death to Mabel, a private in his regiment contacting her to say that he had been killed by a shell. She applied for a widow's pension, being remarkably frank in her dealings with the War Office, making it plain that she and Ransford were unmarried and that, in fact, she was still married to someone else. She was refused a pension and Ransford had made no provision for her in his will.

Mabel married Lieutenant Ashcroft a few months later and applied for a pension on his death, being granted £100 a year and a gratuity of £140. Unfortunately, her first husband now returned from Burma and divorced her. Not for the first time in this study, a war widow's misbehaviour was reported to the authorities by a member of her own community. At a time when divorce was uncommon, the matter was newsworthy enough to be in the local paper, where it was seen by an

Aldershot resident who was familiar with Mabel and her teashop. Mabel's initial defence to the charge of bigamy was that she genuinely thought her first husband was dead. Where she obtained this impression is unknown, as had this been the case his Civil Service pension would have paid her four times the amount she was due as the widow of poor Lieutenant Ashcroft. Mabel Bell was forced to admit the fraud and was sentenced to twelve months' imprisonment.

An unusual case of pension fraud concerned Florence Wisher from Liverpool. On the death of publican Henry Crook, Florence presented a marriage certificate to the authorities in order to validate her pension. Only after five years and over £600 in pension payments was it discovered that Florence was not the woman on the marriage certificate. She and Crook had never married, though he had married someone else in 1902, hence the availability of the certificate. On this occasion the court showed some leniency when hearing that the couple had been together for nineteen years and had a 17-year-old son. Crook had insisted Florence use the documentation to make sure she was provided for on his death and the magistrate took the view that she had been very much under his influence, binding her over to be of good behaviour.[12]

Despite the fact that pension fraud cases almost always resulted in prison sentences, it seems that such cases were not always prosecuted. The 1919 report of the Public Accounts Committee revealed that a crime had come to light in which the widow of a naval officer had continued to claim a pension for ten years after her remarriage. She had spent the extra money on her sons' education, and the three boys had all served during the First World War with good records. Despite the fact that the amounts fraudulently claimed must have been significantly more than those cases just listed, the Admiralty had decided not to prosecute her for fear of adverse publicity. The Treasury were not happy with the decision, pointing out that matters of mitigation were for a court to decide after conviction, not for the Admiralty to take into their own hands. One cannot help but wonder if the decision would have been the same had she been the wife of an ordinary sailor.[13]

Other offences that often carried sentences of imprisonment included the concealment of deserters. Aileen 'Queenie' Passmore's husband was killed at the end of July 1916 in German East Africa. Queenie then formed a relationship with a young soldier called Hutton who was serving with the Canadian army. In March 1917, Hutton was absent without leave from his regiment at Witley, and Queenie concealed him at her address. She was prosecuted and fined £5 for her actions, which she claimed were done to 'protect her man', whom she intended to marry.[14] No marriage had taken place by the next time Queenie was in trouble over Hutton, in June 1917, when he had again deserted and the couple were found camping in the woods near Godalming. Hutton had been at large since April, escaping while awaiting sentence for his earlier desertion. Queenie was convicted of concealing him again and this time was sentenced to three months' imprisonment with hard labour. Desertion was a big problem, as the lengthy lists of names appearing in every edition of the *Police Gazette* testify, and no encouragement whatsoever could be given to those who assisted soldiers in the commission of that crime.

For some bereaved women, fellow war widows were the object of their criminality, presumably because they knew these women were likely to be in receipt of pensions with no man to tell them how to spend the money. One such fraudster was Nellie Fairlie of Loch Lomond. Nellie advertised in Glasgow newspapers for a partner to invest in her tailoring business and showed those who responded the workshop concerned and other premises where she hoped to expand the business. Several women saw this as a sound investment and forwarded money to Nellie, hoping to see a little profit. Unfortunately, they saw nothing, as Nellie Fairlie did not own the business, being a mere employee in the workshop she had so proudly shown her victims. One widow had given her £50 and reported the matter to the police. Described as 'an attractive woman of fashionable appearance',[15] Nellie was said to live on a 'luxurious' motor boat on Loch Lomond. Sentenced before the Glasgow Sheriff's Court in September 1923, Nellie Fairlie went to prison for twelve months.

War widows were vulnerable to fraudsters of all kinds and often appear in the pages of the newspapers as victims of crime rather than perpetrators. Bigamy was a crime in which the war widow was often an unknowing participant, as in the case of the unfortunate Ada Taylor.[16] Ada lived in Wallsend and had lost her husband in July 1915. On a day trip to the seaside resort of Whitley Bay in October, she had met a young man called Charles Bell, who turned up on her doorstep a few days later, proposing marriage. Ada declined his offer, feeling it to be too soon after her bereavement to contemplate a wedding, but Bell persisted and they were married in May 1916. The couple had a week of happiness before the police caught up with Private Charles Bell, deserter from the West Yorkshire Regiment. Further shocks were to come for Ada when she discovered that Bell had a wife and five children living in Morley, near Leeds. The two wives appeared as witnesses at the Newcastle Assizes and appear to have been devastated by Bell's dishonesty. Bell claimed that his hospital stays during his military service had robbed him of any memory of his wife and children. His Honour Judge Atkins sentenced Bell to six months' imprisonment with hard labour, remarking that some men found it difficult to *forget* that they were married.[17]

Widows were particularly vulnerable to fraudsters who offered to intercede with the pension authorities to ensure that the fullest allowances were obtained. The burdens of running a household and the reticence often shown by widows in dealing with authority figures must have made such offers very tempting. One such criminal was Harry Harland, who took money from a war widow called Elizabeth Richardson in 1922.[18] Elizabeth had lost her husband at Gallipoli in 1915 and was receiving a pension for herself and her three children. It seems that her portion of the pension had been suspended for some reason and Harland represented himself as the man who could have it restored in full. Of course, this would require expenditure on his part and money for trips to London to deal with the authorities in person. Mrs Richardson handed over £30, which Harland no doubt spent on himself as he had never been in touch with the Ministry of Pensions at all. He was convicted of the fraud and sentenced to twelve months in prison.

The frequency of official visitors to the average war widow made it easier for fraudsters to flourish. Accustomed to the knock on the door from the health visitor, war pensions committee investigator, church worker, school attendance officer or Soldiers' and Sailors' Families Association representative, widows were less likely to question someone's credentials if they presented themselves as from some official body. The evil James Clifton took matters to the extreme. Turning up at the house of widow Annie Newick, Clifton claimed to be from the War Office, looking for lodgings. When Mrs Newick said she did not take in lodgers, he changed his story and said that letters against her had been received at the War Office and he had come to investigate. He then repeatedly attacked the terrified woman. With her two young children in the house, Mrs Newick was too afraid to escape and it was the next day before she was able to raise the alarm.

The casualty lists published during the war and the in memoriam pages of the local newspapers gave fraudsters a source of information that was often ruthlessly exploited. It was not unknown for a stranger to turn up at the house of a bereaved family and claim to have served with the dead man. The fraudster would often claim only hospitality, but sometimes money was wheedled out of the widow, ostensibly to pay for a train fare or some other expense, usually with the solemn promise that the money would be returned once whatever temporary difficulty said to be ailing him was overcome. Needless to say, the cash never materialized and most victims were too embarrassed to report the matter to the police. Where men had been reported missing in action, the opportunities for fraud were even greater. A number of individuals both in Britain and abroad targeted anxious families desperate for news about their missing relatives. Some were petty small-time criminals trying to make a little extra money, whilst others operated on a much larger scale. John Jackson was in the small-time category, though his actions were particularly heartless. A private in the Royal Army Medical Corps, Jackson contacted Eleanor Ruffell on seeing a report that her husband was missing on the Western Front. He claimed to be a friend of George Ruffell, and offered to go and find him if Eleanor would pay his expenses to do so. Four pounds was duly handed over, but no enquiries were made on her behalf. When brought to trial in September 1918, Jackson said in evidence that a fellow soldier had told him George Ruffell was dead. Eleanor immediately collapsed in court, this being her first news that this was the case. Jackson was sentenced to three months' imprisonment.[19] George Pugh, aka Leonard Hardy, also targeted the families of the missing. In November 1919, he approached a widow in Romsey claiming to have information about her husband and her brother, both of whom had been reported missing in action. Pugh/Hardy claimed to be a sergeant major sent from an Edinburgh hospital to collect Millie Webber and take her to Scotland for a tearful reunion with her wounded brother and shell-shocked husband, Launcelot. The circuitous route to Edinburgh involved much lending of money to the good Samaritan until Millie was penniless and wiring her parents for more. By now the rest of the family realized this was a fraud and had detectives waiting to arrest Pugh in Edinburgh. Pugh was a career criminal who admitted to several similar offences around the country and was sentenced to five years' imprisonment at his own request.[20] Millie's husband never returned home.

A man calling himself 'Dr Arthur Harrison' had a grander vision. He operated an organization named the Army Educational Bureau, which sent out flyers offering to trace missing soldiers for a fee. Once the money was forthcoming, the good doctor was not, and hundreds of families appear to have been taken in. In June 1916, the War Office was forced to put information in the newspapers warning relatives not to have any involvement with the Army Educational Bureau, and by August the *Police Gazette* was asking for sightings of Harrison to be reported to them so he could be apprehended.[21] Harry Whiting of Kew Gardens was charged with fraud for running a scam called the MMA Company, sending out circulars to the families of missing officers, offering to trace them for a sum of three guineas up front plus an extra two for expenses. Whiting had made £114 from the fraud before he was caught and convicted, being sent to prison for four months.[22]

Sometimes widows paid the ultimate price for an association with an unsuitable man. Such was the case with poor Sarah Brookes. Sarah had been widowed in 1917 when husband Leonard was killed in action in Belgium. By 1926, she had been in a relationship with Edward Leatherland for two years. At twenty-eight, he was ten years her junior. During an argument, Leatherland killed Sarah by fracturing her skull, using two bottles and a piece of stone. He then walked to the nearest police station and told them what he had done. Facing trial for murder, a sympathetic jury found him guilty of the lesser charge of manslaughter instead. The trial judge felt they had been incredibly lenient and it is hard to avoid the conclusion that the verdict was one on Sarah Brookes' lifestyle as much as Leatherland's culpability.[23] She had dishonoured her dead husband with this illegitimate relationship. Edward

Leatherland escaped with fifteen years' imprisonment. Sarah's death left three children motherless.

The cases that brought war widows to the notice of the courts illustrate the standards imposed on their behaviour over and above the general population. Widows were always seen in relation to their connection with men, either their deceased husbands or rogues who had now led them astray. Where some leeway was given to a widow guilty of a crime it was often made explicit that this was entirely on behalf of the dead husband, in honour of his sacrifice. The defendants themselves appeared to understand the operation of this convention, often specifically citing their husband's service to the country by way of mitigation. Those widows who did not honour the memory of the deceased serviceman, either by failing to safeguard the hero's children or by engaging in illicit relationships with other men, were punished severely. Widows seen as being overly influenced by stronger male personalities were treated more leniently, but where it was clear that they were acting entirely under their own direction, no mercy was shown by the courts.

Chapter 8

Religion and Spiritualism

'Bow down thine ear O Lord. Hear me; for I am poor and needy.'

The established Church faced serious challenges during the First World War, both practical and theological. Whilst many people clung to their religious faith in a time of deep uncertainty, just as many others found the Church's teachings no longer made sense of a world where such indiscriminate slaughter could take place. A decline in religious observance was a trend that had started well before August 1914, but the war undoubtedly led many to question their faith and to seek alternatives.

Many widows did find solace in their religious faith, of whatever denomination. Eliza Booth's husband Norman was not a churchgoing man and put his faith in socialism instead. When he was reported missing, the distraught Eliza leaned heavily on the services of the local vicar of Rastrick, in both spiritual and practical terms. Although the couple's eldest child, Ethel, had been baptized, her two young brothers had not. When Norman was confirmed as dead and Eliza gave birth to a new baby girl, she had all three children baptized at the same time. She was now head of the house and it was her decision alone.[1]

Traditional religious faith could not offer answers that satisfied everyone. A letter from the chaplain of her husband's battalion was often the first contact a widow would receive from a religious figure in her bereavement. The idea that dead men were now in a better place and free from pain and suffering was frequently offered to widows as a consolation. Writing to Sally Blakey in 1916, Alexander Spence, the chaplain to her husband's battalion, said:

> I get such brave letters from home every day from wives and mothers who have lost their loved ones and yet are happy and resigned because they know that their dear ones are safe with God from all the troubles and cares of the world. It is touching to hear of your children asking for their daddie but you must tell them he is in heaven and still is loving them and watching them though they cannot see him.[2]

Chaplains often had little practical knowledge of the man concerned, meaning that their attempts at consolation fell a little flat. Spence wrote that he had heard that

David Harkness Blakey was a fine soldier, but 'I did not know him very well as I have only been a little time with this battalion.'[3]

The religious knowledge of men at the front was often limited to snippets they had picked up in Sunday school. Anglican chaplains were often amazed and disappointed at the lack of engagement ordinary soldiers had with their professed religion. Julian Bickersteth, chaplain to the 56th Division of the British Expeditionary Force in France, wrote home to his family in 1916 that for many men, religion was just a name with no real connection with their lives.[4] Back in England, similar views were being expressed in print by Artifex in the *Manchester Guardian*, who wrote: 'The war has revealed, as nothing has ever done before, the weakness of the Church and the failure of organized religion as expressed in all the denominations to guide and inspire the nation.'[5]

If the ordinary soldier found it difficult to engage with religious teachings, the overwhelmingly upper-class Anglican priesthood sometimes found it difficult to understand the lives of the working-class soldier and his family. The Archbishop of Canterbury betrayed his ignorance of working-class families in his opposition to allowances to unmarried wives. He gave evidence to the Select Committee on Pensions in 1915, decrying the lack of distinction in separation allowances between the married and unmarried wife of a soldier: paying out to unmarried 'wives' encouraged immoral behaviour and undermined the Church. He argued that any payments to unmarried wives should be guided and supervised as they had already shown themselves to be morally suspect and were therefore more likely to waste their allowances.[6] One of the Church establishment's bright ideas was that unmarried wives shouldn't be able to collect their allowances and pensions from the Post Office, but should have to pick them up from somewhere that could offer them moral guidance.

The established Church appeared to have little to say to the average working-class family. The Anglican Church, with its prohibition on saying prayers for the dead, appeared to have a particular doctrinal void as far as the bereaved were concerned. This refusal to ease the suffering of those grieving for lost relatives by a specific prayer was a big issue, with many priests refusing to deviate even slightly from Church routine. The Catholic Church, where prayers for the dead had always been an integral part of the doctrine, seemed better equipped to provide solace. The churches undoubtedly did perform an important role for some of the bereaved. Priests in some parishes were very proactive in visiting the families of those serving, and in areas with large numbers of casualties, this work could be time consuming and difficult.[7]

The introduction of separation allowances and widows' pensions arguably helped reduce the influence of the Church on the wives of soldiers at the front.

One of the key functions of the Church in the late nineteenth and early twentieth centuries had been its social work in the community in the form of charitable donations of one kind or another to those in need. The introduction of school meals for children, old age pensions and the National Insurance Scheme provisions had to some extent eaten away at the work of the churches by the outbreak of the war.[8] Widows' pensions can be seen as a further step in this direction.

If the established Church was failing to satisfy the needs of a nation at war, this did not mean that people were unwilling to believe in forces greater than themselves. The big questions of life brought into sharp focus by the national emergency meant an increasing interest in all things spiritual, despite the fact that such matters may lie outside of the boundaries of traditional Church teachings. Several writers have noted the superstitious nature of the average Tommy, with a strong belief in fate and symbols of luck.[9] If the man at the front believed such things, the woman at home often did too.

Private John Starkie had a premonition that he would not come home to his wife Sophia and his two young children. Starkie was an army reservist, who had survived some of the toughest battles of the first year of the war. On his last leave home to the mill town of Mytholmroyd in Yorkshire, he had insisted on having a photograph taken of himself with Sophia and the children so she would have something to remember him by. Starkie died in August 1915, not on the Western Front, but by drowning in the Thames in a boating accident.[10]

The idea that her husband may have foreseen his own death played on the mind of Annie Chambers (née Allard) for the rest of her life. George Allard had been called to the frontline trenches unexpectedly the night before a planned attack. The soldier who gave Annie details of her husband's death told her that George had insisted on his platoon singing *Abide with Me* the night before they went over the top. She knew her husband was not religious, so this behaviour was out of the ordinary for him. She could not bear to hear the song again. 'I could howl my eyes out when they play that. ... Whether he had a premonition I can't bear that.'[11]

Margaret Forster of Sunderland believed very strongly in fate. Interviewed many years after the war, she was still able to cite the case of a bank manager who, in an attempt to spare his son from battle, managed to have him employed at Palmer's Shipyard in Jarrow instead of joining the army. When the Germans bombed Jarrow on 15 June 1915, Palmer's took a direct hit, killing seventeen people and injuring many more. The bank manager's son was among the dead, whilst others stood nearby survived unscathed. Margaret's response was that this was fate – 'I said, they have to die.'[12] She took the same view of her own husband's death, saying that she had dreamed of receiving the letter giving her the news three Fridays running before it actually arrived.

Ethel Cove and her husband Wilfrid had no belief in the supernatural. However, Ethel's wartime experiences led her to question this position. Having enlisted under the Derby Scheme before the formal introduction of conscription, Wilfrid Cove sailed for France in August 1916 as a gunner in the Royal Artillery. He was particularly close to his two daughters, regularly writing to his 6-year-old, Marjorie, and carrying their letters and drawings with him at all times.

Writing after the war, Ethel recalled that a few months after Wilfrid left, their usually reliable grandfather clock stopped working. In late February 1917, Wilfrid's bathroom shaving mirror crashed to the floor. On reporting this to her husband, he mocked and told her to 'Hang it up and carry on.'[13] A few days later, his favourite painting also fell from the wall, smashing the frame. This time, Ethel was alarmed and did not tell her husband. On 1 March 1917, Wilfrid received a shrapnel wound to the head, which, though not serious, did necessitate a hospital stay. Feeling something of a fraud on seeing the badly wounded patients around him, Wilfrid asked to be discharged so he could return to his battery. On 5 March 1917, he wrote home that he had been lucky in the location of the wound and was confident that he would eventually return home safe and sound. He reminded Ethel that her motto was 'Every cloud has a silver lining.' On 7 March 1917, Gunner Wilfrid Cove was killed by a direct hit from a German shell.

Ethel Cove had not been unduly worried about her husband's wound, but that day her mood abruptly changed.

> On March 7 however I had an awful restlessness, and distinctly remember kneeling on the floor to write to a friend. Next morning my little girl, who was then nearly six, said 'Mummy, I had such a funny dream last night. Daddy came to the bedroom window and beckoned. He was dressed all in black, and the bandage on his wounded head was black too.'[14]

Later that same day, confirmation of Wilfrid's death arrived in the form of a letter from his immediate superior. Ethel was distraught and confused.

> Why that small child should have been visited by such a gruesome apparition, I cannot understand; nor what prompted my baby girl of three to sing, on that morning of March 8 when I was particularly upset – 'There's a silver lining thro the Dark Clouds Shining.'[15]

Ethel Cove put no specific supernatural label on her experiences, simply writing it up as 'A "Weird" War Story'. However, increasing numbers of people were starting to believe in the supernatural, from premonitions to signs from their loved ones after death. Reports of hearing familiar footsteps on the stair to apparitions of the dead soldier were widely reported. It may be in many cases that these experiences were mere symptoms of grief rather than genuinely supernatural occurrences. A post-war survey found that 14 per cent of widows claimed to have seen their husband after his death and another 39 per cent reported to feeling his presence in some way.[16] Peter Marris found similar data in his 1950s sample, with half of those widows having a belief that they had seen or heard their husband after his death.[17] He also noted that a number of his widows were bitter towards the Church as they could not reconcile its teachings with their loss.

The combination of an increasing interest in the supernatural and the perceived failure of the established Church led to a massive boost for spiritualism. Originating in America, spiritualism became very popular in Britain from the middle of the nineteenth century. The oldest spiritualist church in Britain was established in Keighley in 1853 and still exists today. By the end of the century the appeal of spiritualism had declined, partly from the exposure of many exponents as fraudsters. Those who retained an interest sometimes did so in the name of scientific enquiry. The Society for Psychical Research was founded in 1882 specifically to make investigations in relation to spiritualism and associated supernatural phenomena. Sir Oliver Lodge, physicist and principal of Birmingham University, was a prominent member of the society. The association of figures like Lodge with spiritualism took it beyond the realms of folk religion to being potentially seen as a legitimate form of communication with the dead.

Spiritualism could be a comfort to the bereaved and a palliative to those going to the front. Spiritualist magazine *The Light* summed up the movement's appeal in this time of crisis:

> If we could be sure of what lies beyond the grave, and if the knowledge were comforting, how much more willingly and cheerfully would men die for their country, and how much more contented and happy would the relatives of those dead warriors be if they knew their loved ones were still alive, though physically dead, and were not lost to them forever.[18]

The death of Sir Oliver Lodge's son, Second Lieutenant Raymond Lodge, in 1915 made his interest more personal than scientific. He and his wife were desperate for communication with their son, and through the medium Gladys Osborne Leonard, achieved their goal. Lodge wrote his famous book *Raymond* in 1916, where he claimed to have had direct contact with his son, who now existed in a form of heaven known as 'Summerland'. Gladys Osborne Leonard was guided by an Indian spirit called Feda and performed readings for a number of writers and celebrities at the time. The book sold out several print runs and provoked literary responses from spiritualists and opponents of the practice for years thereafter. The revelation that whisky and cigars were available in heaven caused particular debate. Despite Lodge's professed scientific approach to the subject, his critics accused him of gullibility where fraudulent mediums were concerned.

Sir Arthur Conan Doyle was another high profile advocate of spiritualism, having been involved with various psychic societies since the 1880s and being a regular contributor to *The Light*. As with Lodge, the loss of a son, Kingsley, in 1918 turned Conan Doyle's interest into something much more personal. Conan Doyle was a believer in spiritualism for the rest of his life, despite being the victim of several clumsy frauds including the Cottingley Fairies photographs. Conan Doyle dismissed accusations that their own personal loss had led him and Lodge to abandon their objectivity as 'clumsy lies'.[19] Both Lodge and Conan Doyle engaged in regular sell-out lecture tours to spread their beliefs around the country and abroad.

The scale of losses of men both dead and missing led to many ordinary people seeking answers from the other side rather than the War Office. In 1917, the Spiritualists' National Union had 200 branches nationwide. The appeal of spiritualism was across all classes and geographic areas; there were three active spiritualist societies in South Shields on Tyneside whilst the London borough of Kensington was reported to have 118 listed mediums within its borders. Women were particularly prominent in spiritualist activity, both as mediums and as subjects. This reflected their position as chief mourners within the family, either as mothers or as widows.

Clare Sheridan's stockbroker husband Wilfred obtained a commission in the Rifle Brigade. He was convinced he would not return from the war, even picking out a spot in the village church for the location of his memorial. His fears were realized when he was killed at the Battle of Loos in September 1915. After attending a memorial service for the Rifle Brigade at Winchester Cathedral, Clare felt she needed to communicate with her husband. She consulted a medium in Notting Hill who had been mentioned by Sir Oliver Lodge in *Raymond*. Through the medium's Indian guide, Clare received communication from Wilfred and from their daughter Elizabeth, who had died in infancy. Wilfred told her that she and her two living children joined him on the other plane when they were asleep and returned to their own world every morning. Though believing that the messages were genuine, Clare Sheridan found the communications 'undeniably unsatisfactory, exasperating rather than comforting'.[20] Her attendance at sittings ceased when, on one occasion when she had taken her son to speak to his father, Wilfred had been rude to her in front of him, criticizing her plans to take the family to live in Turkey.

After the death of John Lethem in December 1917, his family struggled to cope with the loss. His mother found his death particularly difficult to bear, being obsessed with thoughts of his final minutes. Though the family were religious, sometimes attending services twice on Sundays, traditional religious doctrine could not ease Mrs Lethem's mind in any way. The family turned to spiritualism to provide some consolation. George Lethem, John's father, was a newspaper editor and one of the founder members of the National Union of Journalists. He had a particular interest in all aspects of psychic research and shared his studies with the rest of the family. By July 1918, the family were holding their own small séances at home, with John's parents, sister Ella and widow Gladys all trying to make contact with the dead soldier. The experiments really took off when the family gave up their Leeds home and moved to Glasgow, where George had become editor of the *Daily Record*.[21] The Lethems took advantage of some well-known practitioners of spiritualism being active in the city at the time, including William Phoenix and William Jeffreys. A mixture of trumpet séances, psychic circles, private readings and attempts at automatic writing occupied their days and nights to the extent that Ella Lethem recorded in her diary: 'I see I shall have to have a special book for séance reports.'[22] The effect on John's widow Gladys is unrecorded, but the communications with her dead son greatly improved the mood of Mrs Lethem. George Lethem wrote a number of articles on spiritualist subjects, from spirit telephones to an account of the life of a medium. He eventually gave himself over completely to his belief in spiritualism, moving to London with his wife to become editor of *The Light* in 1931.

Ella Lethem's soldier fiancé, Douglas Crockatt, also took part in the séances and sittings and had avidly read *Raymond*. Douglas described the book as 'glorious – like a Second Book of Revelation if true'.[23] The *Daily Mail* took a different view, describing it as 'Sir Oliver Lodge's Spook Book – half a guinea's worth of rubbish'.[24] The same newspaper that was quick to condemn Lodge and his colleagues was equally quick to promote stories of superstition and coincidence from the front without criticism.

The press often reported prosecutions of spiritualists, usually accompanied by giving them the label of 'fortune tellers' or 'crystal gazers'. Fortune telling with the assertion that the predictions were true was an offence. Mediums were prosecuted under either the Vagrancy Act or the Witchcraft Act and were regularly at odds with the police before the war. Though it might have been supposed that the authorities had better things to occupy their time with a nation at war, a number of spiritualists were sent to prison for their activities during the conflict. 'Fortune telling' was seen as bad for morale on the home front. Horace Leaf, a medium of some renown who himself was subject to prosecution, wrote after the war:

In the eyes of the law there appears to be no such thing as psychic phenomena, and whoever exercises psychic gifts in any form may be said to
come within the condemnation of the law.[25]

Women, and especially the wives of soldiers, were seen as particularly vulnerable
to fraudsters. Undercover female police officers were used to entrap mediums into
making predictions that could cross the line into illegality. The manner in which
the press reported such cases betrayed a prejudice not only against spiritualism,
but against women. Those prosecuted were very often women, as were their customers, who were portrayed as foolish and weak willed.

Beatrice Mary Smith, aka Madam Zenobie, was plying her trade in fortune telling in London in 1916, where she earned as much as £23 a week, according to the
police. A cook before she went into the clairvoyant business, Madam Zenobie was
seeing twenty to thirty clients a day for private readings, most of them relatives of
soldiers at the front. Madam Zenobie told the court that she had bought what she
referred to as 'the business' six months earlier for the sum of £50. The presiding
magistrate fined her £25 and pronounced that there would always be people gull-
ible enough to be taken in by this kind of thing, most of them women.

Both backstreet operations and established spiritualist churches had seen an
increase in attendance since the start of the war. The mainstream spiritualist
movement had no time for fortune telling, which they saw as playing no part in
the serious pursuit of spiritualism. In 1917, *The Light* decided to no longer accept
advertising from mediums as they could not vouch for each person's authenticity.
That year saw a large number of prosecutions of mediums, many of whom were
running businesses like that of Madame Zenobie, but some of whom were supported in their claims to genuine mediumship by their clients. In January 1917,
Madame Brockway, an American medium, was prosecuted in London for having
given predictions to undercover journalists. An ordained minister in a spiritualist
church in America, her case was supported by a number of relatives of men serving
with the forces, including a Justice of the Peace from Ireland. The Reverend Carew
Hervey St John Mildmay testified that he believed her to be completely genuine.
Despite these testimonials, she was convicted and fined £50, with a recommendation that she be deported. Her counsel had stormed out of court halfway through
the hearing, complaining that the magistrates were not prepared to listen to his
arguments.

Whilst fines were the usual punishment, some clairvoyants, mostly women,
found themselves serving sentences of imprisonment. Martha McClure had been
the medium in charge of what seems to have been a typical meeting of twenty-eight
women at a local Christian Spiritualist Church in Liverpool, where a collection of

two pence per person was taken and raffle tickets sold to benefit soldiers at the front. Women often brought items belonging to their lost loved ones to enhance the spiritual connection and sometimes paid extra if any information was actually given to them. With the help of evidence from undercover female police officers Martha was sent to jail for a month. Raids and prosecutions became so numerous that a protest meeting was held by spiritualists in London in May 1917 against the persecution of mediums. The campaign to repeal the antiquated laws used was unsuccessful and clairvoyants continued to be taken to court throughout this war and the next.

The demands of total war even reached into the spiritualist world: in 1917, *The Light* announced that Ouija boards and crystals were now not obtainable until after the war, their makers being engaged in war work.

Occasionally the medium herself was a war widow. Eileen Garrett, one of the most famous mediums of the 1930s, started to fully develop her psychic abilities during the First World War. Having divorced her first husband due to his adultery, she started to run an officers' hostel in London, where she met her second husband. When he proposed marriage, Eileen was certain that he was not going to return from the war alive. After his departure for the front, she had a vision of his death, watching him being blown apart before her eyes. She subsequently received the news that he was dead and that his body could not be recovered. Eileen joined a spiritualist circle and began to work with the British College of Psychic Science to develop and test her gift.[26]

Ada Bruce had been widowed in 1924 when her husband Arthur died of a condition caused by his war service. Ada moved from London to Essex, where she became a member of the Conan Doyle Memorial Church in Leigh-on-Sea. Ada and her children settled in nearby Westcliff, where she took in a fellow spiritualist as a lodger. Twice-weekly séances were held at the house, with collections being taken from the attendees. Ada found herself in difficulties with the Ministry of Pensions in 1932 when accusations were made that her lodger was actually her lover. The fact that she held herself out to be a spiritualist was also presented by her accusers as another example of inappropriate behaviour. A member of the Local War Pensions Committee reported that 'for monetary benefit she and the man hold séances in the locality and the widow tells fortunes.'[27] As we have seen, the telling of fortunes was a criminal offence, so the writer chose these words carefully.

In February 1939, Ada's spiritualist business was exposed by a lawsuit from the executors of the estate of Marjorie Dodd. Marjorie had worked in the Civil Service until she fell from a bus platform in Leigh-on-Sea in 1934, sustaining severe injuries. Following the accident, she became a believer in spiritualism and began to attend Ada Bruce's healing circle on a regular basis along with her two sisters. Ada, through her spirit guide, a North American Indian called Grey Feather, encouraged Marjorie to seek compensation for her injuries. Eleanor, Marjorie's sister, explained that when Grey Feather came through to the séance, Ada would go into a kind of trance and speak in a different voice. When a £1,500 settlement was agreed with the bus company, Grey Feather told Marjorie that she should pay Ada £400 for her part in proceedings. The money was duly paid and Ada went to Australia on two extended holidays with her bounty. Marjorie Dodd died and her executors sought the return of this money on the basis that it had been obtained by fraud and undue influence. The judge ruled in favour of the plaintiffs, stating that undue influence had been used on the Dodd sisters to obtain the money. Interestingly, he made no ruling that Ada's spiritualist healing was fraudulent, saying that whilst he had suspicions, he could not rule on anything other than facts. Partly as a result of owing this considerable sum of money, Ada Bruce was declared bankrupt in October 1939.

The Anglican Church establishment opposed spiritualist practices. They believed that, despite the Christian basis of most spiritualist churches, the movement was a direct threat to the authority of the Church. Arthur Foley Winnington-Ingram, Bishop of London from 1901 to 1939, had long been an opponent of spiritualism, claiming that it sent people insane. Nevertheless, the popularity and seriousness with which the subject was treated during the war compelled him into further investigation. In 1919, in a sermon delivered on All Saints' Day, the Bishop declared that he had now studied all available books on the topic and spoken to many people who believed they could communicate with the spirit world. These investigations had not changed his mind and he claimed that he had not found anything that had given any real information on life after death. He considered the practice dangerous to certain classes of people, saying that whilst Sir Oliver Lodge and Sir Arthur Conan Doyle may be unaffected by their experiences, many – by implication, mostly women – were not. He said that he knew one woman who had 'quite lost her mind' over involvement in spiritualism. The official position of the Catholic Church was the same as their Anglican counterparts, despite Catholic ritual having more than a hint of the supernatural about it. Catholic priests condemned spiritualism for being evil, subversive to the teachings of the Church and likely to cause mental illness in those partaking in the practice.

Some priests publicly acknowledged that if there was an afterlife and the soul of man survived, there must at least be a possibility that such souls could communicate in some way with those in the living realm. Several Anglican ministers expressed their outright belief in spiritualism, including Reverend Charles

Lakeman Tweedale, the Vicar of Weston, near Otley. Tweedale believed his own house was occupied by spirits and wrote several books on the topic. He also established the Society of Communion as a dedicated organization for spiritualists within the Anglican Church. Reverend A.J. Waldron, Vicar of Brixton, was another avid student of spiritualism and declared himself a believer in communication with the dead. In 1920, Waldron wrote a play about an unmarried mother who wanted to marry the spirit of her dead lover.

Despite the end of the war, the topic of communication with the dead was not resolved to the Church's satisfaction. The Church Congress discussed the matter in 1919, showing how much of a concern the rise of spiritualism had become. By 1935, the Bishop of London, though still claiming that spiritualism was 'very dangerous, dishonouring to the dead and a waste of time for the living', was now imparting some kind of psychic ability to the medium, saying that he believed they possessed mind reading powers and this was how they were able to give convincing messages to the bereaved.[28]

The prominence given to the Church in the post-war peace celebrations and remembrance events is sometimes cited as evidence that the established religion did regain its footing by the end of the war. However, remembrance rituals were arguably more to do with ritual itself and less to do with religion. Events for Peace Day and the first anniversary of the Armistice were designed to be secular, paying lip service to the large number of non-Christian soldiers who had fought and died on the Allied side. There was no blueprint to follow for such events as this scale of sacrifice had never taken place before. The churches offered a semblance of ritual that could be roughly fashioned into a nondenominational ceremony to demonstrate thanksgiving and remembrance. During the war, Anglican parishes had co-opted aspects of Catholic tradition into their daily routine; the proliferation of war shrines, for example, had more in common with Catholic pilgrimage. Armistice Day ceremonies were similarly patchwork affairs, with some aspects coming from the Church and others from sources outside. The minute's silence came from a one-off event in the Boer War, not from the Archbishop of Canterbury. The whole concept of the Unknown Warrior ceremony did not come from the Church and much of the press coverage around that event was arguably more in tune with spiritualism than Church doctrine, with the suggestion that the dead could be perceived as taking part in the event being a common feature of reports. This was taken to the extreme in 1921, when Estelle Stead and Ada Emma Deane's 'spirit photographs' appeared in the press, purporting to show the faces of the dead in clouds around the living at the Cenotaph. Amazingly, it took three years of such ceremonies before the photographs were confirmed as fakes. Many of the so-called spirit faces belonged to people who were very much alive and had recently had their photographs printed in the newspapers, thereby allowing the fraudster to clip them for her 'spirit' composition.

The Bishop of London acknowledged in 1915 that the Church had shown 'many a weakness and many a shortcoming' since the outbreak of war.[29] These weaknesses and shortcomings opened the door for people to seek other sources of spiritual guidance and support. Preaching a sermon at the memorial service to the London Rifle Brigade in June 1915, the Bishop told mourners that their relatives had died for the freedom and for the honour of their womenfolk. If that was not consolation enough, dead soldiers had 'gone to a life that a young man can enjoy'[30] in their passage to heaven. He told the congregation that God had made a world on the other side of the mortal realm where their relative would be happy. It is not surprising that many would see the logic in being able to communicate with that world and see no conflict with Christian doctrine in so doing, regardless of the views of the established Church. Spiritualism was often closely aligned with religious faith, not set against it. Many of its followers sought confirmation of the main doctrines of the Church, not the destruction of religious faith. Meetings at spiritualist churches often started and ended with familiar hymns and some even had their own choirs. Spiritualist churches engaged in fundraising for the war effort, just like ordinary churches and chapels, and often did philanthropic work in the community in the same way.[31]

Interestingly, after the Armistice the press did not appear to be as hostile to mediums, perhaps because of the sheer number of people who expressed a belief in some kind of communication with the dead, or perhaps because the imperative to preserve order and equanimity on the home front no longer existed. George Lethem wrote a number of articles in the 1920s on subjects such as the life of a medium, psychic photography and the spirit telephone, which would have been unlikely to have reached the final editions during the war. Looking at Ada Bruce's case, it is unthinkable that a judge in 1917 would have taken the approach that Justice Hallett did in 1939, refusing to make a decision that her clairvoyant business was fraudulent. In the 1930s, the spiritualist movement was more popular than ever, and, in Peter Marris's 1950 study, many of his widows still visited clairvoyants for guidance and messages from their dead husbands.

Chapter 9

Returning Heroes and Post-war Deaths

'He gradually faded away like a plucked flower.'

Robert Spoors was a hewer in a coal mine, a very physically demanding job. In October 1914, he joined the Northumberland Fusiliers, leaving his pregnant wife Margaret at home with their 2-year-old daughter. He served for the next four and a half years, spending time in France and Italy as well as on home service. Demobilized in January 1919, the man who returned to his family was quite different to the strapping miner who had enlisted. Margaret would later testify that 'His nerves were gone and he was far from the same man he was before enlistment physically. He gradually faded away like a plucked flower.'[1] Robert was receiving a disablement pension from the army in the sum of £2 3s 4d per week to support his wife and three children. When he died in January 1920 at the age of thirty-three, Margaret Spoors was refused any part of that pension.

The pensions that had been payable to disabled men were not given to their widows in their entirety after their death. Firstly, a man had to be in receipt of a pension of at least 40 per cent disability, and secondly, the widow had to prove that his subsequent death was due to his war service. The widow was then entitled to a specific portion of her husband's pension, depending under which article of the Royal Warrant an award was granted.

In 1924, the original stipulation that a man must die within seven years of the illness or injury sustained during his war service was removed. The Royal Warrant of 1924 now had a two-limbed clause, Article 17, which allowed the widow of a disabled man to claim a portion of his pension on death if the conditions specified in the article could be proved to exist. Article 17b said that a widow could have a pension if:

> it is certified that the death of her husband was **wholly due** to the nature and condition of the disability in respect of which the said pension or allowance was awarded, such nature or condition **having resulted directly from his war service.**

A successful claim by a widow under 17b would entitle her to two thirds of her husband's disability pension.

If the claim was refused, it was open to the Ministry to decide that she qualified instead under Article 17a if her husband's death:

> was **materially hastened** by the condition of the pensioned disability or disabilities as **resulting directly from the continuing effects of war service.**

A 17a grant would result in the widow receiving half of her husband's pension. If neither clause was held to apply, the Ministry of Pensions would not accept liability.

A significant number of men who may have been entitled to pensions never made a claim. Others who were initially granted pensions tired of attending medical boards to have their level of disability reassessed, thereby relinquishing their entitlement. The widows of these men were now left without a claim against the Ministry of Pensions unless they could prove a continuous medical history of the complaint, leading to their husband's death.

The introduction of conscription in 1916 was the catalyst to the eventual widening of liability under the two limbs of Article 17. Men who had no aptitude or desire for military life now were left with no choice over joining up and army medical officers were ever on the lookout for shirkers. The pressing need for manpower led to large numbers of men being admitted to the armed forces who were not really fit for the job. Only 6.5 per cent of men called up in 1916 were rejected on medical grounds,[2] an astonishingly low number. The health classifications of those who were conscripted were also suspiciously good, with many being put down as 'Class A' when they were far from that. In a parliamentary debate of 1917, it was suggested that there were many as 100,000 men who had been taken into the armed forces while unfit.[3] The process of obtaining more men continued with the 'combing out' of non-essential workers from industry and the raising of the higher age limit for conscripts. The fact that these conscripts were older than the average pre-1916 recruit meant that they were more likely to break down under the strain of military service. The state was going to have to make provision for these men and their families at some stage.

The case of Georgina Mathers illustrates the difference between a grant under Article 17a or 17b in financial terms. Her husband Alexander died in 1934 from heart disease, epilepsy and an old skull fracture that he had received on war service. She had applied for a pension under Article 17b, claiming that his death was wholly due to war service, but her claim had been rejected. She was granted a pension under Article 17a giving her £1 a week, i.e. 50 per cent of her husband's pension at the time of his death. She appealed, producing additional medical evidence to a tribunal, which finally agreed her application eight months after her husband died. Her new Article 17b allowance was £1 6s 8d a week, being two thirds of her husband's pension.[4]

The Ministry of Pensions went to some lengths to investigate these cases before accepting liability. In addition to birth and marriage certificates, the soldier's service and medical record, records from any employer, and information from any Friendly Society to which he belonged were checked. Before the introduction of statutory sick pay, the Friendly Society records were the only way of ascertaining whether an individual had taken days off work due to ill health. The Ministry appeared dead set on looking for reasons to disallow a pension claim rather than reasons to accept it. For example, in the case of Lionel Smith, who died of the tuberculosis for which he was in receipt of a 100 per cent disablement pension, the Ministry refused his widow's claim because they decided that 'factors other than the effects of service contributed to his death. There is a history of kidney trouble in boyhood.'[5] Luckily for his widow, a Pension Appeal Tribunal disagreed with that assessment.

The widow must have been married to the soldier at the time he suffered the wound or caught the disease that eventually led to his death. There was a lingering suspicion that women would marry wounded men simply to get their hands on the pension allowance when they died. Only if it could be shown that there was further aggravation to a wounded man's condition after the marriage was his widow entitled to make an application to the Ministry on his death. As with a number of policies of the Ministry of Pensions, this appears to be unfair and arbitrary. Other countries were more flexible, France and Australia being examples where women would be allowed a pension in such circumstances. The difference was that population growth there was a real issue, so every encouragement had to be given to men to start families. Despite the prevalence of the 'Lost Generation' myth, this was not a problem in Britain, meaning there was no such imperative to assure men that their families would be taken care of after their death.

When James Spiers left the army in 1920, he was not in receipt of any kind of disablement pension, despite having received wounds that required an operation to remove shrapnel from a lung. Marrying Elizabeth a year after his discharge, the couple had four children together. In 1930, James was diagnosed with tuberculosis, his doctor claiming that it was a result of his war service. When he later died of the same condition, Elizabeth had no claim to a pension. A friend of the couple sought to intervene with the Minister of Pensions, writing:

> Sir, I appeal to you as a British gentleman to do your best for this poor woman and her young family. This is truly a straightforward and honest attempt to help in a case of real hardship and poverty.[6]

British gentleman or not, the minister was unable to assist.

The starting point for any pension claim was a man's service records. Unfortunately, the information recorded by the army was sometimes incomplete or incorrect. The pressures of war placed a huge strain on the army's administration and their medical officers, meaning that mistakes were made. The Ministry treated all army forms as sacred documents despite the fact that the information contained therein was often inadequate.[7] If men themselves were struggling to put evidence before the tribunals of 1917–18 it is little wonder that their wives were often unable to do so ten or more years later.

Death of a veteran from any kind of chest trouble was sometimes accompanied by a widow's claim that he had been a victim of a gas attack during his service. Annie Rhodes, widow of Private William Rhodes, made her claim for a pension on this basis when he died in 1926. Unfortunately for her, William had been receiving his pension for a gunshot wound to his arm, not for anything to do with the effects of gas. His death from tuberculosis and peritonitis was always going to preclude acceptance of liability by the Ministry. Gas was a new weapon, first used by the Germans in April 1915, so there was little experience of its long-term effects on a victim's health. William Rhodes' doctor illustrated the difficulty he found himself in when asked to offer an opinion on the cause of death. He wrote that he was unable to testify that the man's death was caused by gas poisoning:

> as I consider it impossible 12 months or more after a man is gassed, for a medical man to say definitely that his condition is caused by gas poisoning, but I think it very probable that gas poisoning had a good deal to do with his condition.[8]

Annie's claim was ultimately scuppered not by medical opinion, but by factual research. Looking at Private Rhodes' army record and the movements of his battalion, the Ministry found that there was no evidence of him being involved in any encounters with gas by the time of his discharge from the service.

The doctor in the Rhodes case was not untypical of those mentioned in the existing pension files in that he attempted to be as sympathetic as possible to his patient's claim. These doctors were an integral part of the community in which they lived and would undoubtedly be more inclined to support the family if possible. They would also have seen at first hand the deterioration in their patients, which the Pension Appeal Tribunals could only read about on paper. Death certificates to be found within the files often list the cause of death followed by the words 'due to war service'. Clear tension between the civilian and military doctors is evidenced in a number of Ministry of Pensions' files, with the military claiming that civilian doctors were too soft in their diagnoses.

Widows were not originally able to appeal decisions of the Ministry of Pensions. Men had access to appeals for their pensions from 1917 onwards but, as we have seen throughout this study, the needs of widows were an afterthought. The Pensions Appeal Tribunal established in 1917 was still part of the Ministry of Pensions and acted in what was termed an advisory capacity, dealing only with questions of entitlement for disabled men. Initially, one tribunal travelled around the country but later, local panels were established, consisting of a disabled former soldier, a barrister or solicitor and a doctor. When the right of appeal was subsequently to be extended to widows,[9] proposals were put forward that widows' Appeal Tribunals should have the dependant of a deceased soldier on the panel, but this did not happen. Widows who appealed were not treated in the same way as disabled men; they were not automatically sent a precis of the Ministry of Pensions' case and were sometimes not given full information about their husband's medical history.[10]

A London civil servant's idea of a 'local' panel strained the definition for many claimants, with only twelve tribunals to cover the whole country. Despite Plymouth being a city with a high concentration of widows and ex-servicemen, the local Appeal Tribunal for the South West had been set up in Exeter, even today an hour's train ride away. It is little wonder that many widows found the prospect of an attendance before the tribunal too daunting.

For deaths after service, a widow could only appeal against the refusal to grant a pension under Article 17b. Were her application to be refused for an Article 17a pension, she had no right of appeal. These regulations were much misunderstood, even by those tasked with administering them. It was not uncommon for Local War Pensions Committees to submit appeals on behalf of widows who had no statutory right to one, and even the Ministry of Pensions sometimes sent out letters rejecting the widow's claim under 17a but advising her how to appeal.

The Ministry was fond of pointing out to widows that the fact that their husband had been in receipt of such a pension did not automatically entitle them to a portion of it on his death. The standard letter was worded as follows:

> Your claim has to be determined by the evidence of the actual cause of death, and its connection, if there was any connection, with his war service.[11]

At the Pensions Appeals Tribunals it was apparent that some participants did not understand the grounds on which they were making their appeal. This ignorance sometimes extended to those tasked with representing the appellant. In 1938,

Ellen Mary Smith appeared before the Appeals Tribunal in London, sitting at the Royal Courts of Justice. The intimidating atmosphere was no doubt lessened by the fact that Mrs Smith had hired a solicitor to represent her. Unfortunately, the advocate concerned did not appear to understand the pension regulations, beginning his address to the tribunal by claiming he would have a very easy task as Ellen's husband had been in receipt of a 100 per cent disablement pension before his death. He was brought crashing down to earth by the chairman remarking that 'it was a common fallacy to suppose that the degree of disablement determined the matter of the widow's entitlement.'[12] The solicitor's day got worse when the tribunal disallowed the appeal.

It was not common for a widow to have a solicitor for her appeal hearing. In fact, the involvement of legally qualified representatives in the process was not what the Ministry of Pensions envisaged when setting up the tribunals, claiming that it would 'tend to destroy the informality of the procedure'.[13] The Ministry claimed that every assistance was given to claimants in presenting their case, and that it was the duty of local officials to help. This is a somewhat different approach to that laid out in the Ministry of Pensions' own publication, *The War Pensions Gazette*. In the February 1920 edition, Local War Pensions Committees were instructed to help widows fill in the appeal forms 'if asked', but were told not to encourage what was termed 'futile' action and to maintain a neutral stance in relation to the evidence to be presented.[14] One Local War Pensions Committee reported that they had received a letter from their regional director of the Ministry specifically telling them not to send their principal officers to assist appellants at tribunals.[15]

Rather than formal legal representation it was more common, though by no means universal, to have the widow accompanied at the tribunal by someone from a voluntary body. The British Legion were the most frequent attenders, but the British Red Cross Society are also often mentioned in tribunal cases. In Dundee, the Soldiers and Sailors Dependants Association was very active in supporting widows before the tribunal. With Labour Councillor J.G. Fraser as their representative, the SSDA were reported to be dealing with 100 cases per week in 1924,[16] and continued to appear at tribunals throughout the 1930s. Sometimes the representative was not of much assistance. Isidore Roberts appealed against the Ministry's decision not to grant her a pension on the death of her husband from pernicious anaemia. Mr Bremer from the British Red Cross appeared at the tribunal on her behalf, his sole contribution being to say, 'I never met the deceased – I know very little about the case.' This is all the more unsatisfactory because Isidore was bedridden and unable to attend the tribunal in person. Her claim was refused.[17]

The British Legion did not offer a universal service to widows. Their focus was very heavily upon securing the economic and social position of men returning from the war. The Legion was formed in 1921 from the amalgamation of four other associations who had campaigned to improve the lot of the discharged soldier. Comrades of the Great War was a Conservative organization, whilst the Liberal equivalent was the National Federation of Discharged and Demobilized Sailors and Soldiers. The similarly named National Association of Discharged Sailors and Soldiers had links with the Labour Party, with the Officers' Association being the fourth party in the merger. Though one of the avowed policies of the Legion was 'to guard jealously the right to Pension' for widows as well as ex-servicemen, women were not initially allowed to become ordinary members of the new organization.[18] The uniqueness of a man's wartime experience was a huge part of the ideology of the ex-servicemen's movement – only those who had also served could possibly understand. Assertion of the rights of the ex-soldier often involved curtailing the rights of women, in the field of employment, for example, where the Legion actively campaigned for women to be dismissed in favour of veterans. It is also worth noting that the objective of guarding pensions for widows came last on the British Legion's list of National Objects issued at the organization's inception.[19] Assistance from the Legion for widows at tribunals was patchy and location specific. Some areas had very competent and busy representatives and would take on all cases; others appear to have cherry picked cases they thought they could win, whilst less engaged areas appear to have been reluctant to take on widows' cases at all.

In the early 1920s, a widow's chances of obtaining a pension at first application were around 52 per cent. If she had to take the matter to the tribunal, her chances of success fell significantly. The tribunals heard 4,000 widows' cases in 1922, of which only 1,200, or 30 per cent, were successful.[20] This appears to have been well below the success rate generally of all claimants. Margaret Spoors, widow of miner Robert, was one of the lucky ones, with the Newcastle Tribunal allowing her appeal in 1920.

From 1919 onwards, the Pension Appeals Tribunals were outside of the direct control of the Ministry for the first time. One of the recommendations of the Select Committee on Pensions of 1919 was that there should be a truly independent Pension Appeals Tribunal. Civil servants found it almost impossible to relinquish their grip on the process and kept a close eye on the tribunals to see what percentage of claims were being admitted. The financial consequences of liberal interpretations of the pension regulations were always at the forefront of the minds of the Ministry's employees. In 1920, William Sanger, secretary at the Ministry, issued instructions that cases that went before the Appeals Tribunal must be defended at all costs. Sanger wrote: 'Every decision against the ministerial verdict is a reflection on the way in which we have handled the case, and we ought to be prepared to defend every case which we send to it.'[21] This edict goes some way to explaining the apparent heartlessness of ministry representatives appearing at such hearings for the next twenty years.

In 1920, the Ministry started to compile a list of files where they felt the new tribunals had been too lenient. Tribunals dealing with claims relating to officers were felt to be particularly lax, accused by the Ministry of making decisions on 'sentimental grounds'. Internal memoranda regarding the Officers' Appeal Tribunal and its chairmen are particularly scathing, describing its operation as 'little less than a scandal'.[22] The percentage of officers' appeals that were granted was considerably higher than that of ordinary soldiers – in 1923, 61 per cent of officers compared to 43 per cent of men won their appeals. Officers were at an advantage, both in having the education to present their cases and in being able to afford legal representation and private medical reports. Tribunals were often keener to accept the word of an officer and a gentleman than that of a regular Tommy. Officers were also lucky enough to be able to utilize the services of the 'Officers' Friend' section of the Ministry of Pensions. This was an individual in each regional office who was solely tasked with assisting officers and their families. As far as the civil servants were concerned, they were doing too efficient a job when it came to widows, one official complaining that their 'entirely one-sided advocacy' presented the Ministry's decisions 'in the worst light', prejudicing the tribunal.[23] Figures showed that one Officers' Tribunal chairman in particular was granting 79 per cent of the appeals that came before him, a percentage that could not be tolerated. Various solutions were floated around the Ministry, including setting up a second tribunal staffed with harder personalities and secretly funnelling cases away from chairmen seen as untrustworthy, to the abolition of a separate Officers' Appeal Tribunal altogether. In the end, the action taken was a quiet word in the ear of the offending chairmen, making it clear that they were under very close scrutiny.

Some tribunals were not afraid to contradict the Ministry regardless of criticism, especially when the original decision seemed perverse. Hilda Spencer's husband George had been in receipt of an army pension for tuberculosis when he died in 1929. The cause of death was said to be tuberculosis and anaemia. He had been in poor health since his return from the war and had not been able to take up his former employment in boot manufacturing. When Hilda applied for her share of his pension it was refused on the grounds that anaemia was a separate disease not associated with his war service. The tribunal allowed her appeal, clearly indignant at the Ministry's tortuous reasoning; the file notes, 'Appeal allowed without further question and without the Appellant leaving the Court.'[24]

Sometimes the deceased man himself would prove to be his widow's worst enemy due to statements he had made many years before his death. Oscar Westwood died in 1936 of tuberculosis, the very condition for which he was receiving a pension following his discharge from the army twenty years earlier. Though a number of people wrote to the Ministry of Pensions in support of his widow Elizabeth's claim that this former miner had been perfectly healthy pre-war, his medical records showed that the man himself had admitted to having chest trouble prior to his enlistment.[25] Despite an appeal where she was supported by the British Legion, this proved fatal to the widow's claim. The tribunal agreed with the Ministry of Pensions' assessment that Oscar's two years' home service as a regimental cook were unlikely to have caused the condition that killed him.

As the widow of a 'home service only' soldier, Elizabeth Westwood looks to have found herself in a much more difficult position than would have been the case had her man seen service abroad. The appeal files are full of applications rejected from widows in similar cases. Home service soldiers were often older men who were reservists at the time the war broke out after an earlier period serving in the armed forces. Having been categorized as only physically able to serve on the home front, these individuals were more likely to be susceptible to contracting illness or injury while doing so. Poor living and working conditions, like sleeping outdoors on wet bedding, were more likely to induce a breakdown in the health of such men, which may ultimately have contributed to their deaths.

The Ministry of Pensions and the Appeals Tribunals found it easier to refuse the claims of soldiers who had not seen battle. There was little risk of adverse publicity in dealing harshly with these cases, as cooks and farm workers did not have the same sentimental heroic image as frontline soldiers. This attitude was shown in the treatment of accident cases too, where home service soldiers were at a disadvantage compared to those in war zones. The British Legion and other organizations were less likely to kick up a fuss over home service soldiers who had sometimes spent a fairly brief period of time in uniform. Making a fuss for the widows of such men was even more unlikely.

Whilst the Ministry could accuse tribunal chairmen of making 'sentimental' awards, such criticism could never be levelled at their own civil servants. Mabel S. had nursed her husband for nearly twenty years after his discharge from the army. A former soldier who had been called up again in 1915, Mr S. served with the Territorial Army and was invalided out of the service in March 1917 due to contracting sclerosis. He was subsequently granted a pension for the same condition. His medical notes show that he was in a very poor state of health. He staggered and swayed when walking, trembled constantly and had frequent nosebleeds. In 1924 he suffered a minor stroke. When he died of sclerosis in 1946, Mabel's application for a pension looked to be well founded. A Ministry official dealing with the claim wrote on the file, 'The widow must have had her hands full with her ailing husband,'[26] and expressed the view that 'It would be difficult and illogical to refuse the widow.' But refuse her they did, saying that Mr S.'s war service had not accelerated the natural progress of the disease, hence they had no liability. The Pensions Appeal Tribunal harshly upheld the decision.

In some cases, claims were refused where later medical research would suggest they should have been granted. The case of Private Walter Trask[27] is an example. Walter was an underage soldier, enlisting in the Grenadier Guards in September 1914 at the age of fifteen, though claiming to be nineteen. In November 1915, he was badly wounded by a hand grenade and had to have his left leg amputated. He was evacuated to Netley Military Hospital, where a further operation was necessary. Discharged from the military in December 1916 as being unfit for further service, he was awarded a pension based on 100 per cent disablement. Walter required occasional hospitalization thereafter to deal with issues caused by the amputation. In 1946, more than thirty years after he was wounded, three pieces of shrapnel emerged from his stump.

Walter Trask died in 1959. He had married his wife Olive in December 1919, so by the time of his death, she had witnessed forty years of his struggles with his disability. Olive made a claim for a war widow's pension under Article 17b of the Royal Warrant, namely that his death was entirely due to his war service. The official cause of death was coronary thrombosis, but Olive claimed it was the daily wearing of his artificial leg that had produced extra strain on his heart. Walter had been discharged from the army as a result of gunshot wounds, not heart problems, so the Ministry of Pensions refused her claim. It was up to Olive to prove that Walter's death was connected to his war service and she was completely unprepared for this task. She clearly struggled to complete the appeal forms, filling in the wrong boxes and failing to produce any evidence to support her claim. Having sought help from the local British Legion, the most they did was to ask the Ministry to send her an appeal form. Olive's letters indicate that the Legion refused to assist because she was struggling to obtain evidence from her husband's doctor, who had moved away from her village. She was left completely alone in her battle with the Ministry, and did not attend the tribunal, which was 30 miles from her home. Her appeal was turned down, the medical opinion of the Ministry of Pensions experts that Walter's death was 'unrelated in any way to trauma, including gunshot wounds' being accepted by the tribunal. They opined that amputees were no more likely than anyone else to die from coronary thrombosis and that liability in those circumstances could not be admitted.[28]

It was a fairly common basis of a widow's application where an amputee husband had died of coronary complaints to claim that the strain of an artificial limb had caused extra pressure on the heart. Refusal of the pension in those cases was equally common, though it seems that the widows were prescient in making a connection between the two conditions. In 1979, an American Committee of Veterans' Affairs Report highlighted the link between leg amputation and subsequent cardiovascular disease sometimes many years after the original injury. The Ministry of Pensions in Britain set aside forty-nine previous refusals of pensions to widows as a result of this research. No one appears to have written to those who made applications many years before to see if their claims could be re-examined in the light of this new information. Olive Trask survived her husband by twenty-four years, living all of those years without the war widow's pension to which she was probably entitled.

Like Olive Trask, many widows were ill-prepared for the task of taking on the Ministry of Pensions. No doubt some simply accepted the refusal of their pension as they could not face taking the matter to a tribunal. The forms that were required to submit an appeal were daunting, and it was up to the widow to produce evidence that supported her claim. Some widows were indignant at having to provide information they had already given to the authorities many years earlier. Caroline Ridley made a claim on the death of her husband Henry when she was in her seventies and refused to have her forms countersigned by a Justice of the Peace. A visitor from the Ministry reported, 'She states that she will not let anyone know her business for a paltry fifteen shillings a week and would rather die in the gutter than ask anyone to sign the form.'[29] Caroline Ridley told the official that the Ministry 'knew fine well' that she was Henry's widow and if that was not good enough she would have no more to do with it.

Not many widows showed the tenacity of Elizabeth Stout of Aberdeen, who lost her husband Robert in 1920. Robert Stout was from Lerwick in Shetland, where his family ran the Post Office. He had an inauspicious start to the war when he was arrested for spying, one of forty workers briefly imprisoned in November 1914 after an unfounded suggestion that naval messages had been intercepted. He then served in the Royal Engineers, putting his telegraphy experience to good use. When the war ended, he re-enlisted, being posted to Istanbul. His death in April 1920 was a mystery. He had allegedly gone missing from his unit a few weeks earlier and Elizabeth was then informed that he had died of acute alcoholism. Her application for a pension was duly rejected. Not prepared to accept this state of affairs, she appealed to the tribunal, who also rejected her claim. With the help of the Aberdeen branch of the British Legion, Elizabeth instructed a pathologist for a second opinion. Robert's body was in Istanbul and, eventually, a pathologist ruled that he had died of valvular heart disease related to his war service. Armed with this finding and the support of a number of MPs, Elizabeth was able to finally convince the Ministry of Pensions that she and her daughter were entitled to a pension. The process had taken ten years from the date of Robert Stout's death.[30]

In some widows' cases, the Ministry of Pensions sought to go behind the original decision made on the man's disablement pension. Within the department these files were classified as 'cases of erroneous entitlement', the belief being that the pension granted to the man should never have been given. When the question of revisiting those cases on a man's death was raised in 1925, the decision was to make no policy decision, as usual, and deal with matters on a case by case basis. In 1937, less shy of attracting adverse publicity and with a smaller number of widows to deal with, the Ministry decided on a procedure to be followed. Instructions were given that wherever a disablement pension had been granted without reference to the man's full service records and medical history, a widow's application must undergo extra scrutiny. The Ministry's medical assessors would have to be satisfied that her husband had been entitled to *his* pension before she could fight for her share. Instructions were sent to pensions officials that a widow's claim could be challenged if there was fresh evidence available about a pre-war disability, if the original decision was 'demonstrably incorrect and should not be allowed to stand', or where medical opinion now suggested that the original decision was wrong.[31] This seems a particularly cruel trick to pull almost twenty years after the end of the war when more widows, due to their advancing age, would be unable to support themselves by working and were less likely to remarry.[32]

An example of the operation of the policy comes with the case of E.S. and her husband F. F. had served twelve years in the navy as a younger man and was recalled in 1915, serving throughout the war. In 1919, his behaviour became increasingly odd. He claimed to see lice everywhere and was prone to making strange pronouncements. Found to be mentally unfit, he was sent to the Ministry of Pensions hospital at Ewell, in Epsom. Proximity to the famous racecourse seems to have excited F.'s imagination further, as he was constantly telling the hospital attendants that he was due to ride Lady Lavington's horse in the Derby. He was diagnosed as suffering from general paralysis of the insane (GPI) and in 1921 was granted a full disablement pension by a Pensions Appeal Tribunal who accepted that his condition had been caused by war service.

E. brought him home from the hospital that year on the suggestion of the doctors. After fourteen days she had to take him back as he was just too difficult to look after. She clearly harboured hopes that his condition would improve, and had to be told by his doctors in a letter of 1923 that this was not the case. The Ewell superintendent wrote, 'Your Husband's condition will get worse as time goes on, and [we] think it better to tell you this.'[33] Now categorized as incurable, F. moved from

Ewell to the Surrey County Asylum and then 'home' to the Wiltshire Asylum. After six years the medical officer there certified that F. was never going to be fit to be released. He died in the asylum in 1939.

General paralysis of the insane was caused by the contraction of venereal disease, often many years earlier, which gradually manifested itself in symptoms of mental instability and, eventually, death. GPI had been the subject of a debate in the medical profession during the war, with one school of thought stating that it could never be caused by service or even aggravated by it. Others said that as the number of people with syphilis who subsequently died of brain infections or insanity was small, there must be other factors in the deaths of the men suffering from GPI, one of which could be war service.[34] In 1917, the second opinion prevailed, meaning that F. was a beneficiary of the policy and the Ministry of Pensions accepted responsibility. After two decades of austerity and in the midst of another world war, the climate had changed.

E. was refused a widow's pension by the Ministry. She appeared before the Pension Appeal Tribunal in London, where the chairman was at great pains to explain that just because someone had decided that F. was entitled to a pension did not mean that she was going to get a share:

> I want you to understand that your case must be decided afresh. ... Before you will get a pension you must satisfy us that the condition at death was due to the direct result of your husband's service. I don't know why GPI was given as the result of service. We have to satisfy ourselves that he was properly pensioned for GPI. ... GPI is never caused by service. Service may make it worse ... that, however, will not be sufficient for your claim to succeed.[35]

Noting that the original tribunal decision in F.'s favour had not been unanimous, the new body also said that they did not know the reasoning behind the grant, clearly suggesting that it had been 'erroneous'. The Ministry of Pensions' claim that F. did not die of his war disability was accepted by the tribunal, who disallowed the widow's claim. E. had no one to accompany her to the hearing other than her daughter. The Ministry of Pensions' official sent to argue the case reported: 'The widow showed great distress and told the chairman that it was not until she had received the papers that she was aware of what was the cause of her husband's death. She appeared to be an intelligent woman.'[36]

It is doubtful that any degree of intelligence would enable her to understand why the state now did not want to take responsibility for the maintenance of her and her family after her husband's lengthy service.

The imperative for the Ministry of Pensions as far as the Treasury was concerned was clearly to save money. The only way of doing this was to scrutinize all applications for pensions and refuse as many as possible. This task was made easier by the introduction of widows' pensions under the National Insurance scheme in 1925. Though this would only apply to wives of insured men, it did provide an alternative for some women to trying to jump through the hoops required for a war widow's pension. A widow could not have both pensions at that stage, so her receipt of a civilian pension would not only assure the Ministry that she was being maintained in some fashion, it may also act to discourage her from appealing if her war widow's claim was rejected. If the amount she was to receive in total as a war widow would rise only slightly from the basic widow's pension, many women would surely not consider an appeal to be worth the trouble.

In 1973, Annie Hankey applied for a war widow's pension in respect of the death of her husband Richard. He had suffered severe facial injuries during the war and had been in receipt of a disability pension. However, he had died in 1927 and it was forty-seven years before his widow made her application. Richard had not died of his war wounds, but was killed in a fight. On the face of it, it would seem like a simple case to refuse. Annie's argument was that her husband's war experience had so changed his nature and behaviour that it led him to putting himself in this volatile situation, directly resulting in his death. Applying this very modern concept to a 50-year-old case posed some interesting questions for the pension authorities.

Richard Hankey was serving with the Coldstream Guards in February 1915 when his jaw and collarbone were fractured by shell fragments and he was hospitalized for most of the next year. A medical board in April 1916 revealed the severity of his injury, the board noting that '[A] portion of jaw and collarbone is missing and also loss of fourteen teeth.'[37] His appearances before successive medical boards give some idea of the severity of his injury. In January 1919, it was noted that he could not open his jaw wider than an inch. In November 1920, he reported that two pieces of bone had come away from his jaw a few months earlier. He was described as having 'a considerable deformity'. A year later, he explained to the board that 'an ordinary dinner of meat and vegetables will take about an hour to be eaten.'[38] Annie Hankey claimed that the injury had other effects too, saying that her husband 'took brain storms'.

Her pension application was refused by the Department of Health and Social Security, successors to the Ministry of Pensions. They claimed that, other than his jaw injury, Richard Hankey's general health was not affected by his war wounds.

Unfortunately, Annie died before the appeal, but the torch passed to her daughter, Margaret, who sent a series of letters to the authorities. She wrote that she and her siblings had suffered badly in their childhood and that her father's wound had caused him to become 'mentally unbalanced and addicted to drink'.[39] His face was so disfigured that he could not bear to look in a mirror. Annie was unable to obtain any life insurance for her husband due to the state of his wounds and was left destitute on his death. She had to pay for his burial and could afford no more than a pauper's grave. According to Margaret, her mother approached the British Legion for help and received none. She then lost the baby she had been carrying when her husband died.

> The baby was also laid to rest in a pauper's grave so she never approached them again and worked till she was over 70. I could not say there was any British justice here. Compassion and dignity is what every serviceman or ex-serviceman should be shown if they are willing to lay down their life for their country. My father's case should not be judged on how he died, but the reason why.[40]

Two years after the original application, a tribunal ruled that the death of Richard Hankey was not caused or materially hastened by the effects of his war service. Annie's posthumous claim for a widow's pension was denied. The family's application was more about the restoration of Richard Hankey's reputation than the payment of a pension. When her father's service records were sent to her, Margaret Hankey replied: 'Your documents are all I need. Thank you for proving my father was a man, and a soldier.'[41]

Wives who were fortunate enough to have their husbands return alive from the war were not financially secure if the man subsequently died. Though the husband may have been in receipt of a disablement pension due to injuries sustained in war service, the issue of that pension to the widow was not an automatic right. The Ministry of Pensions' attitude towards widows was much less favourable than that shown to disabled men. Any benefit of the doubt previously given to their husbands was ruthlessly removed when it came to applications by widows. Bereaved women were faced with a battle to pick their way through the sometimes confusing regulations in order to prove their entitlement. Many no doubt found the prospect of an appeal too daunting to contemplate, especially as there was no right to representation before the tribunal, which might sit some considerable distance from their home. Though the British Legion undoubtedly helped some widows, there were many others who had to battle alone, with less chance of success before the tribunal than a disabled man. Searching for any loophole to refuse the widow's claim, the Ministry spent a considerable amount of time and effort in fighting these cases, often many years after the Armistice. Having sometimes spent years caring for their ailing husbands, these widows were left in a worse financial position than if their men had died in action.

Chapter 10

Unworthy of our Royal Favour
Widow's Pension Forfeiture Cases

*'If the dead could only speak I would have my name
cleared of all lies.'*

From their inception, separation allowances and pensions were subject to forfeiture should the woman's behaviour be deemed immoral or reprehensible in some way. Successive Royal Warrants maintained this power and the notion of worthiness was inherent within the pensions and allowance system. The wording 'worthy of our Royal favour' proved to be a gossips' charter in relation to widows, leaving women open to intrusive and embarrassing investigation by the authorities.

The First Ministry of Pensions Annual Report in 1918 set out the approach taken by the department and its affiliated bodies. Describing the forfeiture investigation as a 'careful and sympathetic procedure',[1] the Ministry explained how the Special Grants Committee had responsibility for such investigations. Once a complaint had been received, it was passed to the Local War Pensions Committee for further enquiries to be made. The police force for the local area was usually involved, sometimes alongside the local clergy. The report praised the police for their 'admirable tact and discretion' in making these enquiries. Unofficial sources were also consulted, including the local shopkeeper or random neighbours, who would be spoken to by the Local War Pensions Committee visitor to see what they knew about the widow's circumstances.

The Ministry expressed their desire that the woman be given the opportunity of meeting the charge, but the method by which this was done left much to be desired. It was felt to be enough to send full particulars of the complaint and of the general nature of the evidence in support of it to the secretary of the Local Committee 'in order that some suitable person may visit the woman and hear what she has to say in her own defence.'[2] The woman herself, therefore, was never furnished with the details of the evidence against her and her response had to be mediated through a third party, often a lady visitor with very different ideas on respectability and appropriate behaviour. It was not until 1921 and the report of a committee empanelled to investigate the administration of the Ministry of

Pensions that a widow was given the right to make a written statement on her own behalf in such cases and call her own evidence to rebut the allegation.[3]

Forfeiture cases saw widows being defined again by their relationship to men, in this case to their dead husbands. The same principles used to determine the forfeiture of separation allowances were also used in cases of widows' pensions. The principle that the state was acting to fulfil financial obligations in lieu of the absent husband was relied upon to the extent that it was felt to be inherently reasonable to remove that support in cases where the husband himself may have disowned his wife. Separation allowances and pensions could be removed if a woman was felt to be 'generally unworthy', which was defined as 'generally immoral', or where she had been convicted of running a brothel or seriously neglecting her children. In such cases, the presumption was that the pension would be withdrawn. In other cases, the attitude of the husband towards his wife's misbehaviour was a determining factor in her keeping her allowance; if he forgave her, then the payments would continue. Clearly this placed widows at something of a disadvantage as their own husbands' views were not so easily sought. However, the Ministry felt that this route was still open to widows, stating that any evidence that he would have forgiven her if he had not died 'is welcomed by the committee as affording an opportunity of extending leniency in their decision.'[4] In one case where forfeiture was proposed, the fact that the widow had been threatened with removal of her separation allowance while her husband was alive but that she was at his bedside when he died was cited as evidence that he must have forgiven her and that, therefore, removal of her pension for the same offence was not necessary.[5]

If the SGC were satisfied that there had been misconduct on the part of the widow, their powers included complete forfeiture of the pension, suspension while closer supervision took place, or the administration of the pension in trust for the widow. Administration could include vouchers being given to the widow instead of cash, or accounts set up at certain shops on her behalf. This would involve great embarrassment to the widow as it would be obvious to shopkeepers and neighbours that some kind of censure had taken place.

The number of investigations into widows' misconduct is startlingly high; in the financial year 1920–21, 3,502 new cases came before the committee, followed by 3,209 the following year.[6] The number of widows in receipt of a pension in 1921 appears to be in the region of 174,000, meaning that one widow in every fifty-four was subject to an investigation. Of the new cases before the committee in 1920–21, 1,161 were subject to forfeiture. The following year the proportions were even more unfavourable to widows – from the 3,209 cases, 1,361 pensions were removed, whilst 1,007 were continued but in administration. Once reported to the committee, the odds were clearly stacked against a widow coming out with her pension intact.

The number of women investigated and the percentage of pensions subsequently withdrawn is particularly shocking given that such standards were not applied to disabled male war veterans. In a number of exchanges in the House of Commons in late 1919, it was confirmed by the Minister for Pensions, that men's pensions were now 'a right and not a grace'[7] and could not be removed for criminal offences committed by veterans, other than treason. On the recommendation of the Select Committee on Pensions of 1919, the War Pensions Act 1920 established that pensions were also a statutory right for widows and children, but always subject to the relevant forfeiture provisions in the Royal Warrant. No one would take away a man's war pension because his behaviour was below par; for a war widow it was a constant threat.

It should be said that attempts to draw general conclusions from the forfeiture files at the National Archives are inevitably hampered by the very few that remain. A great number were destroyed and there are others that remain sealed for years to come to protect the names and reputation of any living relatives, particularly illegitimate children. With that note of caution, it can be said that many features of the files that still exist are remarkably consistent, particularly with regard to the imposition of middle-class norms on working-class families. Nowhere are the class tensions inherent in the supervision of widows laid bare more clearly than in those files that deal with cases of proposed forfeiture.

The primary reason for the removal of widows' pensions appears to have been for cohabitation with another man. Of the fifty-nine pensions that were removed by the SGC in June 1923, forty-one were taken due to cohabitation.[8] The rules stated that if a widow remarried, she would be eligible for a gratuity of two years' pension (later reduced in 1917 to one year) in lieu of her pension. Any children of the deceased soldier would still be eligible for their allowances as the new husband was not expected to support another man's children. Some women made a conscious decision not to solemnize new relationships by marriage so that they could continue to benefit from their pensions long term. Others were in the unenviable position of being with men who could not marry them for one reason or another, often because they were still married themselves. Such women enjoyed the worst of all worlds. They could not marry their new men as divorce was beyond them and they were therefore unable to avail themselves of the remarriage gratuity payable to other women. If they reported their new living arrangements they would lose their pension completely and, it seems, often irrevocably.

In a society where divorce was expensive and rare, cohabitation had been a recognized feature of working-class communities before the war. After the war, however, those in receipt of a war widow's pension found that living together without marriage could have dire financial consequences if brought to the attention of the authorities. It is unsurprising, therefore, that working-class communities would produce a large number of forfeiture cases.

The fishing town of North Shields on Tyneside was a hotbed of illicit relationships if one correspondent to the Ministry of Pensions was to be believed. In 1924, the Ministry received a series of letters about war widows in the town. An anonymous informant, who later signed herself as Mrs Duffy, wrote to report the behaviour of a number of her neighbours who were consorting with other men while living on their widow's pension. Mrs Duffy herself was a war widow who had lost her pension for cohabitation and could see no reason why others should not suffer the same penalty. She wrote: 'I admit myself some of us have went on disgraceful and I admit deserving to lose mine, but don't let them laugh at our downfall when they are no better.'[9]

She named a number of women who were misbehaving, claiming that the local pub was the place to track them down. 'The Clock Vaults, Wellington Street at 10 pm do not lie.'[10] Ominously, against each name in this letter is a pencilled reference number, indicating that the Ministry of Pensions took her seriously and started investigations in these particular cases. Thankfully for the local community, despite claiming that there are 'thirty or forty' such widows she knows, Mrs Duffy restricted herself to naming just a handful.

One of these women was Margaret Potts, widow of Trimmer Robert Potts, Royal Navy, who had drowned in August 1915. Mrs Potts lived in a one-room house with her three children and, according to Mrs Duffy, a man called James Knight. Margaret Potts told the investigating visitor that Knight was nothing but a lodger, and that she slept elsewhere at night to avoid suggestions of impropriety. She supplemented her pension by taking in washing, earning three or four shillings a week. In her favour, the visitor reported that her three children were well cared for, her eldest being employed as a greengrocer's errand boy, earning eight shillings a week to add to the family pot. Given the unlikely logistics of Mrs Potts' living arrangements, the highly likely outcome of the investigation would have been that her pension was removed. However, before the matter was concluded the unfortunate Mr Knight left the house and died. This left the fortunate Mrs Potts still holding her pension, though it was now to be administered in trust. There appears to be no good reason behind this sanction other than to mark the SGC's disapproval, as there was no suggestion that the widow was misusing the pension money. Given the nature of the allegations made by her neighbour she was no doubt grateful to retain any pension at all.

Sometimes the informant to the SGC was a family member, usually a relative of the deceased soldier, unhappy at the way the widow was living her life. In Mary

Jane Kelly's case her mother-in-law reported her to the authorities for living with another man. Indignant at accusations that she had behaved improperly, Mary Jane denied cohabitation but accepted having a relationship with a man called Ratcliffe, intending to marry him. During the 1921 investigation she wrote:

> I am keeping company quite honourable, I don't keep a bad house or go about with men or bad company. I deny any man or woman before God any misconduct or adultery of any kind.
>
> I think I suffered enough when I lost the best husband in the world for I am only a girl myself and now I have to battle alone. I will close now, my heart is broke.[11]

Despite her protests, Mary Jane Kelly's widow's pension was removed. Unlike many widows, she had the resources to cope on some level, as she was in employment herself, working at the local mill as a four loom weaver, earning £2 5s a week. After two appeals supported by the Local War Pensions Committee and six months of satisfactory visitors' reports, her pension was eventually restored in November 1921.

Fifteen years later, an examination of the Voters' Lists sparked off a further investigation – one Mary Jane Kelly was listed as a resident in a house with Norman Ratcliffe. The SGC sprang into action again, dispatching investigators to interrogate the neighbours. Mary Jane was found to be running a fish, chip and tripe shop with Ratcliffe. A neighbour in the locality told the visitor that the two were not married. Another neighbour reported that he went to 'Norman's' when he was short of cow heels and that Norman's 'missus' helped in the shop.

Mary Jane Kelly told the visitor that far from being supported by Ratcliffe, she was supporting him, providing him with free board and lodging in exchange for helping in the shop. Ratcliffe himself rather unhelpfully disclosed that he had lived with Mary Jane intermittently for ten years. Directed to appear before the Local War Pensions Committee in March 1936, Mary Jane explained that Ratcliffe, a miner, was laid off during the 1926 coal strike and had been unable to get steady work since. In 1934, the mill she worked in closed down and she spent £75 – her life savings – buying the fish, chip and tripe shop. The plan was that they would marry if the business were successful. Despite this plan, she told the committee that they did not live together as man and wife and that Ratcliffe shared a bedroom with the lodger.

The committee had some sympathy for Mary Jane, feeling that she was duped by Ratcliffe. 'The committee are of the opinion that she has been victimized by the man, who has been living on her pension.'[12] The SGC were not quite so generous, no doubt feeling that they had been duped for the last fifteen years, and Mary Jane Kelly's pension was permanently removed. The case does have a happy ending in one respect – Mary Jane Kelly and Norman Ratcliffe eventually married in 1942.

Sometimes widows were their own worst enemies, bringing unnecessary attention to themselves resulting in the withdrawal of their pensions. In a case that would have been cheered by the Charity Organisation Society, the widow of Private Rogers, already in receipt of a pension, shot herself in the foot by applying to the Admiralty for a gratuity in respect of a different man. With the increasing bureaucratization of government departments and cross-checking of data, the Admiralty wrote to the Ministry of Pensions to bring the fact to their attention. The SGC investigated and within a month decided that Mrs Rogers should lose her pension. She wrote to the committee, protesting their decision: 'If the dead could only speak I would have my name cleared of all lies.'[13] She also named some other miscreants in the local area, and the SGC endeavoured to find them, to no avail. Mrs Rogers was supported in her protests by her local British Legion, though their explanation of her position in the letter sent to the Ministry of Pensions stretched credulity to the extreme. The Legion claimed they had investigated her association with the second man, by whom she had a child, and that 'the woman was taken advantage of whilst she was in a fainting fit and knew nothing of the matter until some seven months later.'[14] Mrs Rogers was eventually told she could have her pension back, though administered until her behaviour proved satisfactory.

Once a woman had sinned as far as the SGC were concerned, it was very difficult for her to be absolved. It was open to the committee to reinstate pensions on further application, as happened in the Rogers case. The Ministry of Pensions 4th Annual Report to 31 March 1921 claimed that in 381 cases in that financial year, pensions previously removed were restored after further investigation. However, the existing forfeiture files show some very harsh decisions that were not rescinded when a widow's circumstances changed at a later date.

When Queenie Passmore was sentenced to a term of imprisonment in 1917, Holloway Prison duly informed the Ministry of Pensions that they had a war widow in their custody and the SGC unsurprisingly withdrew her pension. Given that she had concealed a deserter in that difficult year of the war, it was impossible for the authorities to show Queenie Passmore any mercy. Less logic applied to the subsequent refusals to reinstate her pension. Queenie's initial appeal, made on her release from prison, was easily rejected, as enquiries suggested that she was living with a woman recently convicted of running a brothel. Twenty-two years later, she wrote to beg for the return of her war widow's pension, pleading that she could no longer work and was 'beaten'.[15] Queenie explained that she started a new life after her release from prison, obtaining a position as a domestic servant, which she held for eight years. After two operations, she was now lame and blind in one eye, and could no longer support herself. She had tried to struggle on without assistance as 'I have felt so ashamed, but rest assured, my wrong I did all those years ago I have been doubly punished, and now fear for the future compels me to ask for your help.'[16] She was now fifty-three years old and had committed no further offences since 1917. The SGC again refused her application. One committee member returned their papers in the case with the notation 'Mostly sympathetic', but this dissenting voice did not save Queenie's pension.

A similarly harsh case concerns a woman who was living with a married man who was unable to secure a divorce. In 1922, 'A Friend to the Man's Children'[17] wrote to the Ministry of Pensions to report that the man in question was living with a war widow and her children while his original family were struggling financially without him. An investigation was commenced, during which the widow confessed. Given the stark choice of relinquishing her pension or her man, she chose love over money and her pension was immediately suspended. Due to the fact that four of her children were still entitled to their allowances, visits from the authorities continued every six months and she always received glowing reports. Cleanliness was next to Godliness as far as the lady visitor was concerned and the fact that the woman's house was said to be 'spotless' was always quoted in her favour. By 1925, her relationship with the married man was over. The widow wrote to the SGC to plead for the restoration of her pension, saying: 'Surely I am entitled to my pension back which was for the loss of my husband for fighting for his country, not for his wife's behaviour. Surely he did not die for me to be left destitute.'[18]

The SGC were unmoved and refused her application. They also refused further applications in 1929, 1931 and 1934, twelve years after the original report of her misconduct was made.

In cases where widows' pensions were restored, the women concerned remained under the scrutiny of the authorities. When Sarah Clarke's pension was removed, it left her in severe financial difficulty. She herself wrote to the SGC to report that she had been forced to sell a number of belongings, including the bed on which she and her son slept. After numerous appeals and the intervention of her MP, her pension was restored, albeit under administration and strict supervision. Sarah Clarke had to submit to visits from the Local War Pensions Committee four times a month, at all hours of the day and evening. Her pension was eventually restored to her direct.

A lifestyle that fell short of middle-class standards was often punished by removal of a widow's pension. Sarah Clarke suffered partly from being seen as the kind of 'camp follower' army wife of the Victorian age. She had married her husband when he was stationed in Ireland and had followed him around the country thereafter. She still lived near the barracks after his death and supplemented her income by doing washing for soldiers, who were frequently at her house, attracting the attention of the anonymous informant. Though her lady visitor did not recommend forfeiture in her case, powers higher up had taken a dim view of her lifestyle and had acted accordingly.

Anna Anderson's lifestyle appears to be no better or worse than that of most of her neighbours, but because she was a war widow, it was used to eventually remove her pension.[19] In 1923, Anna fell out with her lodgers who then made a complaint about the widow 'misconducting herself' with a man called Wiggins. The police investigated and produced a less then favourable report about Anna Anderson, claiming that she was 'frequently seen in public houses and when the worse for drink is quarrelsome and abusive.'[20] However, as far as her association with Wiggins is concerned, there was never any evidence that it was anything other than a platonic friendship. Anna's children were well looked after and she was described as a hard-working woman. Despite the fact that there was no evidence of cohabitation, the Local War Pensions Committee recommend that her pension should be paid in trust, and the SGC obliged. After twelve years of further scrutiny, with no evidence ever provided that Anna was in a relationship, her pension was taken away completely. Anna Anderson had done nothing other than enjoy a drink from time to time and have a platonic friendship with a man, but the SGC's view of her lifestyle saw her left without a pension and without any adequate explanation as to why.

It is noteworthy in a number of forfeiture cases that the recommendation of the Local War Pensions Committee was at odds with the decision of the SGC. This was a great source of tension between these two parts of the pension administration. Ethel Wood, secretary of the London War Pensions Committee, outlined the difficulties in evidence before the Select Committee on Pensions in 1919.[21] Asked for her opinion on forfeiture cases, she described the whole basis of the work as 'absolutely unsatisfactory'.[22] She was unhappy at the way in which the SGC directed the Local War Pensions Committees to investigate such cases, and would then override their recommendations without explanation. She also felt it was 'thoroughly un-British' not to give an accused woman the chance of a personal hearing:

> Take a wife first. You get a letter from the Ministry which says perhaps that information has been received that Mrs So and So, the wife of a certain soldier, is guilty of immoral conduct, and you send that down to the unfortunate local sub committee. That Committee does not know

whether the Ministry have received an anonymous letter or whether the police have given information or whether somebody knows that a man is living with the woman. They may have to send to a woman they have never seen before to ask her whether she is guilty of immoral conduct and if she has been guilty she will not admit it. What I think is so awfully unfair is that you do get cases where an unpleasant neighbour or some-body makes a purely spiteful accusation against a woman and on paper the facts may look black, and that woman does not get any chance of coming up and putting her own case.[23]

The damage to relations between the accused widow and the Local War Pensions Committee were also very much on her mind. 'Now, if it is not true, and she hap-pens to be a nice woman, she hates that committee for the rest of her life.'[24] Her own opinion was that in cases of proven immorality, the pension should be paid in trust for a specified period to enable the widow to get her life back on a footing that would meet with the Ministry of Pensions' approval. Despite her enthusiasm for voluntary work, Ethel Wood was clear that investigations should be carried out by paid staff, not lady visitors.

A further concern for Mrs Wood and her colleagues was the potential hard-ship caused to children in such families if the widow's own pension was removed. Immorality by the widow would not result in forfeiture of her children's allow-ances, with the result being that the whole family would now live on this lesser amount of money. This particular topic would cause something of a revolt by the Local War Pensions Committees. The view of the Local Committees was that the SGC routinely ordered forfeiture for misconduct cases,[25] an allegation that the SGC denied, saying that each case was considered on its merits and that their 'set-tled policy'[26] was to avoid forfeiture wherever possible. The cases reported where widows did have their pensions taken away belie this assertion. The consensus amongst the Local War Pensions Committees involved in this protest was that widows must be given more opportunity to rectify any errant behaviour without having their pensions completely removed.

The Liverpool War Pensions Committee felt strongly enough to set up a special subcommittee in 1922, forwarding proposals to the SGC to solve these problems. The resolutions that were forthcoming had the children at their heart, stating that it was more important to look after their welfare than it was to punish a woman for misconduct. Liverpool proposed that no widow should have her pension removed without the opportunity to have it administered in trust for a period first, and that unless her conduct was bad enough for the children to be removed from her care, or she could be proved to be an 'unmarried wife', her pension should never be taken. Liverpool had a significant success rate where they administered pensions – of 120 such cases in the eighteen months prior to the letter, only two women subsequently had their pensions removed.[27]

The SGC would not accept these proposals. Their reply denied enthusiasm for removing pensions, claiming that 'isolated offences are never met by forfeiture.'[28] As far as the welfare of the soldier's children was concerned, the SGC 'with great reluctance feel bound to express the view that the proposal to continue to maintain unworthy widows because of the children should not be accepted.'[29]

However, the SGC did not always practise what it preached. The case of Mrs Squire was one example.[30] Though refused a war widow's pension on causation grounds, Mrs Squire was granted a special allowance by the SGC due to the fact that she had five children and exceptional hardship would be caused to the family if no payments were made at all. Mrs Squire was cohabiting with a man called Toye, and her portion of the special allowance was removed for that reason in 1922. The Forfarshire War Pensions Committee did not want the family given anything at all, writing to the SGC that: 'The continued payment of the Special Allowance for the three younger children was likely only to encourage Mr Toye in remaining a member of the household and failing to exert himself to find work.'[31]

The SGC continued to make the payments.

The conflicts with the SGC caused members of the Aylesbury War Pensions Committee to threaten their resignations in a case where they had suggested administration, not forfeiture, where a widow was thought to be consorting with another man. Their own investigation had shown that she was a woman 'of weak intellect'[32] who had been taken advantage of by this individual and had three pensionable children who would be caused a significant degree of hardship by a reduction in the family income. The man himself had now left the area and the widow was seriously ill and unable to work. The SGC removed her pension and refused several appeals by the Aylesbury Committee. The family were said to be living in a state of 'semi-starvation' and, as the widow had two illegitimate children, the local Poor Law Guardians had refused to assist unless the whole family entered the workhouse.[33] The Ministry of Pensions was unrepentant, writing to the Aylesbury Committee and making their position very clear. George Chrystal, secretary to the Ministry, wrote that this was a matter of 'common decency':[34]

> To many of these war widows, the temptation to forego the marriage ceremony, and so retain their pension until they are found out, must be considerable. Are we to add to it by decreeing that, even if the facts are discovered, (and often they are not), the woman has only to send the man away to have her pension restored to her?[35]

Chrystal instructed the Aylesbury Committee to toe the line, not wanting an impression created that forfeiture applied to 'anything other than a very small minority of our war widows'.[36] As we have seen from the figures on investigations and forfeiture, this statement was not entirely true.

Frustrated by the Ministry's intransigence, some Local War Pensions Committees took matters into their own hands and gave out allowances and gratuities where the rules did not allow them to do so. The East Ham Committee found themselves at odds with the Ministry of Pensions for being too generous. East Ham covered a working-class dockland area of London where Sylvia Pankhurst and her East London Federation of Suffragettes had been very active in relief work of all kinds during the war.[37] The League of Rights for Soldiers' and Sailors' Wives and Relatives, of which Pankhurst was an early member, were represented on the East Ham War Pensions Committee, along with a number of trade unionists. East Ham were circumventing regulations in respect of medical certification of disabled men and giving grants for items beyond their remit, including boots for widows and children. In 1919, the East Ham Committee was suspended while an investigation took place. This caused a great deal of ill feeling in the local area and a protest march consisting of disabled veterans and widows made its way to the Ministry of Pensions. A marcher told a reporter, 'The Local Committee was prepared to give us justice, but the Ministry of Pensions has stopped its banking account.'[38] The Ministry's investigation concluded that there had been no dishonesty on the part of the committee – they were trying to provide for their constituents and if the regulations seemed inflexible, they ignored them. The Ministry took into account the fact that East Ham was a very poor area without the ability to raise as much in the way of charitable donations to fill the gaps in the system as a more prosperous part of the country may have done. Nevertheless, all committee members were suspended for twelve months and eventually resigned.

Widows who had their pensions stopped and now had to seek employment found themselves at a significant disadvantage in the labour market. To add to the existing prejudice around working women, these widows often suffered the indignity of prospective employers questioning them about their pensions and the reasons why they were removed.[39] Frank responses were unlikely to result in job offers and local gossip got around quickly. Indeed, the mere fact of an investigation was often very damaging to a widow's reputation, despite the supposed 'tact' of the authorities. In one case where the widow lived in a small village in South Wales, even the visitor to whom the investigation was entrusted appreciated the difficulties. Stating that word was sure to get out once enquiries were made with neighbours, regardless of their discretion being sought, the officer in this investigation concluded that it was a case of 'give a dog a bad name and it will stick'.[40]

As far as the SGC was concerned, once a woman had a bad name, it certainly stuck. Rose Knight's pension was initially removed in 1924 for misconduct with a married man called Horace Porter, after an anonymous letter was received by the pension authorities, this time from someone who signed themselves simply as 'Disgusted'.[41] During the subsequent investigation, Rose told the visitor that she had met Porter when working at a shoe factory. He had pretended to be a single man and allegedly seduced her. Once Rose was pregnant, Porter revealed that he was married, and she claimed at that point to have resolved to have nothing further to do with him. The child, born in 1920, had unfortunately died. Enquiries revealed that the situation was not quite as clear cut as Rose portrayed, and she was still having her meals at the Porter residence. Her domestic arrangements did not find favour with the visitor and it was recommended that her pension be forfeited. The SGC obliged accordingly.

Six months later, Rose applied to have the pension restored, again claiming to have severed all ties with Mr Porter. A visitor's report now showed that she was living at a different address to Porter with a respectable landlady and, crucially, not eating meals at Porter's house. The report said that she now lived 'a quiet life' and only went out to go to work or if accompanied by her landlady. The SGC were prepared to reissue the pension to her on these favourable reports, initially in trust in September 1925, then after two years of supervision, restored to her direct in 1927.

As we have seen in earlier cases, despite the restoration of the pension, widows continued to be under surveillance of one kind or another. Like Mary Jane Kelly, Rose Knight was betrayed by an examination of the Voters' List ten years after the first anonymous letter. The Voters' List showed that she was not registered at the address she had given the Ministry of Pensions and was listed as Rose Porter. A visitor was entrusted to make the relevant enquiries and went to the address, being directed to 'Mrs Porter's' by a neighbour. Rose was there and at a loss to explain why she was known locally as Mrs Porter. She claimed that she moved in with Porter 'to keep the house tidy', was out from 7.00 am to 7.00 pm every day and did not cook the man's meals. The visitor wrote, 'I noticed the woman was very agitated and had changed colour.'[42] When told that she could go before the committee and explain herself, Rose replied, 'I don't want to go before the committee, I will go and get drunk.'[43] Her pension was suspended and when nothing further was heard from her, was removed permanently.

One of the most remarkable files from the forfeiture cases involves Ada Bruce, our spiritualist widow in Westcliff-on-Sea.[44] Mrs Bruce's husband was a skilled clockmaker pre-war and had been discharged with a disablement pension. Unfortunately, Mr Bruce's health was permanently broken and he died in

January 1924. Given the nature of his civilian employment, his widow was able to supply the necessary evidence to qualify for an alternative pension.

In 1930, the Ministry of Pensions received the now familiar anonymous letter accusing Ada Bruce of living with another man. A report was requested from the Local War Pensions Committee, the conclusion being that the man was simply a lodger, and no further action was taken. Two years later, another letter was received, this time signed by a war widow who lived a couple of houses up the street from Ada. This woman had lost her husband at Gallipoli in May 1915 and clearly felt strongly that Ada was not adhering to the high standards required of a war widow. She claimed that Ada and Mr Cusden, the 'lodger', shared a bedroom in the three-bedroomed house, the others being occupied by Ada's three children. The police were asked to investigate. Ada denied the accusation of impropriety and said she needed a lodger to make ends meet. The police described her as a 'church worker' and said her mode of living was 'quite respectable'.[45] The SGC were again content to take no action.

Unfortunately for Ada Bruce, a woman on the Southend War Pensions Committee had it in for her and two short months after the SGC decision, the matter was raised again. Having investigated very recently, the SGC were initially not prepared to reopen the matter. Mrs Jefferies OBE, Ada's nemesis, would not take no for an answer and two months later made a further complaint. She claimed that the war widows of Westcliff were up in arms over Ada Bruce's behaviour and that action must be taken. It was not only her association with the lodger, but also her involvement in spiritualism that demonstrated she was an unworthy widow. The 'church' for which Ada was a worker was the Conan Doyle Memorial spiritualist church, not the local Church of England establishment. Mrs Jefferies did not accept that Ada needed a lodger's rent money to get by, intimating that a woman of her class should be able to manage quite well on the income she was already receiving. An inquiry officer was again sent to Westcliff.

Ada was spoken to by the inquiry officer after arriving home in a stylish touring car driven by a lady friend. The officer – a man in this case – remarked that she was 'very smartly dressed in a fashion superior to what one would normally expect of a woman in her position'.[46] Interestingly, considering the later court case against Ada, he noted her ability to speak in a very different, masculine voice. Ada spent fifteen minutes upstairs retrieving her pension book then offered to show her visitor the bedrooms. She appears to have spent her time upstairs rejigging things to make it look as though Cusden had his own room, throwing men's clothes haphazardly around. The officer was not convinced by what he saw as a charade. His opinion was that the evidence showed she was cohabiting with Cusden, 'who has been responsible for initiating her into the mysteries and practices of spiritualism, and, in my opinion, in the process has turned her into a very capable dreamy looking actress and humbug.'[47] Once again, a man was seen as leading a war widow astray.

Ada appeared in person before the Southend War Pensions Committee, dismissing the allegations as malicious gossip. Ten people subsequently provided references to state that Ada was an upstanding member of the community. However, it seems that a good number of them actually knew very little about her, having simply attended séances at her address. One of Ada's regular customers told the investigator that 'as the widow is quite good looking and attractive, she could find a much better man than Cusden if she was that way inclined.'[48] The report noted, '(Her description of the widow as good looking and attractive is corroborated by the Inquiry Officer.)'

The number of forfeiture cases now being dealt with were considerably fewer than in the immediate post-war years, and it may be that the SGC had softened their approach as, when considering the evidence in some of the other forfeiture files, Ada Bruce would have seemed the ideal candidate for permanent sacrifice of her pension. The amount of money she received from various sources was referred to several times by informants, the clear implication being that the genteel inhabitants of Westcliff thought that this was a woman who had got a little above her station in life. The referral of Ada Bruce to the authorities appears to be more to do with class than morality. Whether the SGC felt the complaints were local jealousy, or whether they were impressed by Ada's character witnesses, the surprising result of the investigation was that the widow kept her pension.

Though statistically a very small sample, the remaining forfeiture files do exhibit attitudes towards widows that we see represented elsewhere in their brushes with authority. A widow was not treated as an individual in her own right and was defined by her relationship to a man. The level of surveillance to which widows were subjected is remarkable and would no doubt have been impossible without the great volunteer army working for the Local War Pensions Committees. In 1927, there were still 17,000 voluntary workers under the auspices of the Ministry of Pensions.[49] A poison pen letter from a neighbour could destroy the financial basis on which a family was surviving. The police and the Church often joined forces to act as agents of the state in such investigations, causing widows a great deal of public embarrassment notwithstanding the outcome of the enquiry. Local gossip was taken seriously even when provided by women who had already proved themselves to be dishonest as far as the SGC were concerned. Members of the Local War Pensions Committees tasked with investigating were sometimes the source of that gossip themselves. Class bias was rife, whether that was disapproval of a certain lifestyle because it was not the middle-class ideal, or whether, as in the case of Ada Bruce, a woman was to be punished for having pretensions to respectability. There was clearly an appetite for such work amongst those responsible for administering widows' pensions; in 1929, the SGC offered to assist the Mercantile Marine in investigating claims of unworthiness in respect of widows under their administration.[50]

Widows were often on their own in fighting such allegations, with the British Legion not well represented in the surviving forfeiture files. Using the Voters' List to catch widows out was a particularly low tactic, using the widows' exercising of one hard-fought right to find evidence to remove another. There was no right to a judicial hearing of any kind and no independent body to which the widow could appeal; the SGC's decisions were final. It is no surprise that a significant proportion of such investigations resulted in the loss of a widow's pension. Where women were seen as the dupes of unscrupulous men, the authorities found it easier to restore their pensions or give them the benefit of the doubt. Women themselves, as with those who appeared before the courts, seemed to pick up on this attitude and present themselves as deceived and misled by men to whom they had become attached. A widow's pension was never considered as an absolute right and the SGC, despite their protestations to the contrary, were only too keen to take it away, often permanently.

Chapter 11

Widows and Emigration

*'I find Sydney an ideal climate and should greatly miss the
sunshine if we returned home.'*

The Salvation Army had been running an emigration programme for teenagers
since 1903, with thousands of young men heading across the seas for new lives
in Canada and Australia. In 1913, this scheme was extended to include widows.
Starting with a grant of £1,000 from General Bramwell Booth, the founder's son
and successor, the emigration scheme was designed to give widows a fresh start in
the Dominions. The Salvation Army's own literature described how hard life was
for widows in Britain and expressed the view that 'material and moral disaster'
lay in wait for those who were too weak for the struggle. Settling a family in the
Dominions was said to cost less than it would to maintain them in Britain on Poor
Law relief. A further motivation for the scheme was supplied by the concept of
there being 'surplus women' in the population of Great Britain, which was an idea
that had been around since the 1850s. The greater preponderance of women over
men in the population was felt to be an issue that could be resolved by encouraging
women to emigrate to parts of the Empire where the gender balance was skewed
the other way. This was not simply about rebalancing the numbers. It was felt
that a feminine influence was much required in the rough and ready outposts of
Empire. It was seen as a patriotic duty to emigrate and take British culture and
refinement overseas. General William Booth had been particularly keen on the
emigration schemes and was described by the Salvation Army as 'one of the greatest empire-builders of his time'.[1]

In the first six months of the scheme's operation, ninety-three widows took
advantage of the Salvation Army's assistance to leave Britain, some receiving financial aid and others paying their own way but using the organization's connections
and hostels to help establish themselves. Some widows were given outright grants,
but most were advanced loans that had to be repaid with 5 per cent interest. The
Salvation Army were particularly keen to have widows go to Canada, where it was
claimed there was a great demand for female employment and that 'all round the
conditions are healthful and stimulating'.[2] The organization was long established

in Canada, with Women's Welcome Hostels around the country where émigrés would be received and would stay until they had homes of their own. The Salvation Army also assisted in finding employment opportunities.

There was a lot of competition in the field of assisted migration, with many charities and other organizations arranging passage for those who wished to try their luck in another part of the Empire. Dr Barnardo's had been sending children abroad for decades and there were other competitors for the Salvation Army's adult migrants. One of these was the British Women's Emigration Association (BWEA), established in 1884. The BWEA felt it was the duty of British women of 'good stock' to go to help civilize and populate the Empire, and viewed the Salvation Army as a rival and inferior organization. The BWEA assisted passage schemes were to encourage women to emigrate to work often as domestic servants, even if such a role was beneath their perceived social status in Britain. The idea was that these women would be fulfilling their patriotic duty while living a healthier outdoors lifestyle. Opportunities for social mobility were felt to be more numerous in the Dominions for the right woman. Domestic servants were a class of workers of which Canada and Australia had a shortage. The reasons for the 'servant problem' in the Dominions was the same as in Britain – women preferred factory or shop work, which was better paid, more sociable and seen as less demeaning than being in service. Regardless of the diminishing appeal of the job, it is estimated that 170,000 British women went to Canada ostensibly to be domestic servants from 1900 to 1930.[3]

The First World War slowed emigration at once due to the dangers involved in making a transatlantic voyage and the fact that the navy requisitioned a large number of passenger ships for troop transport. The war added a new hazard for Empire settlers, as described in the notebook of Miss Butchard, a chaperone for a party of BWEA migrants arriving in Canada within days of Britain's declaration of war on Germany. Her diary entry for 7 August 1914 reads:

> We are all very thankful to have come safely to the end of our voyage; in addition to the usual perils of fog and ice, we have had the unusual experience of being in danger from an enemy's ship. I do not know that the "Royal Edward" was actually pursued, though this was the general belief on board, but it is certain that for a whole night we went full speed through a thick fog, with water tight compartments closed and the principal lights extinguished. The Captain would not have run that risk except for a very grave reason.[4]

Despite the dangers, applications to the BWEA for assistance with emigration actually increased in the first months of the war. A number of women were forced to return from their employment in Continental Europe and found themselves jobless alongside the many women thrown out of work by the trade depression that accompanied the declaration of war. These women were prepared to look overseas to secure their future, encouraged by the availability of assisted passages and the golden promises of emigration organizations. This sudden spike of interest did not last and by December 1914, the BWEA had been forced to reduce their office to a skeleton staff of three.[5] They did not give up and continued to publish their magazine *The Imperial Colonist*. The April 1915 edition of the magazine decried the number of women using other emigration agencies and arriving in Canada unaccompanied. The writer said women should use the BWEA 'as otherwise they do not have the advantage of sleeping in a car reserved for women only.'[6]

The minutes of the society's committee tend to contradict the rosy view of the opportunities available in Canada as presented by the Salvation Army and others. In April 1915, the committee noted that it was actually difficult to find women employment in Canada, save for the most well qualified domestic servants, with even those not being in demand in the west of the country. In Manitoba, the farmers' wives wanted help in the summer and paid good wages, but in the winter were not interested unless the girls would take low or no wages. Committee member Mrs Pauncefote suggested that soldiers' widows might take these jobs because if they were getting pensions they could take low wages. The committee seemed to have no qualms about war widows distorting the labour market in Canada as they had been accused of doing in Britain.

In March 1915, the BWEA plans to resettle women in Australia were advertised via a letter in the *Liverpool Daily Post* from Edith Bright of the National Union of Women Workers. Offering opportunities for women and girls who were willing to be domestic servants, the letter explained that only a third of the fare to Australia would have to be paid by the woman in advance, the balance being met by the scheme, recoverable from the woman's wages. In addition, the Queen's Work for Women Fund would pay £1 towards the fare, give the woman an outfit of clothes, and a grant of £1 on arrival. Widows under thirty-five received preferential rates for the crossing but, as was usual to receive any kind of benefit, had to produce proof of their husband's death.

Interest in the scheme does not appear to have been particularly high, with numerous references in the committee's minutes to public meetings on the topic being poorly attended. The committee noted that the Soldiers' and Sailors' Families Association had received a grant of £400 to assist widows who wished to emigrate to New South Wales, but that none had been found who were willing to go.[7] Where war widows did take up offers, they were specifically noted in the committee minutes, for example, a war widow and her boy engaged by a woman travelling to Australia, the fare being advanced by the employer and to be returned from her wages. Another widow appears in the minutes of July 1916, a factory worker recommended by the Leicestershire Committee of the Prince of Wales Fund. The fact that such cases are mentioned would tend to suggest that they were noteworthy due to their scarcity.

In 1916, the Salvation Army announced their new Women's Emigration Scheme, which was open to all women and not specifically widows. An appeal was made to raise £200,000 to fund the scheme, which was intended to pay for 5,000 widows and 10,000 children to make a new start in the Dominions.[8] The Salvation Army received a £50,000 grant from the Prince of Wales National Relief Fund to assist in this work. Stung by the positive publicity afforded to their rival organization in this endeavour, the BWEA fought back, sending leaflets to local relief committees and SSFA branches nationwide to say that they were more than capable of arranging the emigration of widows.[9]

From September 1916 to the end of March 1923, the Salvation Army's figures showed that only 1,769 women and 1,019 children had emigrated using the scheme and £110,000 – less than half the appeal total – had been expended.[10] Again, the Salvation Army figures do not reveal how many of those women were actually war widows. The BWEA's emigration figures tell their own story. In 1913, the association had assisted 1,201 individuals to emigrate. In 1915, that figure fell to a mere 213.[11] The government had decreed that war widows in receipt of a pension would not forfeit that payment if emigrating to another country within the Empire, but, of course, whether that pension would allow a woman and her family to afford a life abroad was a different matter.

The introduction of passports did not help the emigration figures, adding an extra expense to anyone wanting to leave the country. Identification documents had not been required before the war but the need to regulate those entering and leaving the United Kingdom changed international travel forever. By February 1916, *The Imperial Colonist* was reporting that the government had announced that everyone wishing to travel abroad needed a passport. The cost of the document was five shillings and there was also the expense of providing two photographs. If you lived in London you could collect the passport in person, but if not, another five shillings had to be found to pay for the return postage.

For war widows, the cost of emigration was undoubtedly prohibitive. Though the BWEA had told its members that those in receipt of a war pension could have an advance or a commutation of the pension to pay for a sea crossing to a new life elsewhere in the Empire, this turned out to be incorrect. By October 1916 they were forced to backtrack on that advice, using the pages of *The Imperial Colonist* to tell readers that the War Office were now stating that widows' pensions could not be commuted for a lump sum in any circumstances. The most the War Office would consider was an application for an advance 'in special cases'. This is hardly surprising given the determination not to commit to policies that tied the administration into paying out monies. Any commutation would be difficult to assess given that it was impossible to see how a widow's life would pan out and how long the British state would be responsible for her upkeep. The likelihood of death, remarriage or forfeiture on misbehaviour was undoubtedly high.[12]

The BWEA did not give up their efforts and continued to agitate with governments in Britain and abroad to commit to have them commit to facilitating emigration. Letters received from authorities in Canada and Australia were not encouraging as far as opportunities for women were concerned.[13] Assisted passages to Australia and New Zealand had been suspended, as had any migration of domestic servants to South Africa. The cost of fares was now prohibitive. In January 1918, the BWEA met with Andrew Fisher, High Commissioner for Australia. His main aim in speaking to the association was seemingly to have them postpone emigration completely until after the war. Fisher was not keen to have lower-class women flocking to Australia and was not won over by the BWEA's rhetoric:

> With regard to the argument that Australia needed more population, and should do her utmost to welcome women of good British stock, he told us that Australia was quite satisfied with her small population and would far rather have a small and well-to-do population than a far larger one with a considerable percentage of poverty stricken members.[14]

By the time the BWEA met with Fisher, emigration had virtually ceased. On 7 February 1917, the issuing of passports by the British government was suspended completely. It was announced that no women and children were to be granted passports save in very exceptional and urgent circumstances. This even applied to those trying to join relatives already abroad. 'Very exceptional circumstances' proved difficult to substantiate; the BWEA 1917 figures showed that from 256 applications to emigrate only three were granted. Issues of *The Imperial Colonist* now carried a page from the government explaining the position, telling women, 'Your King and Country need you at home for the present.'

Post-war planning was very much at the heart of the Salvation Army's activities. Confident that post-war emigration would be very popular, they anticipated that the sudden expulsion of women from the labour force would stimulate demand to go overseas. However, the reality was that few of those emigrants were actually war widows. Looking at the post-war statistics, on the declaration of the Armistice the Salvation Army announced that they had received 6,000 enquiries about assisted migration. It seems as though 1,979 of those enquiries progressed further, but only sixty-four from that total were war widows. The majority of enquiries appeared to be from British women who had formed relationships with soldiers from Canada and Australia who wanted to follow their sweethearts overseas.[15] The government had announced that passports would be granted to the wives and dependants of living colonial soldiers returning to their husband's country of origin, and to those intending to marry those soldiers if they had been engaged for two years. Women needed to be available to provide a home for the returning soldier before demobilization took effect, hence being granted priority.

The Salvation Army were criticized from several quarters for their schemes perhaps not being as altruistic as their propaganda literature would have the reader believe. The revelation that the poor apprentices brought over as teenagers were asked to repay the cost of their passage caused some consternation. In addition, Canadian authorities grew wary in their dealings with the organization, questioning the quality of the emigrants being provided. Canada had every right to question, as the Salvation Army was receiving a bonus from the Canadian government for every immigrant. The suggestion was that the Salvation Army had too cosy a relationship with the shipping companies, with whom they also had a commercial deal, blinding them to the unsuitability of some applicants. After the Armistice, the Salvation Army asked Canada for a grant of $100,000 to help fund the war widows scheme. The Canadian government declined to make this large donation, though did still fund the work to a lesser degree.

The British government, meanwhile, introduced their own scheme for resettlement abroad in 1919. Leo Amery, chairman of the newly constituted Overseas Settlement Committee, was a great proponent of the 'surplus women' theory. The 1921 census returns showed an excess of women over men in the sum of 1,700,000.[16] The birth rate overseas was felt to be adversely affected by the lack of female migrants and the committee assembled to report on the issue of postwar emigration made clear in their report that they considered female emigration 'to be the essential foundation of all effective Empire settlement'.[17] Free passage to Empire destinations was now offered to ex-servicemen and women but also to those dependants of men who were killed in the war, as long as those individuals were in receipt of a pension. The Salvation Army hit back, offering completely free passage for widows and children of war casualties. Much was made in their literature of the superiority of their emigration schemes as opposed to those of the government, stressing that clients would be assisted throughout the process and seen safely to their final destinations, rather than abandoned at the port of entry, as they claimed was the case with government emigrants. The government scheme, they claimed, 'lacked the personal touch'.[18]

In a summary of fifty widows sent to Canada after the Armistice, the Salvation Army showed that the average age of the widows was forty-three years and eight months – five years older than the pre-war age of emigrating widows. The selection of fifty cases showed only two where the outcome was unsatisfactory, one owing to the widow's ill health and one blamed on the influence of 'friends'. Three out of the fifty widows remarried – a much lower remarriage rate than among war widows in Britain, where the figure was around 40 per cent.[19]

Unfortunately, the Salvation Army's records of individual migrants were destroyed by fire during the bombing of London in the Second World War. However, the organization's many publications included letters from widows who had emigrated, always describing the experience in a positive way. The letter writers are not identified; simply the date of the letter and the country from which it originates. From the eight letters reproduced in the Salvation Army survey *Transplantations*, only one is described as being from a war widow, a brave woman with nine children who emigrated to Australia in January 1922. Research reveals that this is Margaret Browitt from Bolton, who sailed on the SS *Ballarat* with her large family. Margaret's husband Richard was killed at Gallipoli in August 1915 while she was pregnant. The passenger list of the SS *Ballarat* reveals that there were eight children in the family on board, with ages ranging from twenty-two to seven years old. An article in *The War Cry* described her as 'a plucky little woman'[20] and revealed that arrangements had already been made for the family in Bairnsdale, Victoria.

Margaret wrote to the Salvation Army in April 1922:

> Just a line to let you know we are getting more settled in our new home now. I must say it is a beautiful country to live in. I have seen pictures of Australia, but I never thought there was such a place on earth. I only wish all my friends and relatives back in old England could see sunny Australia in reality, I am sure they would want to come out.[21]

She remained in Australia for the rest of her life, dying there in 1935.

The BWEA, now renamed the Society for the Overseas Settlement of British Women (SOSBW), continued its own emigration schemes and, like the Salvation Army, occasionally reproduced letters from grateful emigrants in the pages of its publication. One such widow was Helen Batchelor, identified only as 'H.B.' in *The Imperial Colonist*. Helen was the widow of career sailor Alfred Batchelor who was killed in the HMS *Natal* disaster in Cromarty Firth on 30 December 1915. They had been married less than a year and had a son called Ronald, born in 1916, who never saw his father. By 1918, both of Helen's parents were dead, she had a brother already settled in Australia and may have felt her ties to England were few. She and Ronald sailed to Sydney on board the SS *Euripides* in September 1920, and eighteen months later wrote to the SOSBW to report on her progress:

> After I had been in Sydney one month I obtained a position at a large confectioner's in Pitt Street, where I have been ever since, and I must say I have made good progress, the working conditions being much better than at home.
>
> I find Sydney an ideal climate and should greatly miss the sunshine if we returned home. My little boy Ronald (aged 6) has been attending school for the past year and is greatly improved in every way since our arrival. Taking all into consideration I have no cause to regret making the trip.[22]

Helen came back to England in 1923 for a visit, but returned to New South Wales in 1924 and remained there, remarrying in 1927.

The government's free passage scheme was aimed at resettling 450,000 ex-service personnel, widows and children in the year of its operation. In fact, only 82,000 people in total took advantage of the scheme. The majority travelled to Australia, probably due to the fact that the cost of passage there would under normal circumstances have been further out of reach of the ordinary person. The work continued after the expiry of the original deadline, under the Empire Settlement Act of 1922, with the by now familiar mixture of state aid and voluntarism. The act allowed the government to work with private agencies and charities to encourage emigration and resettle British subjects elsewhere in the Empire. Extra incentives were offered to women who were willing to be domestic servants and training courses were set up in Britain to teach applicants the relevant skills. The Salvation Army were hoping to resettle 250 widows a year in Canada under the scheme.[23] Regardless of such inducements, the figures never reached the levels imagined by the government and its partner agencies.[24]

A survey of ships going to Canada in 1920 shows a cross section of war widows striking out for a new life.[25] For some the move was successful but others soon came home to Britain. Some paid their own passage; others took advantage of the Overseas Settlement Committee scheme. Some had their passage paid by employers in Canada eager to use their expertise whilst others were going to be with family members already in the country.

Minnie Banham paid her own passage to Canada, arriving on the SS *Melita* in March 1920. She was the widow of Second Lieutenant Ernest Banham of

Sheffield, who was killed on 29 September 1918. The couple had been married for only a few months when he died. Minnie had previous experience of Canada, having lived there for a few months in 1911. She obtained work as a bookkeeper in Vancouver, but couldn't settle in her adopted country and returned home to England in 1923.

Jemima Speed was the 40-year-old widow of William Marshall Speed, who was killed on 27 September 1918. She took her three children to Toronto on the SS *Melita*, their passages paid by the King's Fund. Unlike Minnie, Jemima stayed in Canada, dying there in 1942.

Another war widow on the SS *Melita* was Julia Hannah Watson from Bolton, destined for Hamilton as a home help and accompanied by her son James, aged seven. The British government paid for her passage to Canada. By 1923, she had remarried Dutchman Theodore Van Laarhoven and the couple then moved to Wisconsin, where Theo worked in the burgeoning automobile industry. Other war widows who took advantage of the Overseas Settlement Scheme in March and April 1920 included domestic servants Jeannie Lloyd and Elizabeth Ann Bann, nurse Dorothy Hastings and farm worker Emily Flack.

A move to a new country allowed a considerable amount of reinvention of history for some of the female migrants, the opportunity being taken to rid themselves of any stigma that was attached to them back in Britain. It was not unusual for British women to appear on the 1921 census of Canada as 'widows' without any trace of a wedding back in England. Nellie Newell was one example of a woman reinventing herself in Canada as a war widow when she arrived in 1920 with her son. Nellie's birth name was Newell and her son's birth certificate was silent as to the name of his father. She had never married in England. In Canada she attained respectability, eventually marrying her employer in British Columbia, a widower with six young children for whom she had been a housekeeper.

Nora Field appears to be another woman ridding herself of a complicated past by a cleansing emigration. Another passenger on the SS *Melita* in March 1920, Nora had her fare paid by the British government. She was going to Calgary as a housekeeper and had two teenage children with her. She was noted to be joining her parents, who were already in Canada. A search through the records left back in Britain shows a complicated history and a possibly bigamous marriage. Nora married a baker called Alfred Dyte in 1900, father to two of her children and resident of Southampton. By 1911, the census shows that Nora Dyte, a widow, and her youngest child were now living in Smethwick in the West Midlands with a man called Arthur Field, a widower with a young son. On 5 August 1914, Nora Dyte and Arthur Field were married. Field was an army reservist so aware he was likely to be amongst the first to join the fighting. By the end of October 1914, Arthur

Field was dead. Nora was granted a war widow's pension for herself, Arthur's child and her own daughter.

Records suggest that Arthur Dyte, Nora's first husband, was very much alive at the time she married Arthur Field. Dyte would serve briefly in the navy as a ship's cook in 1916 before being invalided out of the service with alcoholic neuritis. The two children Nora had with her as she entered Canada in 1920 were her own daughter and Arthur Field's son. Her eldest son, Victor, had travelled to Canada with other family members some years earlier. The waters are muddied further by the fact that by the time the Canadian census enumerators called on her household in 1921, Nora was again using the surname Dyte, perhaps because it was the real surname of her own children. A move from one part of Britain to another had rid Nora of her alcoholic husband and now a move to another part of the world had changed her history again.

Whilst the majority of widows to be found on the passenger manifests were coming to Canada to work as domestic servants, some skilled workers were in demand and employers were keen enough to pay for some women to migrate. Nellie Cobley, another SS *Melita* passenger, was a war widow and skilled hosiery maker from Leicester. Her fare was paid by Mercury Mills of Hamilton, Ontario, a textile plant built in 1916 that employed over 1,000 people in its heyday. Lily Brown, widow and passenger on a ship arriving in April 1920, was a box maker by trade and had her voyage paid for by the Dominion Paper Box Company of Toronto.

Taking the passenger manifests as an indicator of the level of post-war migration, the number of war widows to be found listed therein is comparatively few. Most of the ships used on the Canadian Pacific Line carried around 1,800 people and widows were scarce amongst the passengers. The majority of emigrants were male and the majority of women on the lists were either single or travelling with their husbands.

It is no surprise that war widows were not clamouring to take up offers from the various schemes proposing emigration. Having lost a husband, no doubt many widows were not keen to also lose the support of their extended family by moving thousands of miles away, however idyllic the destination. Wider family members could be the difference between a widow managing to cope financially and having to resort to charity, with accommodation, monies, food and even childcare to allow the widow to take up employment being vital. Travel was not something that was an established part of working-class life at this time, and the maintenance of friendship and family bonds was very dependent upon geographical proximity. Maud Pember Reeves noted that in the Lambeth Walk district, which constituted her study area, 'A family which moves two miles away is completely lost to view.'[26] One that moved 2,000 miles away was certainly going to be beyond the consideration and assistance of friends and family. In addition, articles appeared in the newspapers periodically during the war to deter emigrants by pointing out that the destabilization of the labour markets in the Dominions meant that opportunities for advancement were greatly reduced.[27] A long and arduous journey overseas, possibly accompanied by small children, was not something that many widows would undertake lightly. Following widows through the passenger lists and into the 1921 census of Canada, it is clear that many were travelling to be with family members who had already made the journey.

Most emigration schemes, as we have seen, were aimed at filling positions in domestic service, a profession in which British women had become increasingly disinterested. A number of women's and labour organizations in Britain expressed objections to the whole idea of exporting British women to act as mere drudges abroad.[28] The average wage of a domestic servant in Australia or Canada may have looked more attractive on the surface, but the increased cost of living in comparison to Britain would have soon wiped out any financial advantage. There was also a deep irony in the plan to resettle widows with children as domestic servants, as many mothers in Britain over the decades had either been refused jobs or forced to have their children reside elsewhere if they wished to be live-in domestics. This certainly remained a problem for those wanting to go to Australia. In 1921, the premier of every Australian state replied to an enquiry from the British government regretting that war widows with children could not be accepted into the country presently without being nominated by friends or family already there. It was stated that employers did not want the widows' children about their own houses. The British letter had tried to present such families as self-supporting, outlining the pensions they were receiving. The Australian authorities had a different view of British generosity in that regard, feeling that the war widows' pensions on offer would not go very far at all in Australia.[29]

The introduction of pensions for civilian widows in Britain in 1925 and the Depression fatally undermined large-scale emigration schemes and the golden age of Empire settlement was dead.

Chapter 12

Remarriage and Remembrance

*'I am very lonely at times. … I am forty-one years of age,
with furniture of my own.'*

The abandonment of Victorian mourning dress for widows was about more than practicality and the national morale. The underlying message of a widow's weeds was that her romantic life was now at an end.[1] Given the loss of life during the war and the emphasis on raising a healthy nation, it was no longer appropriate to be seen as unavailable. The national concern with the repopulation of the nation meant that the widow had to remarry and produce more children, or at least raise the ones she had in a healthy and respectable way, which she was much more likely to do if she was a wife again. The periods of mourning therefore had to come down accordingly, as did the extravagant dress code – a widow *was* available for remarriage.

The Treasury were keen to see war widows remarry to take them off the country's pension bill. A year's pension payment to the bride was a much more financially attractive proposition to the state than supporting a widow for the rest of her life. The pension lump sum available was seen as one of the attractions for a man in marrying a widow. It was often referred to as a 'dowry', cementing the concept of the state's patriarchal control over the widow; rather than being pictured as a husband, the state was now a father, giving away his daughter to her new man with their blessings. The lump sum on remarriage was designed to encourage women to remove themselves from the pension list, though this was denied by George Barnes at the Select Committee in 1915.[2] The committee heard evidence from a number of witnesses who felt that the remarriage gratuity would make war widows a target for 'fortune hunters' and the unemployed. The Lord Mayor of Liverpool described the two-year dowry as 'an inducement to the scoundrel'.[3] The Surrey War Pensions Committee reported that there had been a number of cases come to their attention of men marrying widows for the pension lump sum and then disappearing.[4]

Thomas Moss, of the Lancashire Fusiliers, was the kind of fraudster feared by the above commentators. Moss made a career from bigamously marrying war widows, his first wife having left him and moved to Australia. Seeing a death notice in the local newspaper in Manchester for Private Theo Downing, Moss contacted his first victim, Downing's widow, Gladys. He claimed to have been with her husband at the time of his death on the Somme, and was asked by the dead man to look after her and their two children. The grieving widow was duped and accepted his marriage proposal. A month after the wedding, having taken most of the widow's money, Moss left, claiming he had to return to his regiment in Hull. In fact, he only travelled as far as Burnley, where he renewed an acquaintance with another war widow, Annie McConville. Annie had also been widowed during the Battle of the Somme, losing her husband Edward. She had known Moss for around five years, and believing him to be single, agreed to marry him. Both she and her father gave him money, which he claimed he would return when he received his army pay. The couple married on Thursday and by Monday, Moss was gone, again claiming he had to join the regiment in Hull. Annie did not see her new husband again until he appeared in court charged with bigamy and deception a month later. Moss, who had previous convictions for offences of dishonesty, was eventually sentenced to nine months' imprisonment for fraud and an extra nine months for bigamy.[5]

A war widow was attractive in the marriage market for other reasons in addition to the pension dowry. She may already have her own house and furniture – an important consideration to a man who was still living with his parents – and knew how to cook and clean and take care of her husband. Newspapers hinted at other areas of experience where a war widow had the advantage over a single maid; as *The Tatler* put it, she 'knew the ways of men'. A sexually experienced woman may well have been a more attractive proposition than a virgin for some would-be suitors. War widows were being reported as unfair competition for single women in the marriage market by 1919.[6] In that year, 38,664 war widows had remarried.[7] By 1927, the total figure stood at 98,500 war widows now in second marriages, leaving 246,360 widows still in receipt of pensions.

It was not unusual after the war and into the 1920s for the personal columns of newspapers to seek war widows for remarriage. In 1929, at the height of the Depression, the Mayor of Durham, W.W. Wilkinson, found himself in the unlikely position of marriage broker after receiving a letter from a man in Welwyn Garden City. The *Durham Chronicle* reported that the man was looking for a wife, and having read of the distress in mining districts, was prepared to offer a new start to a Durham woman. The mayor found himself deluged with offers, many of them from war widows. One widow from Sunderland wrote saying, 'I am very lonely at times' and informing her would-be suitor that she was forty-one years of age 'with furniture of my own. I am five feet four inches in height and fair.'[8] The lucky winner was a woman from Pelton Fell, though the mayor had taken it upon himself to matchmake for other couples who had written in, resulting in around twenty further marriages.

For war widows, economic realities played a large part in their decisions to remarry. As already noted, the widow's pension was less than the woman had received in separation allowance while her husband was alive. The separation allowance itself was, for many women, less than she was accustomed to receiving to run a household. Whilst this was a temporary aberration, it was able to be endured in the short term. Once a man had died and the widow was expected to exist on the even smaller pension payments indefinitely, the picture looked very different. Suddenly the bonus of a lump sum and a man bringing in a full-time wage made remarriage look more attractive than a life in widow's weeds. Mary Ann Lamb married a miner who had lived in the next street to herself and first husband Joseph at Trimdon Colliery. Harry Britton had been discharged from the army in 1917 and was back in the mine, earning decent wages. The couple had a registry office wedding in April 1918 and went on to have five children together, in addition to Mary Ann's existing four youngsters. Eliza Booth was only able to pay off the mortgage on her house in Rastrick after marrying again and having a full wage coming into the household. After being presented with her husband's Victoria Cross at Buckingham Palace, Elizabeth Davies faced the reality of bringing up four children on thirty shillings a week. Employment opportunities for women like Elizabeth were scarce in the mining village of Nantymoel, South Wales. In 1918 she married Eli Darby, a coal miner and widower with five children of his own. After her second marriage, Elizabeth paid for the inscription on Corporal James Llewellyn Davies' grave at Canada Farm Cemetery to read 'Ever Remembered by Wife and Family'.

Officials at the Ministry of Pensions were greatly encouraged by the number of second marriages. The cost of the war had been immense, and any way of reducing the ongoing pension bill was to be applauded. Visiting Leeds in September 1919, Sir Laming Worthington Evans, Minister of Pensions, could hardly disguise his glee at the latest figures, proclaiming that 'widows were to be congratulated upon the rate of their remarriage.'[9]

One class of widows who caused the Ministry a significant headache in remarrying were widows in Ireland who wanted to marry their brothers–in–law. Due to an anomaly in the law at the time, it was illegal for a widow to marry her husband's brother. The law applied differentially to men, with a widower marrying his sister-in-law being perfectly legal. This issue caused the Ministry of Pensions considerable difficulty in Ireland, where the Catholic Church allowed such marriages to take place with the permission of the Church authorities. As far as English law was concerned, such marriages were not legitimate, leaving the Ministry with a dilemma – should the Irish widow forfeit her pension because she was now living with another man, or should she be entitled to the remarriage gratuity? The matter came to a head in 1920, when Margaret Field, war widow, married her husband's brother at a ceremony at a Catholic church in Waterford and applied for her lump sum. There followed considerable debate within the Treasury and the Ministry of Pensions as to how to deal with the problem. The most economical solution was clearly to pay such widows a gratuity and be done with them. The legal position was problematic – without a legitimate remarriage, a widow's pension could only be stopped if she was 'unworthy', and there was no power in the legislation for the government to pay an unworthy widow a gratuity. The Treasury had no qualms about declaring widows unworthy, but the Ministry of Pensions recognized the stigma involved and the political sensitivity of the situation across Ireland. The Regional Director for Ireland noted that: 'So far as the women are concerned, they are not informed by their Church, in which they have every confidence, that they are doing anything either immoral or illegal.'[10]

In the end, the Ministry performed their classic fudge for any situation they had not thought of beforehand, granting Mrs Field a gratuity as an 'Act of Grace' and dealing with cases on an individual basis. In March 1921, the Ministry decided to treat these unions as if they were legitimate marriages in the cases of Irish women. English women had to wait until July for equal treatment when marriages to brothers-in-law were finally legalized.[11] However, clergymen of all denominations were still allowed to refuse to officiate at such weddings, meaning that it was not always possible to have these relationships legitimized. In such cases, even widows who tried to do the right thing in marrying their partners would be liable to forfeiture of their pensions without the compensation of the remarriage gratuity. The Special Grants Committee was unsympathetic to these cases where women carried on the relationship without voluntarily relinquishing their pensions, ordering forfeiture wherever they were discovered.[12]

Second marriages did not always work out. In April 1918, actress Ethel Lewis married Henry Hunter, RAF flying ace and recipient of the Military Medal. In accordance with the convention that white was inappropriate for a second wedding, the bride wore pink silk and her mother wore black satin. The couple had a brief honeymoon at the Ritz before Hunter returned to active service.[13] Hunter was part of the Allied force occupying Germany after the end of the war, and Ethel joined him in Cologne. Ethel thereafter lived a jet-setting life, moving between Paris, Italy, Spain and the French Riviera, and was regularly mentioned in the gossip columns, but her romance with Hunter did not last. He deserted her in 1922 and she finally divorced him in 1926, claiming that he had committed adultery.[14] She returned to using her title of the Honourable Mrs Geoffrey Pearson.

At the other end of the social scale, Mary Bennett of Hunslet was the widow of an iron puddler who was killed on the Somme in October 1916. With five children to support, she married Robert Atkinson in 1918. On the day of the wedding, the couple celebrated at a friend's house before the groom disappeared to the pub. He had then gone back to his own house, much to the surprise of his new bride. He never did move in with Mary, who was left high and dry with no more war widow's pension and little money from her new man, to whom she had a child. Appearing at Leeds Magistrates' Court to prosecute Robert Atkinson for desertion, Mary said that the reason he would not live with her was the presence of her children, who would disturb his quiet life. As the magistrate remarked in awarding Mary fifteen shillings a week in maintenance payments, 'Why did he not think of that before?'[15]

In some quarters war widows were seen as disloyal to their deceased husbands by marrying again; others felt that it was the new husband who deserved their loyalty. Columnist Lily Rose Clyne wrote that war widows who venerated the memory of the first husband were not playing fair by their new man. Criticizing a widow who laid flowers on her dead husband's grave on the day of her wedding, Clyne wrote, 'One man in a home is enough. It is unfair to project a dead one into it. The woman who does so is a moral bigamist.'[16]

Of course, some women committed actual, rather than moral, bigamy. Violet Carter had married husband Arthur before the war but had been separated from him for some years. Arthur joined the army in 1914 and was reported missing soon after the outbreak of war. In 1915, Violet married a dairyman called James Wood. When it transpired that Arthur Carter was still alive, Violet was prosecuted for bigamy. She gave evidence to say that a notice of Arthur Carter's death had appeared in the newspaper during the war. Despite her claim that she believed Arthur to be dead, she had signed the marriage register to denote that she was a 'spinster' rather than a widow. Violet was convicted in 1929 but was simply bound over for twelve months. James Wood, the unfortunate second 'husband', later successfully sued her for the return of money and furniture that he had bought for the marital home.[17]

Violet Carter/Wood may have been too hasty in her remarriage, but it was not unheard of for erroneous reports of a man's death to be received. In 1919, it was reported that four men from Leeds who had been reported killed were later reunited with their families thanks to the efforts of the local missing soldiers' and sailors' bureau.[18] As some widows had insisted at the time of their husbands' supposed deaths, the end of the war did result in men being released from prisoner of war camps who had not previously made contact with their families. However, the numbers were never as large as the anxious widows hoped.

There were a number of fictional accounts of such occurrences. Tennyson's poem *Enoch Arden* was fairly well known and dealt with the same circumstance, though set many years before the First World War. *The Tatler* was confident its readership would understand the reference, speaking of husbands having '*Enoch Ardened* into life again'.[19] W. Somerset Maugham's play *Home and Beauty* was a comedy about the same situation, though in real life there was nothing funny about such cases for any of the parties involved.

The Norfolk War Pensions Committee reported a case in 1920 involving the wife of a naval officer.[20] The couple had married after the woman had received news that her first husband had been killed on active service. The new couple had a child together before it transpired that the casualty reports were incorrect. The unfortunate woman resolved to obey her original marriage vows, and her first husband agreed to take her back. Heartbreakingly for the wife, he refused to accept her baby, insisting cruelly that the child be removed from the family home and that she should have no further contact. The woman reluctantly agreed, and the child was eventually adopted by a childless couple.

Winifred Hooper married her husband Pollard in Bradford in 1913. He joined the West Yorkshire Regiment on the outbreak of war. In 1917, she heard that he had been killed, and subsequently married another soldier, becoming pregnant with his child. Pollard Hooper then returned home on leave, not dead at all, but simply wounded. He was understandably unhappy with what he found on his return, vowing to have nothing further to do with his wife. Winifred Hooper was prosecuted for bigamy, appearing in court with her young baby in her arms, but, like Violet Carter, was bound over. Winifred's new husband and father of her child, Gunner Ware, was standing by her.[21]

Edith Gambles received some shock news following her remarriage. She had mourned her husband, Private William Gambles, of the Leeds Pals, since 1918 when he was reported missing, then confirmed as killed. She had been drawing her widow's pension to support herself and her child until she remarried a year later. Two months into the marriage, she was told that her first husband's mother had received a telegram from him indicating that he was on his way home via the army camp at Ripon. Seeking to soften the blow of his wife's remarriage by telling him in advance, his father went to Ripon to find William but was unable to do so. Finally, the sender of the telegram did arrive home, but it was not the man the Gambles family had expected; the original telegram had been delivered to the wrong address. Private William *Gamble* surprised his family, who had not been expecting him. Gamble lived in the same township and also had a wife called Edith. Mrs Gambles, William's mother, was philosophical about matters, saying, 'I should have been glad if it was my lad who had come back, but maybe things are best as they are and there will be no trouble now.'[22]

In the case of Arthur Bird, a mistake made by the Ministry of Pensions brought the attention of his wife to the fact that he was very much alive. This was not exactly news to Annie Bird as the couple had been living together in Glasshoughton since his discharge from the army. What was news to Annie was the name on the marriage certificate sent to her house by the Ministry – it was not her own, but that of a Sarah Jane Brownlees of County Durham. In 1917, while training in the area with the Durham Light Infantry, Arthur Bird had entered a bigamous marriage with this local girl. Poor Sarah Bird had been mourning her husband Arthur, believing him to have died of wounds. Sarah had sent the relevant certificates to the War Office to receive her pension payments for herself and her child. For some reason, the Ministry of Pensions had become confused and sent the certificates back to the real Mrs Bird's home address. Despite his claim that Sarah Brownlees had got him drunk and taken advantage of him, Arthur Bird received three months' imprisonment for his pains.[23]

An example of Lily Rose Clyne's 'moral bigamist' was Ellen Merrifield, a widow who stopped her wedding procession to lay flowers at a monument to her first husband. Gunner Frank Merrifield had gone missing in September 1914 during the Battle of the Marne. Six years later, Edith remarried and left her bridal bouquet on a recently erected Brighton street shrine that listed the name of her deceased husband.[24]

During the war, women had been at the heart of what can be seen as the beginning of a culture of remembrance in the appearance of these street shrines around the country. Often completely spontaneous, but sometimes encouraged by the local vicar as a way of reconnecting the community to the Church, street shrines were originally set up to honour all men from a locality who were serving in the forces. Displays of flowers and bunting would surround a list of the names of men from a street or parish and religious services would take place at the shrines. This movement looks to have become the model for some aspects of post-war remembrance activity. Nevertheless, a widow's place in these kinds of events was not to be taken for granted.

The Peace Day events of July 1919 were envisaged as celebrations for the end of the war as signified by the signing of the Treaty of Versailles on 28 June. A military parade involving representatives of the armies of most of the Allied nations was to take place in London, with entertainments laid on for the crowds, including country dancing, Shakespeare performances and a huge firework display. The Cenotaph, the tribute to the 'Glorious Dead', was a temporary structure made of wood and plaster, designed to be removed after the ceremonies. The only space allocated on the day for the bereaved was a preferential location from which to watch the parade. The official programme announced that 'On the suggestion of her Majesty the Queen the Green Park side of Constitution Hill is reserved for widows, mothers and orphans of officers and men who have fallen in the war.'[25] This was not the prime spot – MPs and wounded officers and men were given better positions.

The debates around the Cenotaph unveiling and the Peace Day celebrations have been well documented.[26] The tensions between commemoration and celebration, money spent on entertainments versus money made available to those affected by the war, saw arguments over Peace Day that were repeated in relation to many war commemoration events taking place thereafter. The *Times* editorial on the day before the event tried to reconcile the discord between celebration and solemnity, asking if there was any comfort to be derived for the bereaved in the festivities. 'We think there is, and that in meditation on it during even the most boisterous hours of tomorrow hostile feelings will disappear and something like a peace of mind founded on pride and thanksgiving will hallow the day.'[27] These debates were also taking place on a local level all over the country, and an examination of events in one particular area demonstrates how these conflicts were played out in relation to the position of widows.

Former Royal Welsh Fusilier Sergeant Charles Derry gave a lecture on his wartime experiences in the town of Todmorden, Lancashire in May 1919. One of his topics was the rush to build war monuments and he appealed to his audience not to contribute a penny to any fund for a memorial statue while one widow was in want. Derry declared, 'It was no use having a handsome stone monument if the children of heroes had to play around it without stockings on their feet.'[28] At the time of Derry's visit, Todmorden council was making arrangements for the National Peace Celebrations, with meetings on the topic being reported in detail in the local newspaper.

One of the responses to Derry's lecture was from Alice Greenwood, widowed in September 1917 and left to raise two children. Alice wrote to the newspaper to protest against the use of her rates to pay for Peace Day fireworks. She outlined the stark reality of the lives of many women in her situation:

> Just any of you, who read this, think what you would do with 33s a week to keep yourself and two children, rent, rates, gas, coal, clothing and food to pay for rates, light, heating, food, and a hundred and one other things that you don't think about till they come.

The offer of a treat for the children at Peace Day was in no way compensation for their loss. She ended her letter, 'Husbands and fathers have died for the State, but the State will be a long time before it is as good a husband and father as the one I have known.'[29]

The Todmorden Society of Discharged and Demobilized Soldiers and Sailors (TSDDSS) had shared a platform with Sergeant Derry at his lecture in May. They were also ambivalent towards the Peace Celebrations, voting against taking part in any military march past as part of the day's festivities. One of their objections was that the day was not going to be a happy occasion for those who had lost relatives in the war, and it would not be pleasant to see those who had returned safely march whilst their loved one was absent. Other voices objected to putting themselves on display for what they saw as another's entertainment. The TSDDSS did approve fundraising for the war memorial, setting a target of £10,000. However, only £1,000 of that total was to be put towards a granite memorial, the rest being used to alleviate distress amongst ex-servicemen, widows and orphans.[30]

The Todmorden Peace Celebrations went ahead on 2 August as the national date of 19 July did not suit local arrangements. Mills closed and there was a procession of around 8,000 people, led by the fire brigade and followed by a brass band and cadets from the King's Royal Rifle Corps. The celebratory aspects of the occasion were very much to the fore, the whole town being decorated in flags and bunting. There was dancing in the park, and, to end the evening, the firework display that so enraged Alice Greenwood. A tea was put on for soldiers who were to receive medals and gold watches from the council for their gallantry. Widows were not invited to this particular event, though one man's fiancée did attend to receive a posthumous award. Later, a more impromptu gathering involved the burning of an effigy of Kaiser Bill outside one of the local pubs. Only two sites in the town drew attention to loss rather than celebration: one was the TSDDSS building, where a holly wreath draped in black surrounded by a Union flag was the central display; the other was Patmos Congregational Church, where a shrine had been set up for the fifteen members of the church who had lost their lives. The Congregationalist's display in particular was described as attracting a great deal of attention, with people laying flowers at the scene. Accounts later presented to the town council for the event revealed that £45 7s had been spent on fireworks[31] – enough to pay Alice Greenwood's pension for thirty weeks of the year.

Two more gatherings in connection with the Peace Celebrations were held in Todmorden in 1919 – a gala in mid-September that was for ex-servicemen only, and finally, the widows, orphans and bereaved parents' events at the end of that month. Judging by the numbers of dependants who attended, many shared Alice Greenwood's views that 'treats' were not what was required. With 600 men from the area killed, a maximum of 400 family members attended the tea party – nowhere near as many as expected. The dependants were given a meal, though not as lavish as that provided to the soldiers back in August, and two separate concerts then took place, one for adults and one for children. It can safely be assumed that Alice Greenwood was not in attendance.

For some women, public ceremonies of remembrance or celebration for the end of hostilities were just too much to bear. War widow Hannah Miller attempted to drown herself in Ramsgate harbour on Peace Day. She was rescued by two pass-ers-by, who just happened to be messengers from the Admiralty, and, harshly, prosecuted for attempting suicide. A doctor testified to the court that the Peace Day celebrations had brought on a severe attack of grief, and, having promised not to try the trick again, the case against her was dismissed.[32]

The dedication of the tomb of the Unknown Warrior in 1920 gave expression to national grief and prioritized the bereaved in a way the Peace Day celebrations had not. The idea of burying an unknown soldier in the nation's most venerated place of worship stood in place of bringing all of the bodies home. The man could be any woman's husband or son, and great secrecy surrounded the selection of the body for this very reason. The lingering resentment towards those who had not volunteered to do their bit found expression in this process – the army had insisted that only a man who fell in 1914 could be honoured in this way. This decision removed the possibility that the Unknown Warrior could be a conscript who had been forced into active service. It also increased the statistical possibility that the body was not one of Kitchener's volunteers, but a man from the regular army. These conditions do not appear to have prevented thousands of people from believing that there was a chance the Unknown Warrior was theirs.

It was eventually agreed by the organizers that bereaved mothers and widows should have first claim on tickets to the ceremony at Westminster Abbey, with MPs giving up their places in favour of these women. Once again it seems that the Queen played a significant role in this development.[33] *The Times* estimated that 36,000 officers and 600,000 men had fallen in France alone and that the num-bers of relatives eligible for tickets would number 2 or 3 million. In the end, only 14,000 applications for tickets were received.[34] Only 1,000 seats were available in the abbey, but space at Whitehall near the Cenotaph and places in the windows of government offices overlooking the route were also reserved for the bereaved. A hierarchy of grief and sacrifice was established with women able to apply for tick-ets if they were in one of the following categories:

Category A = women losing a husband and one or more sons (99 tickets were claimed by such women)

Category B = mothers losing all sons or their only son (7,506 women fell into this category)

Category C = widows (4,042 women were in this group)

Mothers, not mere widows, were at the top of the hierarchy. Tickets were allocated by ballot and newspapers reported that some of the women at the ceremony were clearly from the poorer levels of society.

The funeral journey of the Unknown Warrior from Dover to London was notable for the numbers of people who turned out to view proceedings. People came from all over the country, many making their first trip to the capital. When the coffin reached Victoria Station in London, some women in the crowd were described as 'crying bitterly', whilst others 'held their heads high and smiled'.[35] On this occasion, it seems, expressions of grief were not to be denigrated. It was reported that a baby's cry during the two minutes' silence at Marble Arch was drowned by 'a loud, clear ululating shriek from a woman, which rose and fell and rose again'.[36] Many of those present at the ceremony in Westminster Abbey were weeping at the end of the two minutes' silence.

One million people had filed past the Cenotaph by the time the official days of mourning had passed, and as many had been to Westminster Abbey, where the opening times had to be extended to accommodate the queues. Even so, not everyone was able to conclude their pilgrimage, the queues being so long that many gave up and went home. The popularity of the Tomb of the Unknown Warrior showed the need amongst many of the bereaved for some kind of ceremony analogous to a funeral for their own missing relative. Women were restored to their traditional place at the heart of mourning rituals for the Unknown Warrior ceremonies and were not derided for showing their grief now the national crisis was over.

A trip to London was a journey too far for many widows, but following the end of the war, there was a demand from some families to be able to visit the battlefields to see their loved ones' graves. This was clearly unsafe immediately after the Armistice, with significant quantities of unexploded ordnance lying around the battle areas and a devastated infrastructure with no facilities for tourists. In October 1919, Angela Farmer travelled to the Somme with her brother Wilfrid Ewart to try to find the grave of her husband, Lieutenant Jack Farmer. Ewart later described the experience, noting the large numbers of haphazard grave sites and battle debris they found, including long discarded meals.[37] Despite these unpromising conditions, in July 1919, holiday company Thomas Cook started advertising battlefield trips to the Western Front. Two versions of the trip were originally offered, the 'deluxe' at thirty-five guineas, or the 'popular' at nine and a half guineas. Both prices would be well out of the financial reach of a war widow on the basic rate pension of twenty shillings a week. War widows were not Thomas Cook's target audience as these were trips for the curious to areas of recent battles rather than voyages of remembrance for a dead relative.

Charitable agencies stepped in to provide widows and other relatives with the opportunity to visit their loved one's grave. The Salvation Army were quickly in the market to arrange visits to battlefield cemeteries in Europe, establishing a Grave Visitation Service. By the middle of 1920, they had established three hostels in France and Belgium for visiting relatives. The Army Council gave the organization £25,000 in 1921 specifically for cemetery visits and by April 1922, the number of hostels available had increased to seven. From 1920 to 1923, 18,507 people availed themselves of the Salvation Army's Grave Visitation Service, coming not only from Britain, but from the Dominions too. These visits were a prominent feature of the Salvation Army publications after the war, with photographs of grateful pilgrims on railway platforms and at hostels being widely used.

The British Legion was another agency assisting relatives in grave visitation trips, initially making an arrangement with the Church Army whereby relatives would be directed to that organization for their travel and accommodation on the Continent. The Church Army ran these trips on a non-profit basis and would provide the service free of charge for those who really could not afford the third class rail fares and hostel prices. In the eight months from November 1919 to June 1920, the Church Army helped 5,000 bereaved relatives to visit the Western Front. The Legion itself carried out trips, mostly on a local branch basis, and a national expedition in 1927 was not particularly well attended. The YMCA also continued their wartime work of helping relatives visit the battlefields and graves, running subsidized trips to the Continent.

A small British population grew up around the battlefields of northern France and Belgium, many employed by the Imperial War Graves Commission. Some of these individuals were ex-soldiers who now made their living conducting tours of the battlefields and cemeteries. As with any commercial opportunity, there were those who exploited visitors, some of whom may never have travelled abroad before this sacred trip. As H.A. Taylor noted in his 1924 review of the former battlefields, 'the Continental visitor is often an unsophisticated person, and the Pilgrim to the War Graves a simple soul, ignorant of foreign ways and the value of foreign money.'[38]

Exploitation was not reserved for those who were brave enough to make the trip across the Channel. Unscrupulous firms and those simply seeking to exploit what they saw as a legitimate commercial opportunity would scan the obituary columns of the newspapers and send out offers to bereaved relatives for all kinds of remembrance paraphernalia. The IWGC sent photographs of gravestones of the fallen that lay outside Britain's shores free of charge to bereaved relatives. This was a slow process, leaving a gap in the market for the private entrepreneur to exploit. In 1932, before the unveiling of the Thiepval Memorial, those relatives expecting to see the name of their missing son or husband were sent a photograph of the structure with a request for payment. This had not come from the IWGC, who were forced to publicize this fact in the newspapers. Companies offering to lay wreaths abroad on behalf of relatives sprang up on both sides of the Channel and so numerous were the complaints about their services that the IWGC was obliged to vet and maintain an approved list. The St Barnabas Society was started in 1919 by a New Zealand chaplain to organize trips for the bereaved that did not involve exploitation by commercial companies or unscrupulous individuals. The society took the view that no grave 'can be regarded as truly consecrated until it has been visited by its rightful warden.'[39] Group excursions were organized to various locations, with the more intrepid single visitors being accommodated free of charge in hostels in France all year round.

The largest expedition solely of bereaved relatives to the Western Front was organized by the St Barnabas Society in 1927. The trip was particularly significant as it marked the dedication of the Menin Gate, the first of the great memorials to the missing that would appear on the Western Front. The society produced a memorial booklet, which gives an insight into the nature of these trips. Money was raised to provide transport to Ypres for around 700 relatives, with a further 300, who were unfit to travel, being provided with a memorial booklet as a consolation. As with most reports of remembrance events, the emphasis in the press appears to have been very much on the bereaved parent rather than the widow. The two English women who were chosen to represent the relatives at the ceremony were both mothers, not widows.

The journey was arduous, especially if travelling from outside of the South East of England. There was no overnight accommodation in Ypres, and the bereaved found themselves in direct competition with tourists for local resources. The St Barnabas Society had hired a local cinema as a place for their pilgrims to rest and receive some refreshment during the day, and had to fight off the representative of a holiday company who was trying to bribe the manager to take his clients instead. Some relatives went without sleep for two nights, leaving Victoria Station on Saturday night and returning on Monday, with just a few spare hours in Ypres before the journey home.

Lord Plumer spoke at the ceremony, stating that the Menin Gate was designed to express the nation's gratitude to the missing and its sympathy to those who mourned: 'A memorial has been erected which, in its simple grandeur, fulfils this object, and now it can be said of each one in whose honour we are assembled here today: "He is not missing; he is here!"'[40]

A number of the bereaved told journalists how fulfilled they felt having seen a name on the stone. One woman told a journalist from the *Daily Mail*:

I felt I wanted to kiss my son's name when I saw it … I feel so happy to have seen that name. He was killed in 1914 – 13 years ago – and ever since I have wanted to tread where he trod. I am happy.[41]

The *Daily Telegraph* referred to the memorial as representing 'a sacred sepulchre'[42] to the bereaved. After the ceremony the relatives returned to the memorial privately to seek out the names of their sons and husbands. There was just time for an impromptu service at the railway station, including the singing of *Abide with Me*, before the party embarked on the journey home.

When the British Legion organized a trip to the Menin Gate in 1928, it was originally for ex-servicemen only. The plan was for 5,000 war veterans to be reviewed at the Menin Gate by Sir Douglas Haig himself. Eventually opened to relatives of the deceased, no children were to be allowed in the party, meaning that it was out of the question for many war widows. Another consideration for a widow was the cost – the trip was not free, costing around £4. The widows in the Yorkshire party were paid for by the largesse of Edward Brotherton, Lord Mayor of Leeds at the time of the outbreak of war. The West Yorkshire group comprised over 200 ex-servicemen and only four widows.[43] Ultimately, 11,000 people took part in the British Legion's pilgrimage, including around 6,000 bereaved relatives.

The presence of so many of the bereaved on the British Legion pilgrimage was due to a change in the purely military character of the event, forced by the death of Earl Haig at the end of January 1928. With the decision taken to invite Lady Haig, his widow, to the event instead, the bereaved took a more prominent part than originally anticipated. Her presence and demeanour was commented on favourably in the press. *The Sketch* said that her presence set the right tone of 'modesty, restraint, simplicity and sincerity'.[44] Lady Haig, still in mourning dress, was the ideal representative of the war widow: dignified, stoic and composed. This had been particularly noted in reports of her husband's funeral earlier that year at Westminster Abbey: 'She went quietly to her place in the choir, her tears forced back from her eyes. It was as her soldier husband would have wished.'[45]

Earl Haig had been a prominent figure in the campaign for the fair treatment of war veterans and their families. In 1919, he appeared before the Select Committee on Pensions, giving evidence specifically about the hardships faced by widows. He had handed in a petition from the war widows of Pontypridd protesting about the level of income they were receiving. He unveiled the Swansea war memorial in July 1922 alongside a war widow who had obtained her place in proceedings by the drawing of lots. Earl Haig's funeral was another occasion allowing widows to express grief in a public arena. Despite his concern for war widows, no special place was reserved for them in his funeral procession. A few managed to get inside

Westminster Abbey for the service, but the majority lined the footpaths watching the coffin pass by, many in tears. Services to commemorate Earl Haig took place simultaneously in many towns, including Leeds, where he had been a Freeman of the city. The emphasis in Leeds, as in other locations, was on former soldiers paying their respects, with a march from the town hall to the parish church. Newspapers around the country reported widows attending these ceremonies dressed in black, sporting single poppies and sometimes their late husband's medals. Haig's death had given them an opportunity to attend the nearest thing they may get to a funeral ceremony for their own particular soldier.

Not all widows took part in remembrance related events, preferring to mourn in private. One such widow was Maud Wright, who was living in Headingley at the outbreak of the war with her husband Reginald and 1-year-old son. Reginald was a plumber by trade and had been a partner in his business since 1911. By 1916, he was in the army with the 227th Field Company of the Royal Engineers. In March 1918, his company was forced to retreat in the face of Operation Michael, the German army's last major offensive of the war. Reginald Wright was one of three men who disappeared. Maud received the standard letter a month later indicating that her husband was missing. She then received confirmation that he had been killed in action. She was widowed at the age of twenty-eight, with a 4-year-old son to raise alone.

Maud Wright was very bitter at the loss of her husband. She does not appear to have responded to the standard request from the IWGC for information about him, nor requested a memorial inscription on his headstone. When an appeal was placed in the local newspaper in 1920 for the identities of men to be inscribed on the Headingley War Memorial, situated less than half a mile from the marital home, Maud did not submit Reginald's name for inclusion. Four years after Reginald's death, Maud married Arthur Gray at St Michael's Church, Headingley. The Headingley War Memorial is situated right outside the church. The story does not end there, as a century later, Reginald Wright's grandson, Graham, won a hard-fought campaign to have his grandfather's name placed on the memorial. On 2 April 2017, the newly restored memorial was unveiled with the inclusion of Sapper Reginald Wright of the 227th Field Company of the Royal Engineers.

Remembrance events in the post-war period, far from being unifying and peaceful reflections on four years of war, were full of conflict. They involved conflict between the celebration of a glorious victory, or, in the case of a veteran, of a safe return versus a respectful moment of grief, and conflict between the monies spent on such events and the lack of money spent on the human memorials of the conflict in the form of the disabled veterans, widows and orphans. The celebratory tone of Peace Day did not survive and the commemoration of the day itself was gone from the national calendar by 1920. Armistice Day, and later, Remembrance Sunday became the days of thanksgiving and reflection on the conflict.

Mothers took centre stage in remembrance culture with a love that was seen as purer and more enduring than romantic affection alone. The bulk of the literature on loss during the war was written by parents, not widows. Rudyard Kipling, Arthur Conan Doyle, Harry Lauder and Prime Minister Asquith all wrote of their grief at the loss of a son. Commentators have noted that with the fall of infant mortality, the Great War generation were the first to expect their children to outlive them; the sudden failure of that promise in the form of mass deaths in war was a crushing blow.[46] Women who lost more than one son were particularly feted in remembrance ceremonies, emphasizing a woman's role in creating and raising decent citizens and being prepared to sacrifice them for the good of the country. The rate of the remarriage of war widows also weakened their hold on a position as keepers of the flame of remembrance.

At the ceremonies in London on Armistice Day 1927, it was reported that the first tribute laid at the tomb of the Unknown Warrior was from a war widow.[47] However, the widow's prominent position in remembrance ceremonies was not secure. The Iris Strange Collection at the University of Staffordshire reveals how war widows had to fight for a place in such services in later years. The War Widows' Association of Great Britain had consistently applied for places at the Cenotaph from the date of their inauguration in 1971, and were always refused. In response, the association had started to attend the memorial privately in the days before the official ceremony and lay a simple white cross of chrysanthemums on the Cenotaph. It was routinely removed by officials on the day to allow the dignitaries' wreaths to take priority. The ribbon attached to the cross read, 'From The Forgotten Legion'.

Afterword

Existing histories of First World War widows in Britain have been criticized for concentrating not on their emotional concerns, but on their relationship with the state.[1] The reason for this is that state archives are the main sources of information on the lives of these women. Post-war publishers were not clamouring for war widows to write their memoirs and in Britain there was no pressure group analogous to those springing up in Australia after the Armistice. Our only records of British war widows are, on the whole, a result of their interactions with the state. In a period where grinding poverty was commonplace, the gap between rich and poor immense and the gender divide in all areas of life rigid and enduring, war widows' experiences were not deemed noteworthy, and in many ways were not considered unique. Joy Damousi asserts that this concentration on the financial interactions with the state removes war widows' anger and sorrow from the records of their experience. However, many letters from widows' interaction with agents of the state lay bare their anguish and indignation at their treatment and I have sought to give expression to the voices of these women where possible.

The First World War presented a challenge to the concept that those in receipt of state aid were inadequate in some way. A disabled Tommy could not be portrayed as some kind of scrounger after his sacrifice for King and Country. But for widows, this was a harder path to negotiate and their status depended on their ongoing behaviour, not the simple fact of the sacrifice of their man. Widows with children, especially, found themselves stuck in a no-man's-land of their own – an ideological battleground where maternalism, welfare, work and the politics of remembrance clashed. Surveillance of widows came from two drivers: the traditional scrutiny of the working classes enshrined in the policies of the Charity Organisation Society and exercised through the lady visitor; and the concern for the health of the nation embodied in pronatalism.

Rather than being part of some inclusive community of bereavement, widows were isolated. They were excluded from full membership of veterans' associations, excluded from work in favour of veterans, and excluded from ordinary social interaction at the risk of approbation, local gossip and the loss of a pension. Whilst the upper classes could afford to give up one home to be used as a hospital, working-class women were losing their only homes due to the inadequacy of pension payments and separation allowances. Widows were an afterthought in pension policy, a perceived threat to the ex-serviceman in the jobs market, and a sexual threat to single women in the marriage market. With parents given primacy in remembrance culture and high rates of remarriage, widows became the Forgotten Legion.

Endnotes

Chapter 1

1. Later called the Soldiers', Sailors' and Airmen's Families Association, but referred to as SSFA throughout this book.
2. Jeffrey Cox, *The English Churches in a Secular Society, Lambeth 1870–1930*, (Oxford University Press, 1982).
3. Figure quoted in Ellen Ross, *Slum Travelers: Ladies and London Poverty 1860–1920* (University of California Press, 2007).
4. See Maud Pember Reeves, *Round About a Pound a Week*, (G. Bell & Sons, 1913).
5. Lady Bell, *At the Works: a study of a manufacturing town (Middlesbrough)*, (Edward Arnold, 1907).
6. Pember Reeves, op. cit.
7. *Report on the Condition of Widows under the Poor Law in Liverpool*, presented to the Annual Meeting of The Liverpool Women's Industrial Council on 11 December 1913 by Eleanor F. Rathbone, Hon. Secretary.
8. Clementina Black, *Married Women's Work, being a report of an enquiry undertaken by the Women's Industrial Council* (G. Bell & Sons, 1915).
9. T.J. MacNamara before the Select Committee on Naval & Military Services (Pensions & Grants) 1915 PP 1915a HC 196 (HMSO, 1915, Appendix 1, p.165).
10. Letter from H. Seely Whitby, *Nottingham Journal*, 28 September, 1914.
11. NA T1/891.
12. In 1919 this amount was changed to 2/3rds.
13. Figures given before the Select Committee on Naval & Military Services (Pensions & Grants) 1919 by Sir Laming Worthington Evans, Minister of Pensions, PP 1919 HC 247, pp.83–4, 1979.
14. Sir Charles Harris before the Select Committee on Naval & Military Services (Pensions & Grants) 1915 op. cit., p.14.
15. The high point of separation allowances came in March 1917, when 3,158,100 dependants were receiving payments – see *Statistics of the Military Effort of the British Empire During the Great War 1914–1920*, (HMSO, 1922).
16. See memo from Sir Charles Harris, January 1915, NA T/11891.
17. Eleanor Rathbone before Select Committee on Naval & Military Services (Pensions & Grants) 1915, op. cit., p.102, 1806.
18. Ibid., p.111, 1997.
19. Derek Fraser's *The Evolution of the British Welfare State* (Macmillan, 1973) gives a comprehensive account of these pre-war reforms.

20. *Hansard*, 12 November 1914, 5th series, vol. 68, column 50.
21. Leicester War Relief Committee HRH Prince of Wales's Fund Report, 31 August 1914 to 1 September 1915.
22. *John Bull*, 3 April 1915.
23. *Hansard*, 26 August 1914, vol. 66, c46 Mr Tennant, Under Secretary for War.
24. Colonel Sir James Gildea, *Historical Record of the Work of the Soldiers' and Sailors' Families Association from 1885 to 1916*, (Eyre & Spottiswoode, 1916).
25. Bell, op. cit.
26. Pember Reeves, op.cit.
27. Archbishop of Canterbury before Select Committee on Naval & Military Services (Pensions & Grants) 1915, op. cit., p.153, 2718.
28. Gildea, op. cit.
29. NA PIN 15/1393.
30. Select Committee on Naval & Military Services (Pensions & Grants) 1915, op. cit., p.xii.
31. William Hayes Fisher MP, before Select Committee on Naval & Military Services (Pensions & Grants) 1915, op. cit., p.127, 2282.
32. Ibid.
33. Ibid., p.87, 1544.
34. *Statistics of the Military Effort of the British Empire during the Great War 1914–1920* (HMSO, 1922).
35. *5th Annual Report of the Ministry of Pensions, 1922* (HMSO, 1922).
36. NA PIN 15/1396.

Chapter 2

1. Margaret Forster, Liddle Collection, Brotherton Library, University of Leeds, WW1/DF/148/1/51.
2. Thompson, P., University of Essex, Department of Sociology, Lummis, T., University of Essex, Department of Sociology: 'Interview with Mrs Chambers' in 'Family Life and Work Experience Before 1918, 1870–1973' 7, UK Data Service (distributor), 2009-05-12, SN:2000, Para. 1067. http://dx.doi.org/10.5255/UKDA-SN-2000-1.
3. Capt Michael Heenan, Liddle Collection, WW1/GS/0737.
4. Eve Hammond, Liddle Collection, WW1/TR/03/43.
5. George William Fowler, Liddle Collection, WW1/GS/0576.
6. 'Interview with Mrs Chambers', op. cit.
7. Capt Harold Ackroyd, Liddle Collection, WW1/GS/0002, letter from Pte Scriven dated 16 September 1917.
8. Capt W.T. Dickson, Liddle Collection, WW1/GA/DBC/42.
9. Ethel Mann, née Booth, Liddle Collection, WW1/DF/148/2/7.
10. *Leeds Mercury*, 7 October 1916, and *Yorkshire Evening Post*, 6 October 1916.
11. Ernest Blackburn, Liddle Collection, WW1/GS/0145, letter from Lily Davies dated 18 March 1917.

12. Ibid.
13. Mrs Limon, Liddle Collection, WW1/TR/04/33.
14. For example, the activities of Page Gaston, described in Richard Van Emden's *The Quick and the Dead* (Bloomsbury, 2011).
15. Letter from Lord Mayor's War Information Office, Newcastle to Sarah Blakey, 13 February 1917.
16. *Sunday Post*, 28 March 1915.
17. *Nottingham Journal*, 7 September 1915.
18. Jay Winter in *Sites of Memory, Sites of Mourning* (Cambridge University Press, 1995) has referred to such connections as constituting a 'community of the bereaved', though how long such links were sustained is variable – Lily Davies and Annie Blackburn's correspondence was limited to just three letters.
19. NA WO 363/L229.
20. 'Interview with Mrs Chambers', op. cit.
21. *Daily Record*, 7 November 1917.
22. For the Ackroyd ceremony, see Imperial War Museum – War Office Official Topical Budget 318-2, IWM NTB 318-2. The award to Mrs Davies is at War Office Official Topical Budget 322-1, IWM NTB 322-1.
23. Another ceremony where footage survives – *Pictorial News* (Official) 342-2, IWM NTB 342-2.
24. See Lou Taylor, *Mourning Dress: a Costume and Social History* (Routledge, 2010).
25. 'War Mourning', *The Times* (London, England), 31 Aug 1914: 9. *The Times Digital Archive* web, 25 Dec 2016.
26. 'The White Badge Of Pride', *The Times* (London, England), 29 Aug 1914: 6. *The Times Digital Archive* web, 25 Dec 2016.
27. 'War Mourning', *The Times* (London, England), 2 Sept 1914: 4. *The Times Digital Archive* web, 25 Dec 2016.
28. Letter from Joan Stanton of Hounslow to the *Middlesex Chronicle*, 15 August 1914.
29. For attitudes towards grief in Germany, see Claudia Siebrecht, 'The Female Mourner:Gender and the Moral Economy of Grief During the First World War' in Christa Hammele, Oswald Uberegger, Birgitta Bader Zaar (eds.), *Gender and the First World War* (Palgrave Macmillan, 2014).
30. *The Tatler*, 25 November 1914.
31. Hammond, op. cit.
32. *The Tatler*, 27 January 1915.
33. Even this lengthy mourning period had reduced slightly from the same column's pre-war advice, where heavy mourning was worn for twenty-one months. See 'The Highway of Fashion' by Marjorie Hamilton, *The Tatler*, 21 January 1914.
34. Geoffrey Gorer, *Death, Grief and Mourning in Contemporary Britain* (Cresset Press, 1965) p.4.
35. *The Tatler*, 7 June 1916.

36. Patrick McVeigh, *Look After the Bairns: a Childhood in East Lothian* (Tuckwell Press, 1999).
37. Bell, op.cit., p.77.
38. Gorer, op. cit., and Pat Jalland, *Death in War and Peace – a History of Loss & Grief in England 1914-1970* (Oxford University Press, 2010) are two examples.
39. See, for example, Pember Reeves, op. cit.
40. Interview with Mrs Chambers, op. cit.
41. http://www.army.mod.uk/news/26599.aspx, retrieved 4 May 2017.
42. *Manchester Guardian*, 1 July 1915.
43. Peter Marris, *Widows and their Families* (Routledge & Kegan Paul,1958).
44. Gorer, op. cit.
45. David Clark, *Between Pulpit and Pew – Folk Religion in a North Yorkshire Fishing Village* (Cambridge University Press, 1982).
46. Wilfrid Cove, letter to Ethel Cove from Lt C.E. Carroll, 8 March 1917, Liddle Collection WW1/GS/0375.
47. Capt Michael Heenan, letter from 2nd Lt Manning to Lorna Heenan, 2 February 1916, op. cit.
48. See Jonathan F. Vause, *Death So Noble: Memory, meaning and the First World War* (University of British Columbia Press, 1997).
49. For more information on the British War Graves Association, see Noel Reeves' blogpost on the University of Leeds Legacies of War website https://arts.leeds.ac.uk/legaciesofwar/themes/yorkshire-and-the-great-war/a-leeds-womans-story-the-british-war-graves-association/.
50. *Leeds Mercury*, 23 July 1919.
51. 'Mourning In Portsmouth', *The Times* (London, England), 5 June 1916: 10. *The Times Digital Archive* web, 29 May 2017.
52. *Daily Mirror*, 9 November 1914.
53. Blackburn, letter from Lily Davies, op. cit.
54. Original message printed in *The Gentlewoman* and reproduced in a number of national and local newspapers in January 1915.
55. Blackburn, letter from Lily Davies, op. cit.

Chapter 3

1. Forster, op. cit.
2. Fowler, op. cit.
3. Bell, op. cit.
4. William Angus MD, DPH, *Report on the Health and Sanitary Condition of the City of Leeds for the year 1915* (City of Leeds, 1915).
5. European War 1914 Ladies' Visiting Committee Minute Book, Bradford, minutes dated 15 September 1914, West Yorkshire Archives Service.
6. Select Committee on Naval & Military Services (Pensions & Grants) 1915, op. cit., Appendix 6, p.234.
7. *Sunderland Daily Echo and Shipping Gazette*, 31 August 1914.

8. McVeigh, op. cit.
9. *Morpeth Herald*, 22 August 1919.
10. *Durham Chronicle*, 5 July 1929.
11. Ernest Blackburn, Liddle Collection, op. cit.
12. Appendix 3 to the Select Committee on Naval & Military Services (Pensions & Grants) 1915, op. cit., p.177.
13. Forster, op. cit.
14. Evidence provided by Birmingham Citizen's Committee to the Select Committee on Naval & Military Services (Pensions & Grants) 1915, op. cit., Appendix 5, p.198.
15. This example from Barbara McLaren, *Women of the War* (Hodder & Stoughton, 1917), p.17.
16. Forster, op. cit.
17. Ella Lethem, Liddle Collection, WW1/DF/074.
18. *North Eastern & Daily Gazette*, 19 November 1914.
19. Marris, op. cit., notes that the idea was still prevalent in the 1950s.
20. Select Committee on Naval & Military Services (Pensions & Grants) 1915, op. cit., Appendix 11, p.245.
21. NA PIN 84/20.
22. Forster, op. cit.
23. *Yorkshire Evening Post*, 26 June 1919.
24. City of Leeds Education Committee Report, 1920.
25. *Instructions on the Training of Widows*, Ministry of Pensions, 1917.
26. More unusually, it included work in the piano trade and as swimming instructors.
27. Ibid.
28. Ibid.
29. *Nottingham Evening Post*, 29 June 1914.
30. *Report on the Condition of Widows Under the Poor Law in Liverpool*, op. cit.
31. *Leeds Mercury*, 3 July 1917.
32. Ibid.
33. *Leeds Mercury*, 28 January 1919.
34. *Yorkshire Evening Post*, 10 September 1919.
35. The National Council of Social Service was founded in 1919 from a legacy left by a Capt Edward Vivien Birchall, who was involved in social work in Birmingham before the outbreak of war. The organization is today known as the National Council for Voluntary Action.
36. Lack of complete information on some families reduced the final sample size to 192.
37. Mary Mason, Liddle Collection, WW1/DF/GA/LEE/2.
38. *Annual Report of the Chief Medical Officer for the Board of Education 1915* (HMSO, 1916).
39. *Annual Report of the Chief Medical Officer for the Board of Education 1914* (HMSO, 1915).

40. McVeigh, op. cit.
41. Ethel Mann (née Booth), op. cit.
42. National Council of Social Service *Report on some Effects of Widowhood in Wage Earning Families. Being the result of an Enquiry undertaken in view of proposals now being put forward for the Adoption of a National Policy of State Pensions for Widows* (The National Council of Social Service, 1920).

Chapter 4
1. NCSS Report 1920, op. cit.
2. Ibid.
3. Ministry of Health *Survey of Relief to Widows and Children 1919* (HMSO, London, 1919).
4. *Report on the Condition of Widows under the Poor Law in Liverpool*, op. cit.
5. Ibid.
6. Ministry of Health *Survey of Relief to Widows and Children 1919*, op. cit.
7. Ibid.
8. Ibid.
9. McVeigh, op. cit.
10. *Report of the Walmsley Orphan Homes 1916*.
11. *Our Waifs and Strays*, 1916.
12. Ibid.
13. NA PIN 84/19160.
14. Kathleen Dayus, *All My Days* (Virago, 1988).
15. Joy Parr, *Labouring Children – British Immigrant Apprentices to Canada 1869–1924* (McGill, Queen's University Press, 1980).
16. Mann née Booth, op. cit.
17. Pember Reeves, op. cit.
18. McVeigh, op. cit.
19. *Report on the Condition of Widows under the Poor Law in Liverpool*, op. cit.
20. *War Pensions Gazette*, September 1917.
21. Bell, op. cit.
22. Pember Reeves, op. cit.
23. Black, op. cit., p.3.
24. Appendix 3 to the Select Committee on Naval & Military Service (Pensions & Grants) 1915, submitted by the War Emergency Workers' National Committee, op. cit., p.176.
25. NA PIN 26/18033.
26. Ibid., letter of 10 April 1918.
27. Mason, op. cit.
28. A number of similar initiatives were started in other parts of the country around the same time.
29. *Yorkshire Post & Leeds Intelligencer*, 17 December 1924.
30. Mason, op. cit.

31. *Leeds Mercury*, 15 November 1934.

32. See Appendix 5 to the Select Committee on Naval & Military Service (Pensions & Grants) 1915, op. cit.

33. Ministry of Health *Survey of Relief to Widows and Children 1919.*

34. Ibid.

35. *Leeds Mercury*, 5 February 1919.

36. Miss Gladys Storey's fund existed for just this purpose.

37. *The Times*, 8 July 1918.

38. *The Times*, 15 July 1918.

39. Colonel Hoffman's notes on the City of Bradford War Relief Committee, West Yorkshire Archives Service.

40. NCSS Report, op. cit.

41. Appendix 5 to Select Committee on Naval & Military Service (Pensions & Grants) 1915, op. cit.

42. Figures from *The Royal Patriotic Fund Corporation – a Short History 1854–1954* (RPFC 1954).

43. SSAFA Post-War Circular No. 1, 20 August 1919.

44. The fund was later expanded to include families of men of the Royal Navy.

45. Sailors' Society', *The Times* (London, England), 29 Oct 1917: 3. *The Times Digital Archive* web, 21 Apr 2017.

46. *The Officer*, 1917.

47. *Women's Migration Scheme, The War Cry*, 28 October 1916, Supplement i-iv.

48. *Salvation Army Yearbook 1916.*

49. *Annual Report of the Chief Medical Officer for the Board of Education 1914*, op. cit.

50. *Annual Report of the Chief Medical Officer for the Board of Education 1920* (HMSO, 1921).

51. *Report on the Condition of Widows under the Poor Law in Liverpool*, op. cit.

52. Evidence given before Select Committee on Naval & Military Service (Pensions & Grants) 1915, op. cit., p.124, 2241.

Chapter 5

1. NA PIN 26/21731.

2. Ministry of Pensions *Special Grants Committee Regulations Part 1, Supplementary Allowances, Special Allowances And Grants And Instructions For The Guidance Of Local Committees Established Under The Naval And Military War Pensions Act 1915* (HMSO, 1915).

3. NA PIN 15/1122.

4. *19th Annual Report of the Ministry of Pensions, Part 2* (HMSO, 1936).

5. Barbara Cartland, *We Danced All Night: a Dazzling Memoir of the Glittering Twenties* (Robson Books, 1994).

6. See Clare Sheridan, *Nuda Veritas* (Thornton Butterworth, 1927).

7. *Preston Herald*, 26 February 1916.

8. *Mid Sussex Times*, 28 June 1910.

9. J.A. Spender, *Weetman Pearson, 1st Viscount Cowdray* (Cassell, 1930).

10. NA WO 363/MIS-SORTS80/44 letter of 22 May 1915.

11. *The Tatler*, 7 March 1917.

12. See Millicent, Duchess of Sutherland, *Six Weeks at the War* (London, *The Times*, 1914).

13. *Western Gazette*, 18 September 1914.

14. McLaren, op.cit.

15. See, for example, Olive Dent, *A VAD in France* (London, 1917). This issue of tension between the professional nurse and the VAD is well described in Alison S. Fell and Christine A. Hallett (eds.), *First World War Nursing: New Perspectives* (Routledge, 2013).

16. Thekla Bower, *Britain's Civilian Volunteers: the authorized story of British Voluntary Aid Detachment Work in the Great War* (New York, Moffat, Yard & Co, 1917, p.4).

17. *Illustrated Sporting and Dramatic News*, 15 July 1916.

18. Diana Cooper, *The Rainbow Comes and Goes* (R. Hart-Davis, 1958).

19. *The Sketch*, 13 November 1918.

20. For more on the work carried out at the Queen's Hospital, see the work of Andrew Bamji.

21. Six miscellaneous essays by patients with facial injuries in Sidcup Hospital, Liddle Collection, WW1/GA/WOU/34.

22. *Western Times*, 16 June 1915.

23. Ibid.

24. Founded by the Church of England in 1883 as the Ladies' Association for the Care of Friendless Girls, the organization was largely concerned with steering working-class girls away from prostitution and into more respectable professions, usually domestic service.

25. Capt W.T. Dickson, op. cit., letter to Mrs Dickson from Annie Michie dated 26 April 1917.

26. L.S. Heenan, Liddle Collection, WW1/DF/064.

27. A correspondent, 'Mrs Denzil Hughes Onslow', *The Times* (London, England), 28 Mar 1933: 16. *The Times Digital Archive* web, 19 Mar 2017.

28. McLaren, op. cit.

29. *The Scotsman*, 7 June 1933.

30. *The Tatler*, 30 September 1914.

Chapter 6

1. See evidence of Lt Gen Sir A. Codrington, former member of Pensions Appeal Tribunal, before Select Committee on Naval & Military Service (Pensions & Grants) 1919, op. cit., p.391, 8991.

2. NA PIN 15/1384.

3. NA PIN 26/19164, letter of 13 January 1917.

4. NA PIN 26/19164.

5. NA WO 374/12354.
6. NA WO 339/18421.
7. NA PIN 15/1383.
8. NA PIN 26/21793.
9. NA PIN 26/18965.
10. NA PIN 15/1380, memorandum of 8 October 1917.
11. Julian Putkowski and Julian Barnes note that in 1917 alone, fourteen married soldiers were executed. *Shot at Dawn* (Leo Cooper, 1989, p.206).
12. Sir James MacPherson to Mr J.M. Hogge, *Hansard*, HC Deb, 13 November 1917, vol. 99, cc191–2.
13. Gertrude Farr, IWM 20682 and elsewhere.
14. The other Everills mentioned have no discernible connection to Hanley and are instead remembered on the Tunstall war memorial.
15. See Putkowski & Barnes, op. cit., p.201.
16. NA PIN 15/1399, memorandum of 28 June 1917.
17. NA CAB 24/33/24.
18. NA PIN 15/1380.
19. NA PIN 15/1400, letter from Lord Derby to George Barnes, 9 January 1918.
20. Ibid.
21. NA WO 339/111890.
22. Ibid.
23. Ibid.
24. See Richard Van Emden, *The Quick and the Dead* (Bloomsbury, 2011), and Gordon Small, *The Newport on Tay and Wormit War Memorial* (Tay Valley Family History Society, 2008).
25. Olive Watson, *Suicide in Victorian and Edwardian England* (Clarendon Press, 1987).
26. NA PIN 15/807.
27. Ibid.
28. Ibid.
29. Ibid.
30. Ibid., memo of 8 January 1917.
31. NA PIN 26/21184.
32. NA PIN 15/808, memo of 22 September 1917.
33. Ibid., article 'A Plea for the Widows', *News of the World*, 12 October 1919.
34. Ibid.
35. Ibid., letter from Thomas Ogilvie to Sir Laming Worthington Evans, 22 August 1919.
36. NA PIN 15/810.
37. Ibid.
38. NA PIN 26/19005.
39. *Liverpool Evening Express*, 7 February 1939.
40. NA PIN 15/808, memorandum of 22 September 1917.

Chapter 7

1. *Yorkshire Evening Post*, 9 April 1920.
2. *Buckingham Advertiser and Free Press*, Saturday, 29 November 1924.
3. *Daily Gazette for Middlesbrough*, 1 November 1916.
4. *Daily Gazette for Middlesbrough*, 22 October 1918.
5. *Yorkshire Evening Post*, 13 August 1919.
6. *Leeds Mercury*, Wednesday, 20 August 1919.
7. *Portsmouth Evening News*, 6 August 1923.
8. *Portsmouth Evening News*, 24 March 1923.
9. *Daily Gazette for Middlesbrough*, 29 February 1916.
10. *Yorkshire Evening Post*, 5 December 1919.
11. *Whitstable Times and Herne Bay Herald*, 17 March 1923.
12. *Aberdeen Press and Journal*, 2 September 1925.
13. First, Second and Third Reports from the Committee of Public Accounts 1919, (HMSO 1919, p.31).
14. *Surrey Advertiser*, 16 April 1917.
15. *Aberdeen Press and Journal*, 3 September 1923.
16. *Daily Gazette for Middlesbrough*, 14 June 1916.
17. See report in the *Sheffield Evening Telegraph* of 27 June 1916 for the judge's comment on sentencing.
18. *Hull Daily Mail*, 29 December 1923.
19. *Illustrated Police News*, 26 September 1918.
20. Reports in *Portsmouth Evening News*, 7 January 1920, *Western Gazette*, 5 December 1919 and additional research at www.ancestry.co.uk and www.cwgc.org.
21. *Police Gazette*, 11 August 1916.
22. *Chelsea News and General Advertiser*, 5 November 1915.
23. *Shepton Mallet Journal*, 19 November 1926.

Chapter 8

1. Mann née Booth, op. cit.
2. Letter from Alexander Spence to Sally Blakey, 28 August 1916, courtesy of the Blakey family.
3. Ibid.
4. John Bickersteth (ed.), *The Bickersteth Diaries 1914–1918* (Leo Cooper, 1998).
5. *Manchester Guardian*, 8 March 1916.
6. Archbishop of Canterbury before Select Committee on Naval & Military Services (Pensions & Grants) 1915, op. cit. pp.153–62.
7. See, for example, Charles Smyth, *Cyril Forster Garbutt, Archbishop of York* (Hodder & Stoughton, 1959).
8. See Jeffrey Cox, *The English Churches in a Secular Society: Lambeth 1870–1930* (Oxford University Press, 1982).
9. See Alan Wilkinson, *The Church of England and the First World War*, 2nd edition (SCM Press, 1996).

10. *Todmorden & District News*, 13 August 1915.
11. Interview with Mrs Chambers, op. cit.
12. Forster, op. cit. No bank managers' sons appear among the dead of the Palmer's raid, but there is a man, Thomas Smith, son of the manager of the local Co-Operative store, who could be the person referred to.
13. Cove, op. cit.
14. Ibid.
15. Ibid.
16. See Gerald J. De Groot, *Back in Blighty* (Vintage, 2014).
17. Marris, op. cit.
18. 'The Hero's Death and After', The Views of an Onlooker, *The Light*, 27 October 1917.
19. Arthur Conan Doyle, *History of Spiritualism* (Cassell, 1926).
20. Sheridan, op. cit., p.114.
21. George Lethem was not the only prominent journalist to declare an interest in spiritualism. The great W.T. Stead, who drowned in the *Titanic* disaster, was a key member of the movement, as was Hannen Swaffer, editor of *The People* in 1924.
22. Lethem, op. cit.
23. Douglas Crockatt's diary, Liddle Collection, WW1/GS/0395.
24. *Daily Mail*, 24 January 1917.
25. Horace Leaf, *What is this Spiritualism?* (C. Palmer & Hayward, 1918), p.140.
26. Eileen Garrett, *My Life as a Search for the Meaning of Mediumship* (Rider & Co, London, 1939).
27. PIN 84/8.
28. Diocesan leaflet written by the Bishop of London and quoted in several newspapers of the time.
29. Arthur Foley Winnington-Ingram, *The Church at War* (Wells, Gardner, Darton & Co. Ltd., 1915), p.v.
30. Ibid., p.29.
31. The Greater World Organization of Spiritualist Churches was particularly active in this regard, establishing a women's shelter in Leeds in the 1930s. Winifred Moyes, the founder, had discovered her own psychic abilities during the war.

Chapter 9

1. NA PIN 26/19155.
2. J.M. Winter, *The Great War and the British People* (McMillan, 1986, p.52).
3. *Hansard*, 6 March 1917, vol. XII, col 268–269.
4. *Dundee Courier*, 2 August 1935.
5. NA PIN 26/19129.
6. NA PIN 26/19146.
7. See Sir Edward Parry, *My Own Way – an Autobiography* (Cassell & Co, 1932).
8. NA PIN 26/18278.

9. The War Pensions (Administrative Provisions) Act 1919 extended the right of appeal to widows in cases of claims rejected due to a soldier's misconduct or where the ministry claimed the death was not due to war service.

10. Cases where men had previously suffered from some kind of venereal disease are examples of this, with the widow being 'spared' that information.

11. NA PIN 26/17396.

12. NA PIN 26/19135.

13. *Hansard*, HC Deb, 16 April 1923, vol. 162, cc1698-9W.

14. *The War Pensions Gazette*, February 1920.

15. *Sunderland Daily Echo and Shipping Gazette*, 10 June 1921.

16. *Dundee Courier*, 16 July 1924. The SSDA were an independent group active mostly in Scotland and not affiliated with the SSFA.

17. NA PIN 26/18974.

18. Graham Wootton, *The Official History of the British Legion* (Macdonald & Evans, 1956). This policy changed in 1922, but even then, women were not allowed to be full members of the British Legion, instead forming a women's auxiliary section. See also Niall Barr, *The Lion and the Poppy – British Veterans, Politics and Society 1921–1939* (Praeger, 2005).

19. See Wootton, op. cit.

20. Statistics given by Major Tryon in the House of Commons, *Hansard*, HC Deb 07 December 1922, vol. 159, cc1960–2.

21. NA PIN 15/809, memorandum of 15 June 1920.

22. NA PIN 15/2412, memorandum of 7 May 1920.

23. Ibid.

24. NA PIN 26/19149.

25. NA PIN 26/19401.

26. NA PIN 26/19156.

27. NA PIN 26/19309.

28. Other examples include the cases of Sgt Ernest Perryman NA PIN 26/18832 and Pte Ernest Doyle NA PIN 26/17766.

29. NA PIN 26/18958.

30. *Aberdeen Press and Journal*, 19 April 1930.

31. NA PIN 15/183.

32. In 1942, instructions were issued to the effect that pensions would no longer be refused for widows where the husband's death was wholly due to his war disability, regardless of the Ministry's view of the original pension award. However, erroneous entitlement was still to be argued before the tribunals in cases where the Ministry put forward the case that the husband's disability did not result solely from his war service; the tribunal would still be invited to rule that the original pension award was wrong.

33. NA PIN 26/19138, letter to E.S., 26 November 1923.

34. Peter Barham, *Forgotten Lunatics of the Great War* (Yale University Press, 2004).

35. NA PIN 26/19138.

36. Ibid.
37. Documents re a continued unsuccessful fight for a pension by a 'War' widow, Liddle Collection, WW1/GA/PEN/3.
38. Ibid.
39. Ibid.
40. Ibid., letter to Pensions Appeal Tribunal, 3 May 1975.
41. Ibid., letter to Pensions Appeal Tribunal, 28 May 1975.

Chapter 10
1. *1st Annual Report of the Ministry of Pensions to 31 March 1918* (HMSO, 1918).
2. Ibid.
3. War Pensions Act 1921.
4. *1st Annual Report of the Ministry of Pensions*, op. cit.
5. NA PIN 26/19160.
6. See Ministry of Pensions *Annual Reports*, 1920/1921.
7. *The War Pensions Gazette,* January 1920. The War Pensions (Administrative Provisions) Act 1919 established a serviceman's right to a pension in qualifying circumstances.
8. NA PIN 84/1406.
9. NA PIN 84/30.
10. Ibid.
11. NA PIN 84/19.
12. Ibid.
13. NA PIN 26/18995.
14. Ibid.
15. NA PIN 84/38.
16. Ibid.
17. NA PIN 84/43.
18. Ibid.
19. NA PIN 84/2.
20. Ibid.
21. The daughter of Quentin Hogg, Ethel Wood was a noted philanthropist active on many social work committees in London.
22. Select Committee on Naval & Military Service (Pensions & Grants) 1919, op. cit., p.192, 4526.
23. Ibid.
24. Ibid., 4533.
25. NA PIN 15/1406, letter from West Riding War Pensions Committee, 6 May 1920.
26. Ibid., letter from the Ministry of Pensions, 12 May 1920.
27. Ibid., Report of Sub-Committee of the Liverpool, Bootle and Waterloo District War Pensions Committee.
28. Ibid., Response from Special Grants Committee.

29. Ibid.
30. NA PIN 26/19157.
31. Ibid.
32. NA PIN 15/1406, letter from William T. Harris, Chairman of Aylesbury & District War Pensions Committee, 15 November 1923.
33. Regulations issued to local Poor Law Committees advised that they were not allowed to give outdoor relief to a widow who had given birth to an illegitimate child after her widowhood commenced unless it was an exceptional case.
34. NA PIN 15/1406, letter from George Chrystal on behalf of Ministry of Pensions, 14 December 1923.
35. Ibid.
36. Ibid.
37. See E. Sylvia Pankhurst, *The Home Front: a mirror to life in England during the world war*, (Hutchinson & Co, 1932).
38. *The Globe*, 25 November 1919.
39. NA PIN 15/1406, letter from Bermondsey & Southwark Area Office of Ministry of Pensions, 6 September 1923.
40. NA PIN 84/21.
41. NA PIN 84/20.
42. Ibid.
43. Ibid.
44. NA PIN 84/8.
45. Ibid.
46. Ibid.
47. Ibid.
48. Ibid.
49. *10th Annual Report of the Ministry of Pensions* (HMSO, 1927).
50. NA PIN 15/1743.

Chapter 11

1. Commissioner David Lamb, *Transplantations – the Salvation Army's Women's Migration Scheme 1916–1923* (1923).
2. *The Emigration Gazette*, June 1914.
3. See Marilyn Barber, 'Sunny Ontario for British Girls 1900–1930' in Jean Burnet (ed.), *Looking Into My Sister's Eyes: an Exploration in Women's History* (Multicultural History Society of Ontario, 1986).
4. *The Imperial Colonist*, November 1914.
5. *The Imperial Colonist*, December 1914.
6. Ibid., April 1915.
7. Committee minutes of BWEA, 7 May 1915, Women's Library, London School of Economics.
8. Quoted in *The War Cry*, 17 June 1916.
9. See Committee minutes of the BWEA, October 1916.

10. Figures taken from *Transplantations*, op. cit.
11. Figures from *The Imperial Colonist*, January 1917.
12. The War Pensions Act of 1921 later gave 'any person in receipt of a pension' the right to apply for its commutation, but how many of those appeals by widows were successful is unknown.
13. See *The Imperial Colonist*, March and May 1918.
14. Committee minutes of the BWEA, January 1918.
15. The BWEA reported a similar bias in enquiries to their own emigration scheme.
16. Quoted in *Report of the Overseas Settlement Committee for 1922*, Cmd 1804 XII 1923, p.13.
17. *Report of the Empire Settlement Committee 1917*, Cd 8672, p.28.
18. *The War Cry*, 30 August 1919.
19. *Transplantations*, op. cit.
20. *The War Cry*, 4 February 1922.
21. *Transplantations*, op.cit.
22. *The Imperial Colonist*, December 1922.
23. *Report of the Overseas Settlement Committee for 1922*, Cmd 1804 XII 1923, p.24.
24. Figures quoted in Janice Gothard, 'The healthy, wholesome British domestic girl: single female migration and the Empire Settlement Act 1922–1930' in Stephen Constantine (ed.), *Emigrants and Empire – British Settlement in the Dominions Between the Wars* (Manchester, 1990).
25. Information comes from passenger lists and Canadian immigration forms available via www.ancestry.com.
26. Pember Reeves, op. cit. p.40.
27. See, for example, *The Aberdeen Journal*, 5 October 1915 – 'Emigrants Beware!'.
28. See Brian L. Blakeley, 'The Society for the Overseas Settlement of British Women and the Problem of Empire Settlement 1917–1936', Albion 20 3, Fall 1988.
29. National Archives of Australia, A457, L400/5.

Chapter 12

1. See Gorer, op. cit., for example.
2. See exchange between George Barnes and Dr Marion Phillips of the National Women's Labour League, Select Committee on Naval & Military Services (Pensions & Grants) 1915, op. cit., p.59, 991–992.
3. Ibid.
4. *Surrey Mirror*, 22 January 1922.
5. *Burnley Express*, 18 November 1916.
6. See, for example, *Leeds Mercury* of 23 July 1919.
7. *Leeds Mercury*, 12 December 1919.
8. *Durham Chronicle*, 15 February 1929.
9. *Yorkshire Post & Leeds Intelligencer*, 14 September 1919.
10. NA PIN 15/259, memo of 10 March 1920.

11. Deceased Brother's Widow's Marriage Act 1921.
12. See NA PIN 84/39, for example.
13. *Grantham Journal*, 18 April 1918.
14. It is likely that the 'adultery' was pre-arranged to facilitate a divorce between the two. See NA J 77/2256/693.
15. *Leeds Mercury*, 14 August 1919.
16. *Portsmouth Evening News*, 22 January 1920.
17. *Derby Daily Telegraph*, 3 October 1929.
18. *Yorkshire Evening Post*, 11 March 1919.
19. *The Tatler*, 26 September 1917.
20. *Nottingham Evening Post*, 25 June 1920.
21. *Surrey Advertiser*, 25 February 1918.
22. *Yorkshire Evening Post*, 16 June 1919.
23. *Yorkshire Evening Post*, 2 and 16 July 1921.
24. Reported in a number of newspapers in March 1920, the story had added pathos with the detail that the young widow had nursed her soldier husband, who had eventually died of his wounds. This embellishment was untrue as Frank Merrifield never made it home to Brighton at all.
25. *Official Programme of the National Peace Celebrations 19 July 1919* (HMSO, 1919).
26. David W. Lloyd, *Battlefield Tourism* (Bloomsbury, 2014), for example.
27. 'To-morrow's Pageant', *The Times* (London, England), 18 July 1919: 15. *The Times Digital Archive* web, 21 May 2017.
28. *Todmorden & District News*, 2 May 1919.
29. All from *Todmorden & District News*, 30 May 1919.
30. *Todmorden & District News*, 6 June 1919.
31. *Todmorden & District News*, 26 September 1919.
32. *Yorkshire Evening Post*, 22 July 1919.
33. See Lloyd, op. cit.
34. 'Over 1,000,000 Pilgrims', *The Times* (London, England), 16 November 1920: 14. *The Times Digital Archive* web, 21 May 2017.
35. 'The Last Journey', *The Times* (London, England), 11 November 1920: 14. *The Times Digital Archive* web, 21 May 2017.
36. 'Armistice Day, 1920', *The Times* (London, England), 12 November 1920: i+. *The Times Digital Archive* web, 21 May 2017.
37. Wilfrid Ewart, *Scots Guard on the Western Front 1915–1918* (Strong Oak Press, 2001, originally published 1934).
38. H.A. Taylor, *Goodbye to the Battlefields – today and yesterday on the Western Front* (Stanley Paul & Co, 1928) p.128.
39. *St Barnabas Society Pilgrimage to Ypres 1927*.
40. Ibid.
41. Ibid.
42. Ibid.

43. *Leeds Mercury*, 6 August 1928.
44. The *Sketch*, 18 August 1928.
45. *Hartlepool Northern Daily Mail*, 3 February 1928.
46. See Adrian Gregory, for example, *The Silence of Memory – Armistice Day 1919–1946* (Oxford University Press, 1994).
47. *Shields Daily News*, 11 November 1927.

Afterword
1. Joy Damousi, *The Labour of Loss* (Cambridge University Press, 2010).

Select Bibliography

Anderson, Olive, *Suicide in Victorian and Edwardian England*, Clarendon Press, 1987.

Barham, Peter, *Forgotten Lunatics of the Great War*, Yale University Press, 2004.

Barr, Niall, *The Lion and the Poppy – British Veterans, Politics and Society 1921–1939*, Praeger, 2005.

Bell, Lady Florence, *At the Works: a study of a manufacturing town (Middlesbrough)*, Edward Arnold, 1907.

Black, Clementina (ed.), *Married Women's Work: being a report of an enquiry undertaken by the Women's Industrial Council*, G. Bell & Sons, 1915.

Bosanquet, Helen, *Social Work in London 1869–1912: a history of the Charity Organisation Society*, J. Murray, 1914.

Bourke, Joanna, *Dismembering the Male: Men's Bodies, Britain and the Great War*, Reaktion Books, 1996.

Brandon, Ruth, *The Spiritualists: the passion for the occult in the Nineteenth and Twentieth Centuries*, Wiedenfeld & Nicolson, 1983.

Cartland, Barbara, *We Danced All Night: a Dazzling Memoir of the Glittering Twenties*, Robson Books, 1994.

Connelly, Mark, *The Great War, Memory & Ritual – Commemoration in the City and East London 1916–1939*, Royal Historical Society, 2002.

Cox, Jeffrey, *The English Churches in a Secular Society, Lambeth 1870–1930*, Oxford University Press, 1982.

Dayus, Kathleen, *All My Days*, Virago, 1988.

Damousi, Joy, *The Labour of Loss*, Cambridge University Press, 2010.

De Groot, Gerald J., *Blighty: British Society in the Era of the Great War*, Longman, 1996.

Back in Blighty, Vintage, 2014.

Fell, Alison S. & Hallett, Christine A. (eds.), *First World War Nursing: New Perspectives*, Routledge, 2013.

Fraser, Derek, *The Evolution of the British Welfare State*, Macmillan, 1973.

Gildea, Colonel Sir James, *Historical Record of the Work of the Soldiers' and Sailors' Families Association from 1885 to 1916*, Eyre & Spottiswoode, 1916.

Gorer, Geoffrey, *Death, Grief and Mourning in Contemporary Britain*, Cresset Press, 1965.

Grayzel, Susan R., *Women and the First World War*, Pearson, 2002.

Gregory, Adrian, *The Silence of Memory – Armistice Day 1919–1946*, Oxford University Press, 1994.

Gregory, Adrian, *The Last Great War: British Society and the First World War*, Cambridge University Press, 2008.

Hazelgrove, Jenny, *Spiritualism & British Society Between the Wars*, Manchester University Press, 2000.

Jalland, Pat, *Death in War and Peace – a History of Loss & Grief in England 1914–1970*, Oxford University Press, 2010.

Lewis, Jane, *The Politics of Motherhood: Child and Maternal Welfare in England 1900–1939*, Croom Helm, 1980.

Lomas, Janis, 'Delicate duties': issues of class and respectability in government policy towards the wives and widows of British soldiers in the era of the Great War, *Women's History Review 9*, 2000.

Lomas, Janis, 'So I married again': Letters from British Widows of the First and Second World Wars, *History Workshop*, n38.

Lomas, Janis, *War Widows in British Society 1914–1990*, unpublished PhD thesis, University of Staffordshire, 1997.

Lloyd, David W., *Battlefield Tourism*, Bloomsbury, 2014.

Mandler, Peter & Pedersen, Susan eds., *After the Victorians: Private Conscience and Public Duty in Modern Britain*, Routledge, 2005.

Marris, Peter, *Widows and their Families*, Routledge & Kegan Paul, 1958.

McVeigh, Patrick, *Look After the Bairns: a Childhood in East Lothian*, Tuckwell Press, 1999.

Meacham, Standish, *A Life Apart: the English Working Class 1890–1914*, Thames & Hudson, 1977.

McLaren, Barbara, *Women of the War*, Hodder & Stoughton, 1917.

Meyer, Jessica, *Men of War: Masculinity and the First World War in Britain*, Palgrave Macmillan, 2009.

Murdoch, Lydia, *Imagined Orphans: Poor Families, Child Welfare and Contested Citizenship in London*, Rutgers University Press, 2006.

Nelson, Geoffrey K., *Spiritualism and Society*, Routledge & Kegan Paul, 1969.

Pankhurst, E. Sylvia, *The Home Front: a mirror to life in England during the world war*, Hutchinson & Co, 1932.

Parry, Sir Edward, *My Own Way: an Autobiography*, Cassell & Co, 1932.

Pedersen, Susan Gender, Welfare and Citizenship in Britain During the Great War – *American Historical Review 95*, 1990.

Eleanor Rathbone and the Politics of Conscience, Yale University Press, 2004.

Family, Dependence and the Origins of the Welfare State, Cambridge University Press, 1993.

Pember Reeves, Maud, *Round About a Pound a Week*, G. Bell & Sons, 1913.

Putkowski, Julian & Sykes, Julian, *Shot at Dawn*, Leo Cooper, 1989.

Roberts, Robert, *The Classic Slum: Salford Live in the First Quarter of the Century*, University of Manchester Press, 1971.

Roper, Michael, *The Secret Battle: Emotional Survival in the Great War*, Manchester University Press, 2009.

Ross, Ellen, *Slum Travelers: Ladies and London Poverty 1860–1920*, University of California Press, 2007.

Love & Toil – Motherhood in Outcast London 1870–1918, Oxford University Press, 1993.

Smith, Angela, *Discourses Surrounding British Widows of the First World War*, Bloomsbury, 2013.

Taylor, Lou, *Mourning Dress: a Costume and Social History*, Routledge, 2010.

Todman, Dan, *The Great War – Myth & Memory*, Hambledon & London, 2005.

Van Emden, Richard, *The Quick and the Dead*, Bloomsbury, 2011.

Wall, Richard & Winter, Jay, *The Upheaval of War – Family, Work and Welfare in Europe, 1914–1918*, Cambridge, 1988.

Watson, Olive, *Suicide in Victorian and Edwardian England*, Oxford, 1987.

Wilkinson, Alan, *The Church of England and the First World War*, London, 1996.

Winter, Jay, *Sites of Memory, Sites of Mourning – the Great War in European Cultural History*, Cambridge University Press, 1995.

The Great War and the British People, Macmillan, 1985.

Wollacott, Angela, *On Her Their Lives Depend: Munitions Workers in the Great War*, University of California Press, 1994.

Wootton, Graham, *The Politics of Influence – British Ex-Servicemen, Cabinet Decisions and Cultural Change 1917–57*, Routledge & Kegan Paul, 1963.

The Official History of the British Legion, Macdonald & Evans, 1956.

Archives

The Iris Strange Collection, University of Staffordshire.

Liddle Collection, University of Leeds.

The National Archives – PIN 15, PIN 26, PIN 84 series.

Salvation Army Heritage Centre.

West Yorkshire Archives Service.

The Women's Library, London School of Economics.

Online sources

www.ancestry.com

www.cwgc.org

www.britishnewspaperarchive.co.uk

Index